W9-ANN-005

# Preserving Your Paper Collectibles

## Demaris C. Smith

BETTERWAY PUBLICATIONS, INC.
WHITE HALL, VIRGINIA

Published by Betterway Publications, Inc.
P.O. Box 219
Crozet, VA 22932
(804) 823-5661


Cover design and photograph by Susan Riley
Typography by East Coast Typography, Inc.

Copyright © 1989 by Demaris C. Smith

All rights reserved. No part of this book may be reproduced by any means,
except by a reviewer who wishes to quote brief excerpts in connection
with a review in a magazine or newspaper.

**Library of Congress Cataloging-in-Publication Data**

Smith, Demaris C.
   Preserving your paper collectibles / Demaris C. Smith,.
     p.   cm.
   Includes index.
   ISBN 1-55870-125-7
   1. Printed ephemera — Conservation and restoration. 2. Printed
ephemera — Collectors and collecitng. 3. Paper — Collectors and
collecting. 4. Paper — Preservation.   I. Title.
Z688.P74S63   1969
676—dc20                          89-36139
                                      CIP


Printed in the United States of America

BOMC offers recordings and compact discs, cassettes
and records. For information and catalog write to
BOMR, Camp Hill, PA 17012.

# Contents

**1.** What are Paper Treasures? . . . . . . . . . . . . . . . . . . . . . . . . . . . . 5

**2.** What is Paper? . . . . . . . . . . . . . . . . . . . . . . . . . . . . . . . . . . 13

**3.** What is Being Done to Preserve our Paper Heritage? . . . . . . . 23

**4.** Historical Paper . . . . . . . . . . . . . . . . . . . . . . . . . . . . . . . . . 35

**5.** Postal Items . . . . . . . . . . . . . . . . . . . . . . . . . . . . . . . . . . . . 45

**6.** Prints I: Posters, Maps, & Photographs . . . . . . . . . . . . . . . . . 55

**7.** Prints II: Cards . . . . . . . . . . . . . . . . . . . . . . . . . . . . . . . . . . 81

**8.** Commercial Paper . . . . . . . . . . . . . . . . . . . . . . . . . . . . . . . . 95

**9.** Paper Currency . . . . . . . . . . . . . . . . . . . . . . . . . . . . . . . . . 103

**10.** The Performing Arts: Playbills, Sheet Music, etc. . . . . . . . . . 111

**11.** Newspapers & Magazines . . . . . . . . . . . . . . . . . . . . . . . . . . 127

**12.** Literary Items: Books & Manuscripts . . . . . . . . . . . . . . . . . . 135

**13.** Puzzles, Games, & Children's Items . . . . . . . . . . . . . . . . . . . 143

**14.** Ephemera: Matchbook Covers, Calendars, etc. . . . . . . . . . . . 163

**15.** An Ounce of Prevention . . . . . . . . . . . . . . . . . . . . . . . . . . . 173

   Bibliography . . . . . . . . . . . . . . . . . . . . . . . . . . . . . . . . . . . . 177

   Suppliers, Organizations, and Associations . . . . . . . . . . . . . . 179

   Index . . . . . . . . . . . . . . . . . . . . . . . . . . . . . . . . . . . . . . . . . 181

# 1
# What are Paper Treasures?

A vast amount of paper miscellany is produced in the course of daily living. Much of it appears to be worth less than the paper that it took to make it. Some of it is meant to be discarded after use, and indeed it is. Some of it, now lost to posterity, could have been prized examples of times long past and fragments of now lost lifestyles.

How, then, to know what should be preserved? In addition to items of an obvious historical nature or the usual collectibles like stamps, picture post cards, baseball cards, photographs, books, magazines, etc., there are the less obvious paper collectibles. The little slices of history, the accoutrements of daily living: ledgers, receipts, advertising items, correspondence, railroad timetables, menus, theater tickets, children's drawings and school papers. And on it goes.

## PRESERVING THE PAST FOR THE FUTURE

Why bother to save what appear to be useless scraps of paper? They serve not only to document history, but also lifestyles of that history. History books can tell us what was happening when, but they can't really tell us what life was like. The items used to run a household, carry one's work, educate one's children, and assimilate oneself into a community tell part of the story. The paper items fill in many of the blanks and provide documentation.

Today's society is fortunate in that written records exist of just about every conceivable happening, and many historical documents are still intact. This in no way means that every scrap of paper must be saved for posterity. But it is important to document lifestyles. And people involved in everyday happenings are the nucleus of the lifestyles. Every effort should be made to preserve as much of it as possible while there is still something left to preserve.

Much interest is centered today on the preservation of historical landmarks and the collection, preservation, and maintenance of many items of historical significance and/or collectible interest. Paper items should not be overlooked. They are the record of the present to be joined with the past to ensure a heritage for future generations.

## WHAT MAKES THOSE PIECES OF PAPER VALUABLE?

A letter written by George Bernard Shaw found in the drawer of an old desk. A $1,200 cache of baseball cards found in the attic of an old house. A $1,000,000 collection of musical works by George Gershwin, Richard Rodgers, Cole Porter, Jerome Kern, and other luminaries of their time found in a warehouse.

History could be in the making right under your nose. Would you recognize it? Is your attic or storeroom or basement a repository for an accumulation of old magazines, books, letters, ledgers, photographs, newspapers, stamps, and other paper items? Have you been thinking of "cleaning out that mess one of these days"? Before you do, it may be well to take a second look.

What makes that piece of paper valuable? The answer to that question is: the same criteria that can make any collectible or artifact valuable. Condition. Dates. Names. Signatures. Rarity.

### Condition

With a few exceptions, items in mint or near mint condition are the most sought after and the most valuable. It's always nice to find clean, clear items on good paper, but if it's old enough and rare enough, condition can be a secondary consideration. Standards of condition vary with different classes of items and are dependent upon the origin and the use to which the item was put. Items that were meant to be handled a lot — playing cards, magazines, maps, matchbook covers, and currency — may not exist in mint condition. Worn does not necessarily indicate old, but if it looks old, it may be wise to take a second look. Some postal items are coveted in any condition because of their extreme rarity. Some stamps are even preferred used instead of mint because of the small number that were postally used.

### Dates

Dates can be helpful not only in proving authenticity but in setting monetary value as well. Several items may be identical except for dates, and the dates may be the difference between a priceless artifact and so much waste paper. A stamped envelope canceled on the first day of issue, in most instances, is of more value than one canceled on any other day. Some items are valuable because of the particular era in which they were in use. Confederate Civil War postal and other items are much sought after.

### Names

A well known name speaks for itself. This includes business and organizational names as well as individuals. Genealogy buffs are always after names and more names. A link in someone's family history may be lurking in a list of names of a Civil War battalion or a county register or in other family records. A missing link in the chain of national or perhaps local history could be stored in someone's attic. Names may be a way of authenticating a document thought not in itself significant. Land grants, charters, and other documents signed by local officials may authenticate the history of a community even if the signers' names aren't well known.

### Signatures

Collecting autographs has become an avocation all its own apart from the obvious historical significance. Autograph seekers abound, and most celebrated folk still with us are happy to oblige (Fig. 1). Harder to come by can be the signature and/or the written word of the celebrated but long departed (Fig. 2). Handwritten documents as well as those with signatures affixed are also a kind of signature. Taking pen to paper was once the only way to make permanent records. Even after the advent of the printing press, typewriter, and other mechanical marvels, many individuals still preferred to make the initial copy of a manuscript or document in longhand. Some such items are known to exist. Because of extensive research and knowledgeable deduction, others are thought to exist. Historians and collectors are on the lookout for both. Sometimes a previously unknown item will surface, and nothing whets the appetite so much as a new find, spurring the historian or collector to seek out new areas of research.

### Rarity

Rarity is defined as something remarkable or valuable because of scarcity. What makes an item scarce is the question. Sometimes it's not only how many were made, but how many of those made survived. Most postage stamps are printed by the thousands, and a lot of them survive. That wasn't always true. When postage stamps were first put into use, only governments

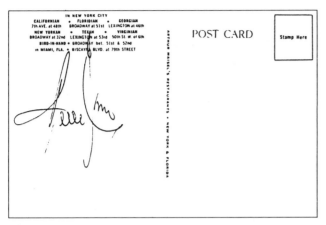

*Figure 1. Autograph of Perry Como on back of post card. (Author's collection.)*

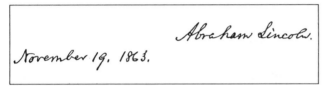

*Figure 2. Facsimile of signature of Abraham Lincoln.*

and high-powered individuals used them, so they were not printed in great numbers. Consequently, some of them are hard to find in any condition and bring premium prices on the stamp market. Political upheavals also contribute to the scarcity of some postal issues. The government in power establishes its own postal services and destroys the previous one. Add to these the mistakes and errors that happen and aren't supposed to be released to the public, but a few slip through. Only one sheet of that U.S. airmail stamp with the airplane printed upside down has ever surfaced.

### Paper

The paper itself may be a determining factor in proving authenticity and in turn value. Paper has its own way of revealing its age. The changes and the progress in paper-making methods can be documented and chemical analysis can be done if necessary to pinpoint a particular era. Certain paper items are victims of the paper-making methods that evolved during the Indus-

trial Revolution. The combination of the machinery and an alteration in the paper content incorporated elements into the paper that caused it to turn yellow and crumble when exposed to certain elements in the atmosphere. In addition, some items are known to have been printed on certain types of paper. Paper varieties exist for some postal issues, for example. Sometimes this was done intentionally. Other times it was necessary because paper supplies were limited, and anything available was used including the paper on the walls. (See Chapter 2 for the history of paper making and a more detailed explanation of the paper-making process.)

### WHAT TO COLLECT

As with other collectibles, the ultimate choice remains in the hands of the collector — whatever piques one's interest or strikes one's fancy or both. What is treasure to one person may be trash to another, but that should not diminish its collectible value. Age is not necessarily a factor. Items of the 1930s, 1940s, and 1950s are being rediscovered. One must also consider the intrinsic value to future generations, if only of one's family. That piece of paper could be a valuable link in the family history or even someone else's family history or the community history as a whole. There seems to be growing interest among cities, large and small, to document their heritage, and one can only guess how much of that documentation is reposing in someone's attic or storeroom waiting to be discovered.

Like most other collectibles, there is an infinite variety of ways to assemble a collection of paper items. There are broad categories such as political items or railroad memorabilia, or a single item such as political posters or railroad timetables. This book will be dealing more with types of paper collectibles than a particular category or item. Because we are dealing with that which can be retained in the home, items must be limited to those that can be stored or displayed in a limited area, and that are in most cases flat as opposed to three-dimensional.

Following chapters will look at each type in turn, describing what makes them collectible and the best ways to preserve them.

## TYPES OF PAPER COLLECTIBLES

### Historical Papers

Historical items of all kinds are much sought after by scholars as well as collectors, but paper items can be the real finds. They provide the positive documentation of our heritage. These papers can include land deeds, town charters and plats, military papers, treaties, proclamations, blueprints of historical structures, letters and manuscripts. Signed documents are most desirable. There still may be a Lincoln letter hidden away in some unsuspecting corner or a handwritten Beethoven symphony or Bronte manuscript.

### Postal Items

Postage stamps have long been sought after collectibles. The hobby has burgeoned into a multi-faceted collectible encompassing a variety of postal items in addition to stamps — postal cards, covers, souvenir sheets, letter sheets, etc. Stamp collectors are among the largest groups of collectors of paper items.

### Prints: Etchings, Lithographs, Posters, Maps, Photographs

Originally an art form, prints — in their many forms - have been adapted for other uses, most notably as illustrations for advertisement and for cards of various kinds. Prints can also be a source of historical documentation. A picture of a long ago personage or happening often can reveal much more than a written description. Original prints should be checked for signatures and other identifying marks which may point to the creators. Currier and Ives prints are among the most sought after of this type of paper collectible. Nothing can be more revealing than an old map when trying to get a line on the migrations of ancient peoples. Written description can be meaningless without a layout of the territory,

even a very crude layout. Some old photographs could turn out to be examples of a well known early photographer. This could include ancestral photos and pictures.

### Cards

Originally an outgrowth of print making and still a facet of that larger encompassing category, cards have grown into an industry all their own with several subdivisions. Collectors like to groups cards under three major headings: advertising cards, insert cards, and souvenir cards. Advertising cards were given away by retail tradesmen or storekeepers to customers or used within the stores to advertise wares. The latter could range to several feet in length. Insert cards were packed or inserted into the wrapper with a product and sold in that manner to customers. Baseball cards in cigarettes, candy, bubblegum, and other products are a prime example. Souvenir cards, in general, are made to be sold and usually have an underlying practical use or purpose. Examples are greeting cards and picture post cards.

Early picture post cards often were issued in sets of six or more, and completing some of those sets can involve a real paper chase. There are categories for these, too, such as animals, transportation, cartoons, etc. Baseball cards also come in many varieties. That $1,200 cache of baseball cards mentioned earlier was discovered by a young man in Augusta, Georgia in the attic of his grandfather's house while it was undergoing renovation. The cards had been distributed by a tobacco company and were gifts to his baseball aficionado grandfather who enjoyed listening to the games on his radio.

### Commercial Paper

This may be the forgotten category of paper items since much of it must eventually be destroyed to make way for the new. Today much more business paper accumulates than in earlier times, and much of it is destined for the paper shredder. Much early paper ended up on the scrap heap, too, but some of it survived. It may not be as easy to find, but it's out there: ledgers, invoices, purchase orders, receipts, advertisements, stocks, bonds, correspondence. The list goes on. Some of it may even go unrecognized. Nice, crisp printed forms or letterheads weren't always used. Plain, folded paper was sufficient. Even if it was meant to be mailed, envelopes weren't always used. That same folded paper was perhaps folded to envelope size, addressed and sealed with wax and posted. That George Bernard Shaw letter was found a couple of years ago in the drawer of an old desk at a manufacturing plant in Memphis, Tennessee. It was written in 1928 to praise a sample of their product — ax handles — which had been presented to Shaw by the company's European representative.

### Currency

Currency, too, is high on the list of collectibles. Like postal items, currency has had its ups and downs in the marketplace and has been at the mercy of political upheavals. Values have fluctuated to the extreme and back again. Some items are so plentiful and so low in value that serious collectors look upon them as so much wallpaper. Others remain elusive even to the most astute collector.

### Theatrical and Entertainment Items: Playbills, Programs, Sheet Music, Brochures, Movie Stills

Playbills and programs are available at practically any stage performance (Fig. 3). First night items are the most coveted, and even more so if they are autographed by the stars. A few motion pictures have even rated programs (Fig. 4). Along with a giveaway there is usually a fancy program available for a nominal cost. Of course, there are other ways to acquire them, though it becomes a bit more difficult once the show is over.

The motion picture and recording industries have spawned a host of paper memorabilia — movie stills, movie press books, movie editions

*Figure 3. Program from Victor Borge conccert circa 1956. (Author's collection.)*

*Figure 4. Program from motion picture,* Around the World in 80 Days, *1956. (Author's collection.)*

of books on which the movies were based, brochures, publicity stills, and any number of items whose main feature was the imprint on them of the image or images of current star attractions. Most of the other paper items mentioned in this book have been adapted for publicity items for showbiz luminaries — prints, cards, phony money, games, paper dolls, puzzles. Even some postage stamps have been issued (most foreign) honoring entertainment figures, including Mickey Mouse (Fig. 5).

*Figure 5. Belize postal issue, Christmas 1956, featuring Disney characters as they appeared in "Saludos Amigos." (Author's collection.)*

Before the advent of sound recording, sheet music was the only way to acquire new compositions. Musically inclined persons were employed by dealers to either play or sing the latest compositions for customers. Much of this sheet music was fancifully illustrated, and certain of it is in demand for the illustrations as much as the music. Any old piano benches lying around? Original manuscripts and musical scores by prominent writers and musicians are coveted. Among the musical treasures in that $1,000,000 collection are some extremely scarce Jerome Kern manuscripts for "Ol' Man River," "Can't Help Lovin' Dat Man," and at least 200 other songs in Kern's own hand plus seventy "lost" George Gershwin songs and thirty Cole Porter manuscripts. They were among eighty crates of music found stored in a movie studio warehouse in Secaucus, New Jersey.

## Newspapers and Magazines

Old newspapers and magazines are sources of a wealth of information about their time, complete with illustrations. Sometimes they may be the primary source for certain types of information, if not the only source. Don't overlook the advertisements either. Often, nothing is so revealing about a certain era as retail sales. What better way to learn the latest fads and fancies of the time? First editions or those of historical significance may be tucked away somewhere waiting to be found. Even that initial issue of *Playboy*, with Marilyn Monroe properly clad on the cover and properly unclad on the centerfold, brings a tidy sum on the current market.

## Literary Items: Books and Other Manuscripts

Bibliophiles abound. Books are collected all kinds of ways. First editions. Favorite authors. Subject matter. References. On and on it goes. Like most paper collectibles, the fun is in the search. Even the most acquisitive collectors may find it difficult to complete a collection. Original handwritten manuscripts are coveted. Who's to say there isn't a Poe or a Hemingway or possibly a Shakespeare opus in the writer's own hand out there somewhere waiting to be found? Book jackets alone are a popular item with collectors. Some book collectors are also of the opinion that if a book was issued with a jacket, it is incomplete if the jacket is missing.

**Children's Items: Puzzles, Games, Paper Dolls, Books, Playing Cards**

Most of these items go through a lot of handling. Finding very early ones in mint condition may be a near impossibility. Finding uncut sheets of early paper dolls also may be difficult as is finding jigsaw puzzles with all the pieces intact. They were meant to be played with, and played with they were. They may not always have been made from the best paper, either. Children's items include paper dolls, activity books, picture books, comic books, simple games, puzzles, and card games. Of course, there is some overlapping because puzzles, games, and playing cards are also made for adults. Many varieties of all of them exist.

**Ephemera: Matchbook Covers, Calendars, Cigarette Packs, Cigar Bands, Bookmarks, Labels, Catalogs, Brochures, Etc.**

The word "ephemera" is of Greek derivation and means "about daily life." These are the common items that one comes in contact with in the course of daily living, items that appear, on casual observation, to be old or quaint or curious but of no particular interest or value. Ephemera is often regarded as throwaway items.

Many of these are advertising items and are relatively easy to collect. Businesses give them away or don't mind if you take them. Some can also be party items, mementos of happy times. Almost everyone has memories of collecting matchbooks or brochures or pamphlets (Fig. 6) to remember a special event, trip, or favorite restaurant. Aficionados extend their collections beyond youthful fancies and indulgences. Early advertising labels are popular collectibles, too. Some of the most sought after are those colorful ones that were attached to wooden fruit and vegetable crates. Cigar bands are labels, too, though many of us remember them as the fancy rings from Daddy's cigars. Bookmarks are available from many different sources. They are used extensively for advertising. Retailers sell them. They are some of the first things children learn to make. Items like catalogs, brochures (Fig. 7),

*Figure 6. Pamphlets and flyers, left to right: Empire State Building, Radio City Music Hall, and Jose Greco concert. (Author's collection.)*

*Figure 7. Variety of homemaking brochures, left to right: "Better Baking" by Home Economics Dept., Procter & Gamble; two Pillsbury's "Communiques." All three circa 1945. Two brochures on sterling, one on Tabasco, one on fine china.*

and calendars were and are direct mail advertisements as well as pick-up items in businesses. Today many types of calendars are sold at retail, and fees are charged for certain types of catalogs and brochures such as those that are limited editions or dated like auction catalogs or those that contain detailed listings and/or fine color illustrations.

Of course, some of these categories do overlap. Paper items seem to be adaptable to so many uses other than their original conception. Historical items can encompass almost any item with a significant story behind it, usually with age as an additional factor. Prints and photos can be used to illustrate ads, greeting cards, post cards, posters, programs, books, etc. Post cards can be greeting cards or advertisements or a means of correspondence. Advertisements can encompass almost anything.

## PAPER AS TREASURE

As with any pursuit, the objective is subject to the whims of the pursuer. In stamp collecting alone, there are almost as many ways to collect as there are stamps. That is probably true of many other paper collectibles. The ultimate direction is in the hands of the collector.

Paper doesn't necessarily have to be old to be collectible. People have been collecting paper memorabilia connected with their favorite personality or subject of interest for some time, regardless of the age of the item. With a contemporary personality or subject, it's possible to amass a collection as things appear on the market. Who among us has not devoured fan publications to seek out photos and information connected with our favorite movie star, theatrical or recording personality, or sports figure, or in more recent years, rock stars, television personalities, and tennis players? What young person, or perhaps young-at-heart person, doesn't have his/her walls plastered with posters of these same personalities? Those who were doing the collecting seventy-five or eighty or even fifty years ago and had the wisdom to keep it intact and pass it on to someone who cared, passed on an unparalleled legacy.

This book is an attempt to steer the collector in the right direction in handling a collection of paper memorabilia and, in the process, aid in preserving potentially valuable paper items.

# 2
# What is Paper?

**P**aper: A thin flexible material in sheets or leaves, made from rags, wood pulp, or other fibrous material, and used to write or print on, wrap, decorate, etc.

## BEFORE PAPER

From the beginnings of the development of mankind, people have always tried in some way to communicate with each other. Speaking was first, then drawing, then printing. Each of these transitions spanned periods of hundreds or possibly thousands of years.

Prehistoric man had no means other than the human voice to transfer ideas, and early on mastered a positive method of oral communication which conveyed intelligible meanings among those primitive tribes by the use of guttural sounds.

With the advent of drawing, there evolved a method of communication that raised man's intellectual powers to a much higher plane than would have been possible through the utterance of vocal sounds only. Even the crudest drawings on the walls of caves required previously untapped ingenuity and facility and employed skills previously unknown to prehistoric peoples. This primitive start led to the development of more workable materials than drawing upon cave walls or in the sand with a pointed stick.

Wood, metal, stone, ceramics, leaves, bark, cloth, papyrus, and parchment were all used as basic surfaces on which to incise or inscribe hieroglyphics and characters.

Lacking more pliable and flexible materials, each of these substances served their purpose for many centuries.

In 250 B.C., the Chinese scholar Ming T'ien invented the camel's hair brush. This innovation not only revolutionized the writing of Chinese characters, but was instrumental in furthering the development of woven cloth as a writing material. Woven cloth, along with the papyrus of Egypt and the parchment of Asia Minor, made the manuscript roll possible — the first form of a book in its true sense.

It was not until many centuries after the development of paper that the first text printed upon paper was completed — the original printing of Empress Shotoku's million "dharani," in 770 A.D. Though this occurred in Japan, its concept was Chinese and made possible only through Chinese ingenuity and influence.

The origins of most crafts that we now take so much for granted are for the most part obscure. This includes felt-making, weaving, ceramics, printing and, most particularly, the methods of early paper-making technique. Though the inventive Chinese craftsmen were imprinting skillfully executed engravings of religious subjects as early as 868 A.D., no delineations of the paper-making craft were rendered until the Sung Ying-hsing woodblock prints appeared in 1634. There was a similar lack of concern in Europe. No pictures appeared until 1568 when in a little book of trades there was an exquisite woodcut of "Der Papierer" by Josh Amman.

Compensating somewhat for the absence of early illustrations from both the East and the West are the efforts of archaeologists who have unearthed actual specimens or original papers embracing the product of practically every century since the invention of paper making in 105 A.D. through its introduction in the Orient and its 800 years of history in Europe. From these fragments and sheets, still bearing impressions of the woven cloth, bamboo, grass, and metal wire molds upon which they were formed, historians of the craft have been able to piece together the actual paper-making techniques employed by those ancient artisans.

Paper should not be confused with papyrus, bark paper, rice paper, parchment, or vellum. True paper is classified as thin sheets made from fibers that are macerated until each single filament is a separate unit. The fibers are then mixed with water and lifted from the water by a sieve-like screen in the form of a thin layer. The water drains off leaving a sheet of matted fiber on the surface of the screen.

Papyrus antedates paper by many, many years. It is a laminated substance made by slicing the plant stalks lengthwise and pasting the thin strips together in much the same way sheets of laminated wood are built up. It was considered less formal than parchment.

Bark paper is made in the South Pacific Islands from the beaten inner bark of the tapa-paper mulberry. It is beaten and flattened and folded again and again. A piece of bark originally barely three inches wide can assume a width of eighteen inches!

Rice paper is really a misnomer. It is not made from either rice or paper. When sea captains and sailors first brought specimens to England and the New England states, the Europeans and Americans thought the material was genuine paper, but they were puzzled as to what material was used to make it. They erroneously called it "rice paper" and the name stuck. It is cut spirally from the pith of the kung-shue plant that grows in the hills of northern Formosa (Taiwan).

The use of parchment for a writing surface also antedates paper. The name parchment is derived from Pergamum, an ancient city of Mysia in Asia Minor. Though it was probably used as early as 1500 B.C., the King of Pergamum (197-159 B.C.) is usually given credit for its invention. It is thought to have been brought about to rival papyrus in Egypt since the Egyptian rulers would not allow papyrus to be exported. Genuine parchment and vellum are made from animal skins.

Parchment is made from the split inner skin of the sheep provided the skin is suitable for so exacting a purpose. Otherwise, it is made into chamois or suede. The outer wool side of the skin is made into strong leather. Vellum is usually calfskin but goat and lamb are also used. The entire skin is usually used. Sometimes vellum may be distinguished from parchment by the grain and hair marks which produce a somewhat irregular surface.

Parchment and vellum are made in similar ways. The skin is washed, rubbed with lime, any hair is removed, the skin is scraped with a curved knife and washed again. It is then stretched and scraped some more to even out the thickness. The final step is to dust the skin with powdered chalk and rub it with pumice. The modern methods for this craft are almost identical to those used by the ancient European parchment makers.

## PAPER'S BEGINNINGS

The date of the first paper making is usually cited as 105 A.D. It was in that year that a man named Ts'ai Lun astounded the Chinese Imperial Court by proclaiming the invention of paper. Ts'ai Lun did not set out to invent paper. He was more interested in ingratiating himself with Her Majesty, and since he was in charge of the Royal Supply Closet, he realized that the best way to do that was to make better, more economical stationery.

It is doubtful that Ts'ai Lun actually invented paper. Historians are inclined to believe he adapted the idea from the artisans of his home province, who had been making rudimentary paper for 100 years. The perfection of the paper-making process was his real achievement. That process was based on a principle which, for all the computerized sophistication and complex machinery of today, has essentially remained unchanged. The Chinese people themselves closely identify Ts'ai Lun with the beginning of paper making.

This early paper-making process consisted of pounding and working a wet mass of short cellulose fibers until they formed a smooth dispersion when mixed with water. Sheets were formed by filtration of the fibers on a flat screen which, upon drying, bonded together as a result of the pounding. As simple as this process seems to be, paper making appears to have been invented only once — in China.

A specimen of what was then considered the oldest paper in the world was found in 1942 by Professors Lao Kan and Shih Chang-ju of the Academia Sinica in the ruins of a watchtower in Tsakhortei, south of the Bayan Bogdo mountains in the modern Ninghsia area of north central China. This fragment, a crumpled ball of coarse, heavy paper on which about two dozen decipherable characters are written, is believed to have been buried by accident when the military post was abandoned during an attack by the western Hsi-ch¢iange tribe around 109 A.D.

In 1957, scraps of thin, yellowish paper were found at a tomb at Pa-ch'iao in Sian, a modern city in Shensi province southeast of Ninghsia. These paper specimens may be older than those found in Tsakhortei, and are believed to belong to the western Han dynasty, 202 B.C.-9 A.D.

## SPREADING THE WORD

The art of all paper making was derived from the Orient, and the Chinese managed to keep it a secret for several centuries. In China, an exalted discovery like paper was the property of the Court. Considering that status, plus China's closed society, it's not really surprising that over 600 years would pass before word of paper making leaked to the Western world. It took the fortunes of war to spread the word.

Samarkand, a city in south central U.S.S.R. near the Chinese and Afghanistan borders, was the first of the outside world to learn of this craft. Among the prisoners taken by the governor of Samarkand on a raid of Chinese territory in 751 A.D. were several paper makers who offered the knowledge of their craft in exchange for their freedom. With its abundant stock of flax and hemp and a ready supply of water from irrigation canals, Samarkand was naturally suited to paper making, and the craft developed quickly. It soon became an important article of commerce.

From Samarkand this craft spread to Baghdad and Damascus and eventually to Egypt and Morocco. The earliest known use of paper in Egypt was 800 A.D. It was probably exported from Samarkand or Baghdad. True paper was made in Egypt for the first time in 900 A.D. employing the Chinese method. For five centuries the Arabs monopolized paper making in the West.

Paper making did not spread to Europe for more than a thousand years following its invention, but once there, paper making flourished. Johann Gutenberg's invention of printing with movable type spurred an ever increasing demand for paper. The Latin Bible, known as the Gutenberg Bible, was the first book known to have been printed with movable type. It's a toss-up whether paper making was introduced first into Spain or Italy. Each has its own claims on it.

The first use of paper in Italy, thought to have been imported from the East, was in the form of a register written by Giovanni Scriba and dated 1154-66. Not until 1276 was another specimen of paper found in Italy. That was the date of the first mention of the Fabriano paper mills.

The Moors introduced paper making when they captured Spain and wasted no time establishing local paper mills. By the middle of the 12th century, the paper-making industry was in two Spanish cities — Xativa (or Jativa) and Toledo.

France and Germany established their first paper mills in the middle of the 14th century. A little over 100 years after that Poland and England established their own paper-making industries. Little by little other parts of Europe and Asia followed suit.

## PAPER MAKING IN THE NEW WORLD

The history of paper making in America can be traced back almost as far as the history of America itself. Like many other items needed by the early colonists, paper was at first imported from Europe. The first book to be printed in the Colonies was the *Bay Psalm Book* in 1640.

The craft of paper making made its way to the Colonies in 1690 when William Rittenhouse and William Bradford established the first paper mill in Germantown, Pennsylvania, near Philadelphia. The same year Benjamin Harris published America's first newspaper, in Boston.

Though writing and scholarship held high priority in New England, it was 1728 before the paper-making industry really started there. That year a group of Boston merchants built a mill on the banks of the Neponset River in Milton, Massachusetts. Paper was made by hand at this and other early mills. It was 1827 before any paper-making machinery was brought to America.

On June 20, 1788, Benjamin Franklin read a treatise on paper making before the members of the American Philosophical Society of Philadelphia. It was later published in the *Transactions of the American Philosophical Society,* and constitutes the only strictly American contribution to the bibliography of paper making which appeared in the 18th century.

In 1840, the first utterings of America's literary voice were heard. Richard Henry Dana published *Two Years Before the Mast,* James Fenimore Cooper wrote *The Deerslayer,* and Poe, Melville, and Longfellow were in the wings practicing their craft. The demand for reliable supplies of quality paper rose sharply.

In 1842, construction started on the Congin Paper Mill, a building which was to mark the beginning of the S. D. Warren Company. Officially, the S. D. Warren Company dates from February 1854, when two Boston merchants of paper and paper-making materials, Dennis Warren and Otis Daniell, purchased the Congin Paper Mill in Westbrook, Maine. The two were partners in the firm of Grant, Daniell & Co. and hoped to assure a steady supply of paper, which they would sell through their Boston company.

## PAPER-MAKING METHODS

Paper lasts well when properly made and properly stored. The first paper was made of rags pounded and worked and combined with water to form a smooth mixture which was spread on a flat screen for drying. The dried fibers bonded together. The first paper makers used a mortar and pestle for pounding.

Excellent, long-lasting paper resulted from the paper-making process which the Europeans learned from the Arabs. These directions were written in 1025: "Soak flax in quicklime, rub with the hands, and spread out in the sun to dry. Return flax to fresh quicklime and repeat the process a number of times. Then wash flax many times to cleanse it of the quicklime. Next, pound flax with a mortar, wash it and put it into molds of the proper size. Care should be taken to have an even thickness of paper. Leave paper to dry. Treat with rice water or bran water or starch. Glazing the surface of the paper is also helpful."

As long as the paper makers adhered to these fundamentals, they made excellent paper. Old books in the European libraries are still in relatively good condition. Gutenberg's invention in the mid-15th century of the movable type press did for paper making what the internal combustion engine did for the oil industry. The demand for paper soared and paper makers began a search for faster and cheaper methods of production. A long and slow decline in the quality of paper was the result. Rags became scarce and wood pulp was substituted. Iron stampers driven by water power were introduced. This not only beat the fibers, it nearly disintegrated them and pounded some of the iron right into the paper. The iron caused oxidation which in turn caused the paper to turn yellow.

In 1798, a breakthrough occurred that brought paper making into the mechanized age and made mass production possible. It was the brainchild of a millhand named Nicolas-Louis Robert, who mastered the principle of the continuous web paper machine, a device capable of forming paper by pouring liquid pulp on a length of wire screen. Unfortunately, Robert wasn't a master of finance and died penniless. The machine was refined and marketed by the Fourdrinier brothers, Sealy and Henry, and the machine still bears their name. The principle that resulted in the Fourdrinier machine still applies, even though paper-making machines have gone through numerous evolutions.

## THE ENEMIES OF PAPER

### Acids

Acids are the archenemy of paper but seem to be used in abundance in its manufacture. Excessive bleaching by early paper makers caused paper to become quite brittle. Chlorine was very cheap to use, and perhaps the damage it could wreak was not fully understood. The breakdown of the chlorine residues was slow but in turn produced a gradual build-up of hydrochloric acid.

### Alum

Alum, which is strongly acid, is almost universally used in paper making for almost all grades of paper. It has many uses in counteracting manufacturing difficulties. One of its functions is as sizing.

### Inks

Throughout documented history, man has experimented with all types of writing fluids and compounds in his search for a substance of clarity, permanence, and ease of use. Inks used by primitive man were composed of dyes made from tree bark and berries. Even blood was tried, but its clotting factors precluded a smooth, even flow or storage, and the exposed bottle tended to attract flies. These early inhabitants also used sepia from squid, octopus, and cuttlefish, but most of these inks proved difficult to store, hard to use, and not at all permanent.

Again, it was the indomitable Chinese who found the solution. Their ink, called "India" or "China" ink, was made from carbon black, water, and gum. It was permanent, easy to store, and convenient to use — everything its predecessors were not. China and Japan still use it today, and engineers, artists, and draftsmen prize it for its color and indelibility.

The Arabs developed a similar ink called "Lampblack." It was made of oil-tar soot, gum, and honey, and manufactured in small cakes which could be dissolved in water to create ink.

Iron gall ink, which was thought to have been used as early as the second century, is the type of most concern to paper conservators. It was a midnight black color when first used, but faded to a rusty brown because of the evaporation of the water in the ink. It closely resembles the black and blue-black inks of today which are made from refined chemicals and preservatives.

Iron gall ink owes it existence to a by-product of the female gall wasp, whose stinging of oak trees and some other types of plants produces an abnormal swelling or "gall." When this gall is dried and powdered and mixed with certain types of iron salts, it produces a durable ink. Iron gall ink is extremely corrosive because of the gallic and tannic acids in its chemical composition. Over a long period of time and under the right conditions — excessive humidity, for example — this ink can eat right through a sheet of paper. Deacidification can stem this destruction.

It was the 11th century before iron gall ink was in common use, and it remained the most prominent writing fluid until the 1860s and the invention of aniline inks. Aniline inks were made from the blue dye of the indigo plant and were water soluble. A benzine derivative is used by modern manufacturers.

## Atmospheric Conditions

Atmospheric conditions can also cause acid accumulations in paper. Sulfur dioxide is present in small amounts in most industrial areas. It is not in itself harmful to paper. But, in combination with small amounts of iron or copper used in some papers, the sulfur dioxide is changed to sulfuric acid which will rapidly destroy the fibrous structure and render the paper brittle.

## Light

The universal destroyer of organic matter is ultraviolet light, and paper is no exception. Light, especially the ultraviolet-laden destructiveness of direct sunlight, causes ink on paper to fade. Reflected light and fluorescent light can also cause fading. Only total darkness forever will completely safeguard paper from the harmfulness of light, but sheets of Plexiglas scientifically designed to filter out ultraviolet rays are available for use in framing a paper item.

## Temperature

Temperature, too, has its adverse effects on paper. Since paper, like wood, is organic, its fibers expand with moisture and contract when dry. Paper exposed to temperatures of 75 degrees or more and humidity of 30 degrees or less dries and becomes brittle. This dry, hot atmosphere hastens the aging process. In light of these facts, is it any wonder what havoc can be wrought from storage in a stuffy attic or storeroom, a damp cellar or garage (Fig. 8)?

## Dust

Dust has a detrimental effect on paper, too. The sharp edges of dust particles penetrate the paper with a cutting and scouring effect, and once embedded, cannot be removed. Dust also carries microorganisms that can infect the paper. They are fungus spores that thrive in a stagnant, humid environment. Treatment for this infection is difficult and demands expert

*Figure 8.. The back cover of a* Life *magazine dated October 8, 1956, which was stored in a basement locker. The basement sprung a leak and water got into the locker.*

advice. A condition called "foxing" may also occur. If the paper contains iron particles, fungus, or both, brownish freckle-like spots can develop in a humid environment. The term foxing is derived from the color of a fox's fur.

## Insects

Some insects are real bookworms, too. Book-lice, silverfish, termites, woodworms, and cockroaches can all be destructive to paper. It's not always the paper they go for. Some prefer the glue used in bindings, stamps, envelopes, and other paper items to any kind of food.

## Man

Inadvertent though it may be, man, too, contributes to the destruction of paper. Each time a piece of paper is handled, it deteriorates a little. Sweat and skin oils contribute to the damage. Any librarian can tell you about the

*Figure 9. Marriage license dating from 1904 showing the ravages of time and attempts to repair it with transparent tape.*

wear and tear on the most used books and show you horrible examples.

Man's penchant for transparent tape and other adhesives, plastic bags, paper clips, staples, and pins is also a contributing factor to the deterioration of paper (Fig. 9). Any one of them alone is enough, but how often are they seen in various combinations?

## WHAT OF THE FUTURE OF PAPER?

Preserving books and other paper items of the future is more a matter of prevention than preservation. The simple expedient to the prevention of the acid paper problem in the future is the use of "permanent" papers. Permanent papers are estimated to have a useful life span measured in increments of hundreds rather than the tens of years of acid papers. The word "permanent" is used as opposed to "acid-free" to distinguish between two types of acid-free paper — "acid-free" and "acid-free buffered." Acid-free paper is free of acid when it is made, but the assurance is not there that the paper will remain acid-free as it ages. Acid-free buffered paper is free of acid, but also contains substantial amounts of an acid neutralizer (alkaline) such as calcium carbonate to neutralize any acidity

which may develop in the paper itself or intrude itself upon the paper from an outside environment. Buffered acid-free paper is preferred for serious longevity and true archival qualities.

Permanent papers must also be free of lignin, the natural cement that holds fibers in their place in the living structure. It is the lignin that causes the quick browning and embrittlement in paper made from unpurified wood pulp. Various methods are used to separate the fibers used in permanent paper from the lignin.

Books continue to be produced by the millions with the acidic seeds of self-destruction built in, compounding problems for the future while failing to provide a permanent record of our present times. The fault is not entirely that of the paper manufacturers who responded to publishing demands for low-cost book papers. Neither does the fault lie entirely with the publishers who responded to public demands for low-cost books. Permanence was not even an afterthought in overall plans for book production.

The solution to the problem, of course, lies in convincing book publishers to use permanent papers. Many university presses are doing just that, but they represent only a small fraction of the total book publishing industry. A recent government study revealed that only 15 to 25 percent of the books published today are composed of acid-free paper which will guarantee their survival beyond the next fifty years. But things are looking up.

Recently, economic forces and anti-pollution laws have increased interest in acid-free paper production. Alkaline papers have been around since the late 1800s, but in limited supply and used primarily for their archival value. Manufacturing was difficult, and there were undesirable characteristics that sometimes caused problems. The processes for making acid-free book paper were developed in the 1940s, but for reasons unrelated to permanence.

Though the problems of disintegrated books have been recognized years before, only in the last thirty years have publishers paid much attention. After a brief outcry from librarians, several publishers did proclaim that from then on they would use only acid-free paper, but except for a few publishers, the practice was short-lived because of lack of commitment and supply shortages.

Not until 1959 was a synthetic sizing agent compatible with the alkaline process developed. This generated a spate of initially cautious conversions. Technological changes to shift to acid-free paper production are expensive. Conversely, plants making acid-free paper produce less pollution to the streams and rivers and less damage to the environment than those manufacturing acid paper. Another benefit of acid-free papers is that because of the calcium carbonate, the paper is inherently brighter and more opaque.

Several paper manufacturers are not routinely producing acid-free (alkaline) book papers at competitive prices. The largest ones are S. D. Warren Company, P. H. Glatfelter Co., and Finch, Pruyn & Company, Inc. Mohawk Paper Mills, Inc. is not far behind them.

S. D. Warren Company switched its manufacturing from an acid to an alkaline base in the early 1950s because mountains of calcium carbonate had been piling up in the yard of one of the Warren plants in Maine, and the company was looking for a way to use this pure white and inexpensive product. At that time, paper permanence did not enter into the picture. It is now producing alkaline papers with a life expectancy of 300 years at a profit, and the cost to publishers is no more than acid paper. S. D. Warren Company now has four plants — in Mobile, Alabama; Muskegon, Michigan; Somerset, in Skowhegan and Fairfield, Maine; and the original mill in Westbrook, Maine. Each has devised it own system, compatible which its location, to maintain high environmental standards for air and water quality.

P. H. Glatfelter Co., the largest supplier of book papers in the United States, maintains three mills — the original mill in Spring Grove, Pennsylvania, the Neenah Mill in Neenah, Wisconsin, and a mill in Pisgah Forest, North Carolina. All of them manufacture papers entirely by the alkaline (acid-free) process. The company also produces papers for business forms, stationery, annual reports, maps, advertising, and many other routine or specialty applications. Today, the art of making quality paper is done in combination with the science of improving the environment. P. H. Glatfelter Company has been an industry leader in meeting and exceeding established standards for air and water quality.

Finch, Pruyn & Company, Inc. has made all its paper alkaline since 1982. In addition to being made under alkaline conditions, these papers contain substantial quantities of calcium carbonate which serves as an acid receptor and neutralizer. Calcium carbonate filler was deemed so important to the quality of their sheets that, in 1984, they built the first on-site plant to produce very high quality precipitated calcium carbonate filler.

Since 1981, Mohawk Paper Mills, Inc., too, has converted its mills to the alkaline process of paper making for all their printing grades.

In all probability, we may not want nor will it be necessary to have all books last 300 years. With most libraries ever-plagued by a space shortage, lesser-used books will be destined for microfilm anyway. Stacks will be replaced by row upon row of microfilm readers. Much library material has already been transferred to microfilm — prime examples: newspapers and periodicals. Students of the future will be more technologically-oriented than ever. Electronic retrieval of information will be the norm for them.

## AN AMERICAN NATIONAL STANDARD FOR PERMANENT PAPER

The National Information Standards Organization (NISO) has developed an American National Standard for permanent paper. The objective of this standard is to establish criteria for permanence of uncoated paper — paper that should last at least several hundred years without significant deterioration under normal library use and storage conditions. By defining permanent paper and encouraging its use, it is hoped that the selection of such paper by pub-

PULP AND PAPER MAKING

BY
THE P. H. GLATFELTER CO.
SPRING GROVE, PA.

lishers will be simplified, and that comparable future preservation problems can be prevented.

In addition, publications printed on paper that meets this standard should observe these compliance requirements:

1. Statement of Compliance: Applicable publications should carry the following statement: "The paper used in this publication meets the minimum requirement of American National Standard for Information Sciences — Permanence of Paper for Printed Library Materials, ANSI Z39.48-1984."

2. Symbol of Compliance: "In addition to the statement of compliance, the symbol given below may be used to indicate compliance with this standard. It is the mathematical symbol denoting infinity set inside a circle."

3. Placement of Statement and Symbol: "The statement of compliance shall appear on the verso of the title page of a book or on the masthead or copyright area of a periodical publication along with the symbol, if used. One or both may also be used in any other position on the product."

4. Use in Advertising, Promotion, Reviews, and Cataloging in Publication: "For all publications that comply with this standard, the statement, symbol, or both, should be used in advertising, promotion, reviews, and publishers' catalogs. Publishers are also strongly encouraged to indicate compliance with this standard when they submit material to the Cataloging in Publication (CIP) program. The CIP data will then include this information as part of the ISBN qualifier."

## PAPER AS COLLECTIBLE

Paper items are among the most neglected of collectibles. Often they are tossed into a box and stuck up on a shelf or in an attic or basement or garage. What a shock and surprise it can be a few years hence when the opened box reveals yellowing shreds or a tangled mass of stuck together pages.

Paper is the fragile collectible. Even cardboard doesn't retain its properties indefinitely. Man made paper as weak as man once made it strong. It has enemies within and on all sides. It has been beaten, mauled, neglected, abandoned, rejected, and left at the mercy of the elements. It is meant to be treated with respect and handled with dignity and grace.

# 3
# What is Being Done to Preserve our Paper Heritage?

**M**an alone, of all the animals, wants to leave his mark on the universe. He wants to believe that his works will live on in perpetuity and add value to the human heritage.

All the monuments, mechanical wonders, and other manmade marvels may live on for generations after him, but they remain just so many piles of stone and wood and metal and plastic without the written word. Structures can give future generations some idea of the environs of their ancestors, but they can't tell the whys and the wherefores, the hows and the whens. It is the written chain of knowledge passed from person to person and generation to generation that connects everyone to everyone else and everything to everything else — the faith, passions, and skills, the horrors and beauties of lost generations.

The written record is a fragile one. Even the most important parts of that record will not be saved by accident, much less the ordinary. Anyone who has any sense of the importance of the continuing human experience must face the problem of preserving the human record. Failure to do so is tantamount to turning one's back on history.

Researchers have estimated that the life span of most paper in institutions and private collections at the present time is, at most, fifty years. Millions of books in our nation's libraries are already falling apart and millions more are

threatened. The catalysts of destruction are built in and increase their destructive force with each passing year — a slow-acting time bomb set to self-destruct before we reach the end of this century.

## PRESERVATION IS NOT CONSERVATION IS NOT RESTORATION

Though each of these terms is interrelated, they are not the same. Each refers to the maintenance of an item as close as possible to its original form, but one refers to before, one during, and one after the fact.

### Preservation — Before the Fact

This term has been used loosely to refer to something saved from extinction by whatever means. Technically, preservation is defined as keeping something in a perfect unaltered condition or maintaining something in an unchanged form; the placing of something in an environment from its beginnings which will maintain it in near mint condition. Obviously, this is an ideal situation, and not usually the norm when seeking out historical artifacts and collectibles.

When some of the most desirable items came into existence, not much thought was given to preserving them. They were made for a purpose, and most were put into daily use. At its beginnings, paper was made and meant only for the use of government officials and the affluent. The common folk not only couldn't afford it, most of them couldn't read and write anyway. Consequently, some documents did survive, if not in mint condition.

### Conservation — During the Fact

This term is defined as preservation from loss, waste, or harm. It is often used in referring to preservation of our natural resources, even though it can pertain to maintaining anything in a state that will keep it from harm or further harm, no matter what its condition.

Paper is one of those items that appears to be able to take care of itself. Unfortunately, many decades passed before the self-destructive elements of paper were discovered. Some of our most valuable items have been rescued from obscurity and must be maintained in an atmosphere that will prevent any further deterioration.

### Restoration — After the Fact

This term is defined as the act of putting something back into its original condition or as near original as possible. Original can be original only once, but there are ways of removing grime, removing wrinkles, repairing tears, replacing missing parts, replacing paint and ink, and giving new life to something that shows the ravages of time and neglect. Depending on the item, most restoration is best left to experts. Special equipment is available for minor repairs, and this special equipment should be used to avoid further damage.

## WHAT IS BEING DONE?

Preservation of printed matter may well be the great forgotten problem of the 20th century. Specialists and librarians have been aware of the problem for some time and efforts have been made, but in some quarters it's almost a case of "too little, too late." Surprisingly enough, scholars, men of affairs, and users of this printed matter are the ones who have passed over the problem. Perhaps the fault is that the problem is so insidious. Houses and buildings and furnishings remain intact while the forces that destroy printed matter do their dirty work.

All papers that ultimately become part of the country's manuscript and archives collections, including bond papers, carbon papers, mimeograph papers, and second sheets, are in little better condition than is the paper used for book production. But paper deterioration is not the whole problem. Many inks, including those for typewriter inks and the dyes used in carbon paper, are subject to fading.

The problem is really a two-headed monster. There is not just the question of how to deal with the materials, the ink, and the bindings. There is also the question of the priorities and techniques of selecting what is to be preserved, of assigning the responsibility for those choices, and for securing cooperation. Needs and opportunities for collaboration must be found before the technological solutions can be used effectively.

## EARLY PRESERVATION EFFORTS

As early as 1898, the then Librarian of Congress, John Russell Young, recognized the problem and tried to effect a change in the copyright law to require book publishers to publish a few copies of each title on good paper, but to no avail.

Early in this century, Harry Miller Leidenberg of the New York Public Library tried to get newspaper publishers to do the same thing, and for many years, *The New York Times* published a rag-paper edition.

The first attempt to solve the paper preservation problem on a nationwide scale occurred in 1962 when the Association of Research Libraries, with a grant from the Council on Library Resources, asked Gordon Williams, Director of the Center for Research Libraries, to study the problem. Mr. Williams did so, in depth, and prepared a detailed report. Though the Association approved the report in 1965 and issued it in 1966, no action was taken on Mr. Williams recommendations for a number of reasons. The entire library community did recognize, however, both the importance of the problem and the validity of Mr. Williams' basic recommendations.

In 1972, a second report was prepared by Warren J. Haas, then Director of Libraries at the University of Pennsylvania and then Vice President and Director of Libraries at Columbia University. The Haas report, in addition to confirming the same basic problems as the Williams report, also pointed to the inherent difficulties in carrying out the course of action proposed by Mr. Williams. Mr. Haas did make suggestions as to how these difficulties might be overcome, and offered some additional recommendations. Once more, for varied and numerous reasons, no national program was established at that time.

## THE LIBRARY OF CONGRESS EFFORT

The Library of Congress and the Association of Research Libraries did hold a meeting in December 1965, as a result of the Williams report, to discuss the need for a national preservation program, and it was agreed that such a program was needed. The Library of Congress agreed to establish it, set no timetable, but began work almost at once. Following this joint conference, the Library of Congress made plans for an expanded and centralized preservation effort. These plans included:

1. Centralization of the total preservation budget to provide more effective utilization of funds, and a more unified budget justification to Congress.

2. Centralization of preservation activities in one office with the exception of those related to the preservation of motion pictures and sound recording which remain under the domain of the Motion Picture Section of the Prints and Photographs Division and the Recorded Sound Section of the Music Division.

3. The establishment of a Preservation Research and Testing Office and a modern conser-

vation-restoration facility under direct Library control to replace the existing restoration activity that was under the supervision of the Government Printing Office.

Operating as the Office of the Assistant Director for Preservation, it consists of five units:

1. The Binding Office is responsible for the preparation of all routine Library binding. The Library of Congress writes its own specifications and awards binding contracts by public bidding. This office's annual budget of more than one million dollars enables the Library to bind some 250,000 volumes each year.

2. The Collections Maintenance Office is responsible for the physical maintenance, care, and cleaning of the collections, and the moving and shifting of the collections in stack and storage areas.

3. The Preservation Microfilming Office is responsible for the administration of the Library's program for preserving the intellectual content of the deteriorated and brittle materials in the collections. Overall, the Library spends approximately one million dollars each year on this microfilming program. The actual camera work is the responsibility of the Library's Photoduplication Service.

4. The Preservation Research and Testing Office is responsible for a research program on preservation problems. These range from the mechanism and chemistry of paper degradation to the testing and evaluation of the supplies and materials used in preservation work at the Library of Congress.

5. The Restoration Office is responsible for the conservation-restoration program at the Library. It provides treatment of all kinds from the conservation of manuscripts to the conservation and restoration of rare books.

The Library of Congress is the world's largest library and has put much effort into perfecting a deacidification cure for its own holdings. Three and a half million items are already too fragile for handling. In the early 1970's, the Library initiated a major preservation program.

Since the onset of its research slightly more than twenty-five years ago, the Library of Congress has concentrated almost exclusively on one chemical method to neutralize acids. Early research indicated that a handful of books could be deacidified by subjecting them to vapors of diethyl zinc (DEZ) in a pressure cooker. However, the system still needs refining, and the Library has been criticized for focusing on this one method and ignoring other techniques.

With the help of the National Aeronautics and Space Administration, in 1982 the Library set up a pilot DEZ plant at the Goddard Space Flight Center in Maryland because Goddard had big vacuum chambers for conducting the test. For the deacidification process, books are stacked in special carts and placed in a closed chamber. The air is pumped out to produce a vacuum. The vacuum and a slight heating reduce the amount of water normally present in paper. DEZ gas is introduced into the chamber continuously at low pressure. It both neutralizes the existing acid and reacts with water to form zinc oxide, which neutralizes future acid. Excess DEZ is recycled out of the chamber and reused. Water vapor is then pumped into the chamber to restore moisture to the books. Estimates are that it will take 50-55 hours to treat books in multiple chambers that hold one to three thousand books each. DEZ and its byproducts are considered non-toxic, but DEZ does need special handling because in liquid form it ignites spontaneously when exposed to air. It is also quick to react with water-forming ethane gas.

Early in December 1985, at the pilot plant, water was accidentally mixed with liquid DEZ which resulted in a fire in the vacuum chamber causing significant but not major damage.

Two months later, on Valentine's Day, a researcher opened a valve in the system which triggered an explosion that blew apart the walls and two doors to the equipment room. Inadvertently, brine had been mixed with liquid DEZ resulting in a tremendous buildup of pressure of ethane in the pipeline. Fortunately, no one was injured and no books were in the chamber during either accident.

Following the explosion, NASA ordered the unit demolished because it could not account for all DEZ believed to be still in the system. Library of Congress officials protested such drastic measures, contending the pipes could be tapped to locate the DEZ. But a week later NASA called in the Army Corps of Engineers to level the plant with explosives.

NASA's report on the accident revealed serious flaws in the management of the experiments. The report pointed out that the crew failed "to follow good practice in the development and implementation of operating procedures," and "a certain amount of improvisation occurred during the operations which preceded these mishaps."

Enter the deacidification process that is now being tested at a pilot deacidification facility at the Texas Alkyls Chemical Co. near Houston. Some experts are of the opinion that the Library's experimental process is encouraging, but the technology has yet to be proven on a commercial scale. The completion of this small-scale facility is enabling the Library to move ahead with an engineering test phase, as preparation for designing the large-scale facility needed to deacidify the Library's collections.

In addition to testing engineering concepts and allowing a scale-up design, this test facility is for refinement processes, evaluating equipment modifications and improvements, and developing quality control procedures. Procedures will also be developed for deacidifying other paper formats, such as maps, folios, and manuscripts. It is also anticipated that Texas Alkyls' experience with the Library of Congress deacidification project will open the doors to future deacidification services needed by other research libraries.

The consensus at the Library of Congress was that the NASA and Northrop Services were lacking in chemical processing expertise, and the Library of Congress should have consulted the chemical industry from the beginning.

The Library of Congress now wants to contract with a private company to build a facility that would use the Library's patented technique for treating deteriorating paper items. A private company would be able to build a facility large enough to process more than the twenty million items from the Library of Congress collections. Collections from university and research libraries could be treated as well. A government-built treatment plant would be able to handle only the collections of the Library of Congress and other federal agencies. Congress would have to approve the licensing plan, under which the money — $5 million - already allocated to build the facility would be used instead to finance treatment of books. The proposal is cheaper and less risky than previous plans, and Akzo Chemicals, Inc., the parent company of Texas Alkyls, has already presented an unsolicited proposal to the Library to build such a facility since the DEZ test facility in Texas is up and running well. At this writing, the Senate is all for it, but it is stalled in the House. It seems that a U.S. Representative, at the urging of a small Pittsburgh firm marketing a system called the "Bookkeeping Process," which incorporates liquid-phase freon, says the Library of Congress plan would hurt other deacidification enterprises.

## THE WEI T'O SYSTEM

The debate goes on between competing methods of deacidifying the paper in books; on one side the Library of Congress, on the other side Richard D. Smith, a book conservator originally trained as an engineer. Smith returned to school when he was in his thirties to study library science. He began development of a deacidification method in the bathtub of his Chicago apartment. His Wei T'o System (named for a Chinese god) is now sold to libraries here and abroad. The system incorporates solvents to impregnate the paper of books with an alkaline agent — an organic magnesium carbonate is nonaqueous and safe for the users as well as for most books. It is, thus far, the only method on the market to deacidify books en masse. Wei T'o's first major customer is the National Library of Canada. Over thirty-four Wei T'o "Soft Spray" installations exist today.

Wei T'o's "Soft Spray" system works like a giant aerosol spray. Its use is so straightforward, almost amounting to pointing and spraying, that ordinary persons can produce professional quality conservation treatments following a brief training period. A steady worker can "Soft Spray" 3 to 3½ (300 page/150 leaves) books per hour. With allowances for interruptions and other tasks, about thirty books per day, 150 books per week, or 7,500 books per year can be treated per person. The cost per treatment is approximately $9.00 per book.

The "Soft Spray" system has three essential components:

1. Delivery system — spray gun, hose connectors.
2. Self-pressurized deacidification spray.
3. Self-pressurized cleaning solution.

A fourth component, a spray booth and exhaust system, the Wei T'o Stainless Steel Bench Top "Soft Spray" Booth, comes complete with 115 volt electric lead, explosion resistant exhaust fans, and five feet of flexible 10″ I. D. exhaust duct, and is ready to install. The booth features two spraying platforms, one for books and single sheets and the other for single sheets only. The cost for the basic equipment is slightly more than $2,000. The deacidification and cleaning solutions are bought by the 4.5 gallon cylinder. Wei T'o estimates that between 2,000 and 5,000 8½″ by 11″ documents can be deacidified and protected against aging with each 4.5 gallon cylinder of "Soft Spray."

## RARE ITEMS
## GET RARE TREATMENT

Few of the millions of items ever drawn or printed are destined for individual conservation. But for items that rate it, preservationists will go to unusual lengths to save a rare paper treasure. Painstakingly, conservators combine the skills of a chemist and the creativity of an artist to restore books, maps, manuscripts, music scores, documents, and photographs. Prime examples are:

### At the Library of Congress —

An old book may get a new, hand-done Binding (Fig. 10) and a custom-made box sporting a small bone hook for closure.

The title may be applied in calligraphic lettering.

Single sheets of a book may be dipped into an alkaline solution to neutralize the acid in the paper, and dried separately on racks.

Small boxes hand-constructed from acid-free paper board encase a series of 1930's children's "Big Little Books."

All of the 1917 editions of *Izvestiia*, the Soviet newspaper's first year of publication, have been encapsulated in clear polyester sheets.

Heat-set tissue mending is also an option (Fig. 11).

### At the National Archives —

A team of conservators care for this nation's most valuable historical documents.

Small holes in an old Civil War document were repaired with a patch that is virtually invisible because the paper was made to match in weight and correspond in watercolor tinting with the original.

A torn black-and-white photograph by Margaret Bourke-White, missing a half-inch square spot on the side, was restored with the recreated missing piece containing just the right amount of gloss and grays.

The most elaborate and costly conservation efforts are centered on the nation's charters — the Bill of Rights, the Declaration of Independence, and the Constitution. Our forefathers had the foresight to write these documents on parchment which has been quite durable over the centuries. Stored in helium-filled cabinets which were sealed in 1952, the condition of these documents is constantly monitored. A high-resolution camera in tandem with a computer measures minute changes in the documents.

### At the Newberry Library in Chicago —

An ultra-modern book stack building was opened in 1982 to maintain 1.2 million books and 5 million manuscripts at a constant 60 degrees Fahrenheit and a carefully controlled humidity. Books must be used only in the building to avoid destructive atmospheric changes.

## PRESERVING THE CONTENT IF NOT THE SUBSTANCE

While all this was going on, other factions have not been idly watching. Experts are of the opinion that for the present, microfilm is the most effective process for saving the intellectual content of the largest number of endangered books while scholars wait to learn whether more advanced technologies such as optical disks are viable alternatives.

The Committee on Preservation and Access, an offshoot of the Council for Library Resources, an influential private advocacy group, produced a landmark study urging that the federal government and twenty of the country's leading academic and public libraries to prepare to transfer to microfilm 3.3 million of the most endangered brittle books in the next twenty years. Each library would preserve 175,000 volumes at a cost of $300 million with roughly two-thirds of that money to come from the federal government.

One result of the report: The federal agency charged with supporting library activities, the National Endowment for the Humanities, recently awarded $1 million grants to the libraries at Yale University and the University of California at Berkeley. The money is earmarked for development of methods for nationwide use in preserving collections. Coincidentally, it will also save 48,000 of the most endangered books in the humanities collections of both universities.

The National Endowment chief, Lynne Cheney, proposed, to a House subcommittee, a five-year budget under which the government's support of preservation activities would triple for the next fiscal year. By fiscal year 1993, the current $4 million allocation would rise to $20.3 million. The bulk of these funds would be used to help microfilm 3.3 million of the most important

*Figure 10. Shaping the spine of a book. (Courtesy the Library of Congress.)*

*Figure 11. Heat set tissue mending. (Courtesy the Library of Congress.)*

volumes in major American libraries and archives.

During the last two decades, many libraries have initiated their own preservation programs, but because of the expense, these efforts are a "Band-aid" approach. Repairing a book, photocopying it, or placing it on microfilm can cost up to $75, while conserving a book in its original form can amount to hundreds of dollars.

More than three billion government documents are housed in the National Archives building in Washington, DC. Included in this collection are items such as census and immigration data, military veterans' pension files, correspondence received by the U.S. Consul in Yokohama during the 1920s, and the water-stained log of a Civil War steamer that was blockading the North Carolina coast — bound as thick volumes, stuffed into file boxes, and packed into metal cases. The crux is that about 530 million of these paper-based records are in deplorable condition. The more heavily used of the documents are deteriorating at a fast clip.

The National Archives and Records Administration (NARA) turned to a panel of the National Academy of Sciences for a solution to the problem. The panel recommended that the best method for saving the papers was photocopying on durable paper or transferring them to microfilm.

Electronic processes for copying and storing paper items in museums and libraries have long been used to retain the content of an item when that takes precedence over retaining the item itself. More and more this material — the history of our civilization — is being contained on magnetic materials. But these materials are subject to their own forms of deterioration as well as to technological obsolescence.

Computer-based magnetic tapes or optical disks are not acceptable options because these technologies are changing so quickly. Videotape, for instance, has gone through at least nine different formats over the last thirty years, and some are now obsolete. Also to be considered is that much of the equipment, hardware and software, used to read these tapes is no longer being manufactured or maintained. In addition to this, tapes can stretch and the binders that fix magnetic particles into place on plastic films can be unstable, so that magnetic files must be recopied about every ten years. Even small-scale physical deterioration can result in large data losses because so much information can be packed into very small areas.

Similar problems exist with optical storage. Reading the disks with low-power lasers that illuminate compact or digital audio disks incurs no damage, but the long-term stability of materials used to coat disk surfaces is not yet known. Estimates of the lifetime of disks is twenty years or less.

By contrast, microfilm life span is similar to that of properly cared for paper which can be hundreds of years.

Recommendations of the National Academy of Sciences panel for the storage of future paper items hinge on the use of acid-free paper. Acid-free paper is also recommended for photocopying deteriorating records.

Another step is to institute a screening process by which the condition of papers can be checked each time an item is used. Materials suffer relatively little damage when properly boxed and rarely used, even if there is a high acid content in the paper. It is the handling and exposure to light and air that do the real damage.

Archives papers are already repackaged into acid-free cardboard boxes. Corroding fasteners like paper clips and staples are also removed. Old government-issue filing folders, so acidic they are known as a file's "kiss of death," are replaced.

## GENERAL RULES FOR PRESERVING PAPER ITEMS IN THE HOME

### Handling

1. Treat paper items with the same respect you would give to any other more obviously treasured collectible.

2. The proper technique for handling paper items is to handle them as little as possible. Each

time a piece of paper is handled, it deteriorates a little.

3. Items that must be handled a lot are best encased in Mylar sleeves of the proper size to avoid further deterioration. Fingerprints, sweat, and careless handling can all leave their indelible marks.

4. Hands should be scrupulously clean when handling paper items. Whatever soil is on the hands can be transferred to the paper permanently. Forgo hand lotions and creams when working with paper.

5. Folded paper items should be unfolded if feasible, but do not force the folds open or try to iron them out. Some paper items are all but impossible to store unfolded. Others may have been folded or creased inadvertently, and it may be necessary to consult experts to render them flat again. That does not necessarily mean all creases, wrinkles, and folds will be removed. Some of them may be necessary for identification purposes or to retain the paper as close to its original state as possible.

6. Whatever appears to be of value is best left as is while consulting experts to verify authenticity and value.

7. Repairs and restorations are best left to the experts, too. Homemade attempts at repairs and restorations have resulted in further damage and deterioration.

## Environmental Conditions

1. Keep paper items dust-free, away from direct light - natural or manmade — and avoid extremes of temperature.

2. The key to the whole preservation process is an acid-free environment. Bad paper against good paper damages the good paper. Poor environmental conditions can aggravate the acid elements in the paper with resultant damage and deterioration. They can also result in fungal infections and insect infestations in the paper and their resultant damage.

3. Create a relatively acid-free environment when displaying, storing, mounting, and framing paper items by using archival quality mats, stor-age containers, mounts, and framing materials. Even if you consult a professional framer, be sure acid-free components are used. Some framers still haven't gotten the word.

## Archival-Quality, Acid-Free Supplies

1. Several manufacturers and distributors specialize in archival-quality supplies — all acid-free — which may be purchased by mail order, however, a minimum order may be required. (See Suppliers of Archival Materials for addresses.)

2. Philatelic (stamp collecting) supplies are acid-free, and many of them are adaptable to other paper items.

3. Dealers in photographic supplies may have acid-free pages, albums, and matting and framing paraphernalia, but check before buying. Some manufacturers are beginning to stock acid-free items, but you better read the small print to be sure.

4. Some dealers in paper memorabilia also stock acid-free supplies. Comic book dealers are an example, but here, too, you better check before you buy.

5. Stationers stock sheet protectors sized to fit 8½" by 11" paper, but they are not all acid-free. Again, check before you buy.

6. For odd-sized items, you'll probably have to go with an archival-quality supplier. Some will even cut to special measurements.

7. Archival-quality materials may cost a bit more because you may not be able to buy just one or two of an item, but chances are you'll need several anyway. And if your paper treasure is worth the extra care, it may be cheaper in the long run. Restoration can be much more costly than preventive measures.

8. Beware of vinyl, vinyl products, and polyethylene bags. They all contain plasticizers and other additives that can damage paper. Some polyethylene enclosures are advertised as containing no plasticizers, but they will have to be replaced after several years because they turn yellow and sometimes get sticky and collect dust.

9. The sheet protectors you see in discount and drug stores are mostly vinyl products and unsuitable for storage of paper items.

## PRE-STORAGE PREPARATION FOR PAPER ITEMS

Before storing any paper item, a careful examination should be made to evaluate its condition and determine the proper storage method.

1. Dust carefully with a soft brush to remove loose dirt and dust.

2. Remove any foreign objects provided they are not part of the work. This includes plastic envelopes or sheeting, newspapers, acidic wrapping papers, cardboard mats or backings, dried adhesive tapes, metal fasteners such as paper clips, pins, and staples, and any other substances that could damage the paper.

3. Check the paper item for any signs of biological infestation by insects and mold before adding to an existing collection.

4. If a work is framed and the framing doesn't meet archival standards, remove the frame from the work if it can be done without damaging it. It may be well to consult the experts if it seems advisable to remove the frame to avoid further damage.

5. Works on paper of poor quality should be isolated from those of good quality to avoid the transfer of acids and other contaminants to the good paper.

6. Oversized works that are fragmented or warped, works with delicate images — pastel, charcoal, or chalk — or works with flaking paint may require special containers or mats larger or deeper than usual, to protect these vulnerable surfaces and preserve any fragments.

## STORAGE METHODS FOR PAPER ITEMS

Paper items should be packed and stored for ease of handling and ease of retrieval to avoid any inadvertent damage.

1. There should be enough room to remove one item at a time without crowding or damaging the others.

2. A simple way to protect paper items is to interleave them with acid-free tissue or, for larger pieces, a heavier acid-free paper. Interleaving sheets should be cut to fit the inside dimensions of the storage container to avoid slippage. One sheet should be placed between each paper item.

3. A greater protection than interleaving is provided by individual folders or enclosures. They provide better support and safety when moving an item since they are heavier and enclose the item. Catalog and other information pertaining to the item can be recorded on the outer surface. Acid-free folders and enclosures are available in a variety of styles and sizes.

4. One of the best methods for providing support and protection for a paper item is to mat it, if the item is appropriate for matting. Mats reduce the risk of damage during handling. (See Chapter 6 for matting techniques.)

5. Once a paper item has been protected by either interleaving with tissue, or placing in folders, mats, or polyester protectors, it can then be stored in a box. Boxes are further protection from light, dust, and accidental damage.

6. Archival-quality storage boxes are available in a variety of sizes, shapes, and constructions. Some are made of lightweight card stock with reinforced corners. Others are made of sturdy corrugated cardboard. The corrugated type is shipped and stored flat and can be folded into a box when needed. The strongest and most convenient type of flat box is the Solander box. It is constructed of heavy board lined with good-quality paper and covered with durable cloth. It has a hinged back which opens flat, making it easier to lift works in and out. The contents of each box can be listed on the exterior of the box to facilitate care and use of the contents.

## HOUSING A COLLECTION OF PAPER ITEMS

1. The ideal housing for storage of boxes of paper items is sturdy horizontal shelving made of enameled steel.

2. Wooden shelving is acceptable if it is first painted with interior acrylic latex to retard migration of volatile contaminants.

3. The boxes will be heavy, so stacking should be kept to a minimum.

4. Map cabinets and shallow drawers can also be used to store paper items, especially oversized or odd-shaped ones and those enclosed in folders.

5. Provision must be made for adequate air circulation for paper items stored in closed cabinets. Air should circulate around the outside of the cabinet, especially under the bottom and behind the back, to retard cold from damp floors and walls.

## PAPER AS HERITAGE

"Not worth the paper it's written on." The paper it's written on may be worth more than is thought, not so much as a tangible asset but for its intrinsic value. These pieces of paper represent links in the chain of our heritage and each link forges a stronger and deeper connection to our past. The connection has never been completely broken, but in some areas it is certainly fragmented.

Who's to know when a piece of paper will surface to fill in one of those gaps? No doubt there are many links yet to surface. Only time will reveal their whereabouts. Much that has appeared has done so more by accident than by design. Someone just happened to look in a forgotten corner, and there it was. Links to our heritage may be found where least expected.

# 4
# Historical Papers

## WHAT IS A HISTORICAL DOCUMENT?

A document is usually defined as written or printed matter containing authoritative information, records, or evidence. Documents can range from a charter to a treaty to a town plat to a military record to a ship's passenger list to a manuscript or letter. Each may establish proof of an event or the existence of a particular person during a certain time period, but not necessarily be of historical value.

Historical documents can be almost anything, including those in the range of a document, although the technical definition is an original or official paper which offers proof or support to an event of historical nature or something related to the event. These can include documents from all areas of the human experience: government, science, the arts, literature, business.

Historical documents usually fall into three major categories:

1. Documents — forms, with blanks, usually filled in by hand. These include papers related to a historical event or papers related to or produced by a public figure during his or her lifetime or for twenty years thereafter. Examples include: contracts, deeds, census rolls, licenses, maps, battle orders, checks and bank drafts, commissions and discharges, birth certificates. These are materials of everyday living — in both the public and private sectors. But, as opposed to throwaway items, these offer signed and dated documentation of a particular lifestyle.

2. Autographs — original papers, written or made in the author's own hand. These include: signed manuscripts, signatures, drafts, letters, works of art — sketches and drawings. Original signed papers are also called "holographs," and these are often more valuable than other signed papers.

3. Manuscripts — generally intellectual creations, for example a piece of writing including essays or written music — the longer and more complex, the better. Manuscripts should be written or typed, not printed. Examples are: book chapters, literary compositions, musical compositions, typed letters. Both signed and unsigned versions may be found, and may include typed papers signed by the author, "holograph" papers, or unsigned, handwritten compositions.

Printed papers such as posters, broadsides, handbills, playbills or programs, and menus may also be classified as historical documents but usually must be of very early origin and/or connected with some historical event. This is also true of first-day covers, inscribed books, and original, signed photographs. All of these are covered in other chapters in detail.

Historical documents, as opposed to postage stamps or post cards, are usually either one of a kind or in very limited editions. Because they are the evidence of a particular event or a history maker's personal experience, they are an original part of the history of man that cannot be duplicated.

Historical documents are as close as we can get to those moments of the past that shaped our destiny. Our knowledge of our forefathers is almost always derived from secondary sources — magazines, books, motion pictures, television. Historical documents offer us firsthand knowledge of our origins through the original thoughts and deeds of our forefathers, bequeathed to us in their letters, documents, and manuscripts.

## COLLECTING HISTORICAL DOCUMENTS

Documents are usually treasured for their contents. They represent links in the chain of history, and the hope is always there that if enough links can be found, a more complete story of mankind will evolve. No doubt there will always be some gaps, but every link narrows the gaps a bit. A pictorial cut or a signature may be the deciding factor in determining actual worth.

Some early documents may be written on parchment. Certificates or deeds on parchment and paper with a high rag content, made prior to 1950, usually are in better condition than items made from paper pulp. Figure 12 pictures a letter dated 1636, the original copy of which was presented to the United States Postal Service as a gift from Swedish stamp collectors in commemoration of a joint stamp issue by the United States and Sweden on January 23, 1986, honoring the hobby of stamp collecting. The year 1636 also marked the first year of activity of the Swedish Post Office. The letter was sent to Queen Kristina, and the text on the front side consists almost entirely of Honorific Titles of the Queen. According to a note on the front side, the letter was delivered to Her Majesty on March 23, 1636.

Official seals were sometimes hand drawn. They were made of colorful wax attached with a paper wafer or imprinted onto the surface by embossing with a press. Territorial seals and any penmanship embellishments are of much interest.

Printed documents, often with pertinent information added in manuscript, were in common use at the turn of the 19th century. Early documents, including factual information about Colonial life, the Revolutionary War, Indians, the West or another subject of historical interest may rate a closer look.

From 1862 on, revenue stamps were attached to documents. Most of these stamps are of little value, but are interesting and colorful additions to a certificate, policy, or deed.

Historical documents will not be so easily found as most other paper items. There is always the possibility of running across a find in some attic or at an estate sale, but a reliable dealer is the most likely source. Today, people are becoming more knowledgeable of the value of paper items, and any documents found in the home or in the process of handling an estate are not likely to end up on the open market.

Original documents can be expensive. Each collector must decide not only what he wants to collect, but also how much of his or her assets is to be assigned to collecting interests. Collecting historical documents can prove to be a rewarding experience both aesthetically and financially, but the rewards will accrue in direct proportion to the care and respect given the documents.

## COLLECTING MILITARY ITEMS

Military items can be a special collection in themselves. During the Civil War alone, a multitude of certificates were issued for honorable service, discharge notification, bounty applications, payments due, invalid pensions, etc. These were printed forms filled in with pertinent information. Some of these documents are prized for their illustrations, signatures, or seals as well as their contents. Add to these a host of other military-related documents. Correspondence, both military and civilian. Letters from the men on the front lines to the folks back home can be very revealing. Messages to and from the troops.

Passes through the lines. Maps and charts of troop movements. Items of the confederacy are probably harder to find than those of the Union since the Confederacy was a bit unstable and often short of supplies, not the least of which was paper.

## COLLECTING AUTOGRAPHS

For some collectors the signature itself is trophy enough, attached to a document or not. If the signature is rare enough, it can be written on almost any scrap of paper, but the most coveted ones are usually part of a document or manuscript of some kind.

Very few living persons live to see their autographs become collectors' items. Exceptions are those who rarely sign their names to any-

thing and appear in public so seldom that one would be hard pressed to even approach them, should the opportunity arise. Greta Garbo is a prime example.

Many collectors assemble very nice collections of autographs from present day celebrities. Collecting autographs of entertainment figures and sports stars has always been popular. Autographs are secured on all types of things: photos (Fig. 13), currency, envelopes, old receipts, note paper, tickets, baseball cards, sometimes on whatever piece of paper is handy. One is not always prepared with the proper accoutrements when the opportunity to secure an autograph in person arises.

One of the most popular ways to secure an autograph is to write to a favorite personality and ask for it. If you want an autographed

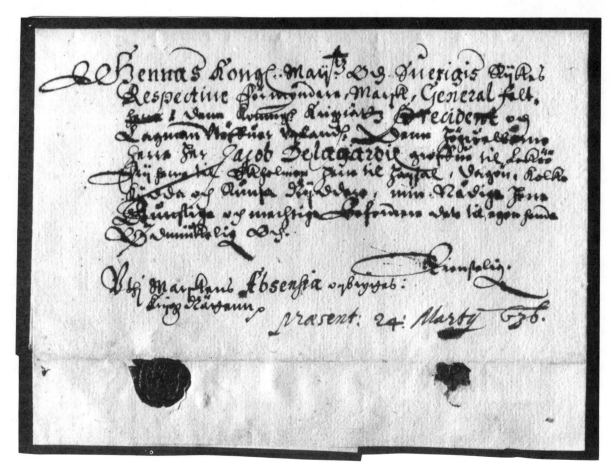

*Figure 12. Facsimile of letter sent to Queen Kristina in 1936 and presented to the United States Postal Service on January 23, 1986 as a gift from Swedish stamp collectors. (Photograph courtesy Swedish Post Office.)*

*Figure 13. Autographed photograph of Ida Lupino, movie actress.*

photograph and assurance that the autograph is the original and not a copy, you can send your own photo. Because they get so many requests, celebrities often sign one picture and then have copies made. Figure 13 is a copy.

Most celebrities do not charge for autographs, but to be on the safe side, ask if any payment is required. At the most, the fee should be a dollar or two, although some sports figures are beginning to charge $5.00 or so and donating the proceeds to charity. Be sure to include a self-addressed stamped envelope of the correct size.

Securing autographs of those no longer with us may not be so easy. However, the signatures of the more recently departed celebrities — from about fifty years ago to the present — are not likely to be too scarce. The exception might be those who had a short life span, and consequently, weren't around long enough to apply their signature to many items. Jean Harlow is an example.

Most of these recent autographs are not likely to be of high monetary value at present. One can only guess about the future, but some of them can increase in value as the years pass and these personalities take their places in history.

For collectors who are looking for investment as well as signature, two factors must be considered: rarity and content.

### Rarity

Rarity has a dual connotation. First, a signature may be hard to find. Second, only a few specimens of a signature may be known to exist. Almost anything signed by President William Henry Harrison will be worth more than for example, a nice, clean, beautifully written letter by Franklin Delano Roosevelt on official White House stationery. The reason: William Henry Harrison lived but a month after his election, and his presidential papers and documents are quite rare. FDR was elected to four terms and his papers are quite common.

### Content

If there should be a choice of more than one item signed by the same person, then content must be considered. As an example, suppose two letters written by General Dwight D. Eisenhower were available. One is written to General Omar Bradley concerning World War II battle plans. The other is written to Mrs. Eisenhower and concerns family matters. Which one is the most significant? The one to General Bradley is because of its historical connotations.

Other factors that may enter into placing a value on an autograph are the condition of the paper the autograph is on, whether it was signed in ink or pencil, and the date of the signing. Usually autographs of United States presidents dated during their presidential terms are more valuable.

## RARE AUTOGRAPHS

The rarest autograph in the world is thought to be that of Julius Caesar, if one could be found for sale. Next to his is that of William Shakespeare. Only six Shakespeare signatures are known to exist, and all are in institutions. Both of these signatures are priced in the millions of dollars.

American historical autographs are among the most popular collectibles, and some of the most sought after are the original signers of the Declaration of Independence. One of the rarest of these signatures is that of Button Gwinnett (Fig. 14). Why? Less than a year after signing this extraordinary document, Button Gwinnett was killed in a duel. In addition, he was not a frequent letter writer. Hence, the astronomical odds against finding anything with his signature on it.

*Figure 14. Facsimile signature of Button Gwinnett.*

The rarest of the signers is Thomas Lynch, Jr. (Fig. 15). He contracted swamp fever while on active duty during the Revolution and was in declining health when he was elected an extra delegate to the Continental Congress. One of his last public acts was the signing of the Declaration of Independence. He was forced to return to his home in South Carolina in the autumn of 1776 when his health continued to fail. Three years later, he sailed to the West Indies with the hope that he could recover his health there. His ship was lost at sea. Only one signed letter by Thomas Lynch, Jr. is known to exist. His signature has appeared in various forms on documents and on the flyleaves of books.

*Figure 15. Facsimile signature of Thomas Lynch, Jr.*

Care must be taken not to confuse Thomas Lynch, Jr.'s signature with that of his father who was also a Congressional delegate. Thomas Lynch, Sr. died of a series of strokes in mid-1776. He was an early and staunch defender of Colonial resistance to England and was sent as a South Carolina delegate to the first and second Continental Congresses. Though his letters are themselves extremely rare, his signature does appear on pre-Revolutionary paper money of South Carolina. There is a blank space for his name on the Declaration of Independence, but he never made it to Independence Hall to sign it. In addition, there was a New York city merchant named Thomas Lynch whose signature resembled that of Thomas Lynch, Jr.

## FREE FRANKS

Another type of autograph collecting is free franks. Originally, the franking privilege was reserved for royalty, but by the late 1500s it was also extended to those in service to the king. The word franc is of French origin and means free. In 1660, England established a post office, and along with it provided for members of Parliament and some of the nobility to send mail free under cover of their signatures. Later, greater restrictions were placed on this privilege because of flagrant abuses. In 1840, with the introduction of the postage stamp, the free franking privilege ended in England.

In 1775, when the Continental Congress was established, one of its first actions was the establishment of postal facilities. Since that was a time of such upheaval, the Congress felt the urgency to develop a system for a rapid and secure means of conveying mail throughout the colonies. That same year, members of Congress and the military were granted the free franking privilege. For the military, it was required that the commanding officers apply the frank. On January 9, 1776, the Post Office began operation. The free frank was extended to a number of government officials in 1782. With a new United States government in operation in 1792, the frank was granted to President Washington, his Cabinet members, members of Congress, and a number of other officials.

The franking privilege was abolished in the United States in 1873 during the administration of President Grant. All the presidents prior to that time had the free franking privilege. Several presidents also had the free frank as Vice Presidents, Cabinet members, or members of Congress. Members of Congress were again granted the free frank in 1891, and it was granted again to Vice Presidents in 1895. Figures 16 and 17 are copies of envelopes bearing the franks of former

Senator Howard H. Baker, Jr. of Tennessee and of Representative Jack Brooks of Texas.

All the First Ladies with the exceptions of Caroline Fillmore, Julia G. Tyler, and Eliza M. Johnson were granted the franking privilege by a special Act of Congress upon becoming widows.

## SIGNATURE COLLECTING

One facet of autograph collecting is a bit like stamp collecting. Though there are great rarities in both fields that the average collector is not likely to ever see, let alone own, a variety of specimens are available at comparatively nominal costs. Just as stamp collectors can buy selected lots of foreign stamp mixtures for $10.00 to $15.00 on up to $50.00 to $100.00 each, autograph collectors can buy signature collections of government officials, politicians, writers, com-

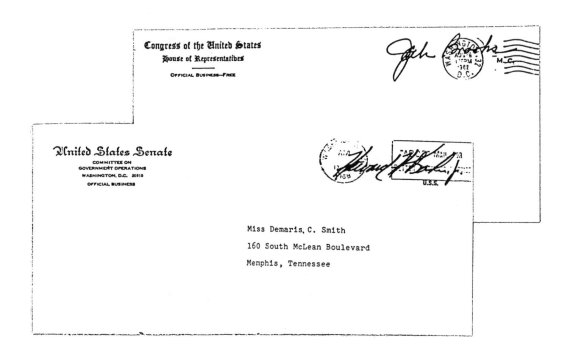

*Figure 16. Facsimile of envelope franked by Representative Jack Brooks, dated August 28, 1962. (Author's collection.)*

*Figure 17. Facsimile of envelope franked by Senator Howard H. Baker, Jr., dated June 12, 1968. (Author's collection.)*

posers, etc. in packs of one hundred at a cost of $50.00 to $100.00 a pack. These specimens are cut from letters and other documents. True, some of these specimens may be unknown to the autograph seeker, just as many stamps in mixed lots are not readily identifiable. Researching these unknowns is an excellent way to learn more about the hobby and perhaps open up new avenues of interest.

## KNOW WHAT YOU ARE COLLECTING

As with other collectibles, it is most emphatically suggested that anyone with a serious interest in collecting historical items take time for some learning along the way. Wise collectors know what they are buying even from a reliable dealer. Facsimiles and fakes of some documents, autographs, and manuscripts do exist, and some are extremely difficult to distinguish from the original. There is also the possibility of happening upon what appears to be a real find when that reliable dealer isn't around. Informed collectors also can be more selective in their purchases. If a collector knows there is a better specimen available, the option is there to wait for something better, especially if a considerable outlay of money is involved. Conversely, the informed collector should also recognize a bargain if one should surface.

## PRESERVING HISTORICAL DOCUMENTS

### Preserving the Evidence

First and foremost, a document is a valuable source of evidence, and it is this quality above all others that is being preserved. Whether printed, handwritten, or apparently blank, the possibility remains that it is a fertile source of information. Besides the written content, tears, holes, creases, folds, alterations, original sewing holes, watermarks, erasures, and traces of seals may all have their stories to tell.

Collectors of yore would often write with a pencil directly on a document the source and purchase price. Thousands of pieces have these notations or dealers' prices and comments such as "very rare" on them. Do *not* attempt to remove these penciled notes. They will not harm the paper and may be of considerable importance in establishing origin. The handwriting of many old-time dealers and collectors is recognizable by many knowledgeable dealers and collectors. These markings are also one of the ways to prove authenticity. Conversely, *nothing* should be written on a document.

Before the advent of the filing cabinet, documents for storage were usually folded and tied up in bundles with string or ribbon. The English government often used red tape instead of string. This was the origin of the term "red tape" as in bureaucratic foul-ups.

Such bundles are still found tied and folded in this manner. Any collector who happens to acquire one of these bundles should, as soon as possible, carefully unfold each piece and place it between two sheets of acid-free paper and on a flat surface for gradual unwrinkling. A weight such as a book may be placed on top provided it doesn't come in contact with the document. Remove all paper clips, pins, ribbons, etc. Wax seals, if intact — a rarity — should be left in place.

### Preserving Methods

The same basic preservation procedures that apply to all paper items apply to historical documents as well, but probably in spades. Dealing with a piece of history is a bit like walking on eggs. Tread lightly.

Proper care and respect for these documents is of the utmost importance to ensure their continued existence. One-of-a-kind and limited edition items especially should be preserved with care. Nothing should be done to an item that cannot be reversed without damage. Nothing should be applied or attached to it that cannot be removed safely. Treatments such as washing, bleaching, or tinting should not be done if they cannot be reversed without harm to the item. Repairs should not be attempted with home remedies. Any existing damage such as foxing, water spots, and that caused by the ravages of time should be subjected to deacidification by a highly qualified restorer.

Whatever must be done in the way of preservation is best kept to the minimum consistent to retain its validity as evidence. The less done to the item, the greater its value as evidence. Repairing is one thing, restoration is distinctly something else.

## REPAIRING DOCUMENTS VS. RESTORATION OF DOCUMENTS

Repairing is a means of forestalling decay and protecting from further damage. Work on a properly repaired document will be apparent but should be unobtrusive. Tears and holes may be filled in neatly with comparable though not exactly matching paper. An observer can clearly tell which is the original document and which is the repair work. The outer edges are left as is, frayed or not. The document is presented as it was found with nothing added or removed. The evidence is saved.

Restoration is the addition of missing elements to bring the item back to what is assumed to be its original condition. Work on a restored document should be invisible as far as is possible. Paper is cleaned. Any holes are filled. Exactly matching paper is used to add margins. Missing borders and writing and damaged images are restored. The whole work is refurbished so that it is all but indistinguishable from an untouched original.

Most collectors prefer repairing where possible rather than restoration. Reversibility is the one underlying principle in the repair of items as opposed to restoration. Restraint is the order of the day. Generally, the collector is advised to let well enough alone and leave repairs and restoration to the professionals.

One other reason for leaving well enough alone is that many forms of treatment, aside from the most urgent first-aid repairs, are more or less for cosmetic effect. The temptation is to smooth out folds and wrinkles which are in reality part of the lifetime of the article and essential

components of evidence. The primary purpose of preservation is to keep the evidence intact.

## STORING DOCUMENTS

An excellent and accepted way to protect documents is to store them in acid-free sleeves in a three-ring binder. Museum quality folders are also available if you prefer the file cabinet method of storage, but do encase the documents in acid-free sleeves. If the document consists of several pages, remove all paper clips and staples, and store each page in a separate acid-free sleeve.

Do not put anything else in the sleeve with the document. The temptation arises to put anything related to an item in the same sleeve or folder as the item. Newspaper clippings are glaring examples. Don't! That is an excellent example of putting bad paper next to a sheet that is infinitely better. The bad paper will bleed onto the good and result in staining and the ultimate ruin of a document.

As an added precaution for more important documents, it is suggested that a typewritten page containing a complete transcript of the document and pertinent information concerning it — existing copies, repairs, known publications, public exhibitions, the address of the dealer if applicable, etc. — be placed in a facing sleeve. Biographical information and a picture of the signer might also be included.

Acid-free hinged lid document cases are also available. These sturdy, durable, and attractive cases are of one-piece construction with exclusive locking tabs for easy assembly without glue, tape, or staples. They are available in either letter or legal size and can accommodate file folders.

## KEEPING RECORDS

If the document was purchased from a dealer, retain the correspondence relating to it along with the bill of sale. Reputable dealers will provide a sales slip on which the document is listed along with a description. Also included should be a statement guaranteeing authenticity. A reputable dealer will not object. If one does, take your business elsewhere.

If the document is not purchased from a dealer, retaining all receipts and information about it may be doubly important. Before considering purchase, secure as much information about the document as possible from the seller — former owners, statements of authenticity, how it has been stored, any repairs, etc. The seller, reliable though he or she may be, may not be available a few years hence to provide information or verify any information given at the time of purchase. If the seller can't provide any information, it may be advisable to have the document authenticated by experts, especially if the purchase involves a considerable outlay of money. Keep in mind that the sellers of anything want to move the merchandise, and if luxury items are involved, the sellers may "gild the lily" a bit.

## FRAMING DOCUMENTS

An extremely valuable document should not be framed or displayed. As mentioned in Chapter 3, light, especially direct sunlight, can fade the ink on the document. Reflected daylight and fluorescent lighting can also cause fading. A more contemporary document — a signed letter or an autographed picture of a favorite personality — is a better choice.

Framing techniques are not difficult to master, but for some the framing shop is the answer. Observe a few precautions when entrusting a paper treasure to a framer.

1. Insist that only museum-quality, acid-free materials be used for the framing process.

2. Explain carefully to the framer that transparent tape, masking tape, or any other kind of tape should not be used. Museum-quality adhesives are available if needed.

3. Particularly point out that the document or photograph should not be pasted down in any manner — not even to prevent wrinkling or buckling, nor should it be cut or trimmed in any way.

4. Instruct the framer that anything framed with the document — engravings, plates, illustrations, photos — should not be allowed to touch the document.

If the do-it-yourself method is preferred, the first step in the framing process is to devise an attractive layout that will display the document to the best advantage. A careful balance of matting and frame and any illustrations and name plates is necessary to enhance the natural beauty of the document.

Next, cut matting pieces from museum-quality materials and arrange them according to the layout to check the result. Then put the document, illustrations, and plates in place and affix with museum-quality materials. Special cloth tapes and adhesives are available to hold the document and matting in place without damage. The matting boards should be thick enough to keep the document from touching the glass or the frame and allow for some air circulation. All board backing should be of museum-quality materials, too.

The matted document is now ready to be fitted with a sheet of glass. A sheet of Plexiglas which is scientifically designed to filter out ultraviolet rays is the best assurance against fading, and it should be cut to fit over the matted document. The document is now ready to be placed in a coordinating frame.

Obviously, preserving historical documents is not inexpensive, but an exceptional document deserves nothing less than the best. Those who collect museum-quality documents should be able to give them museum-quality care.

## HISTORICAL DOCUMENTS AS COLLECTIBLES

Other paper collectibles verify lifestyles. Historical documents are verifiable evidence of our existence — as a people and as a nation. Without that documentation, our history books would be akin to myths and fairy tales — interesting stories without foundation. Collecting and preserving historical documents ensures a heritage for future generations.

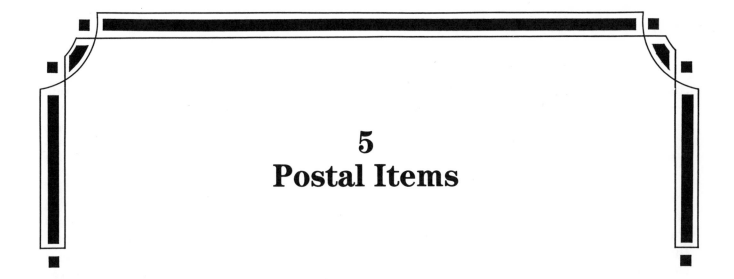

# 5
# Postal Items

## THE BEGINNINGS OF THE POSTAL SYSTEM

Man's efforts to establish some sort of system for the delivery of messages coincides roughly with his first efforts to create writing surfaces a bit more transportable than the wall of a cave. The advent of written records, governments over extensive territories, the concentration of populations in cities, and the specialization of occupations signalled the need for an efficient means for transmitting messages.

The word "post" is defined as a fixed station or position and stems from the Latin term *positus*. A series of stations or delivery routes was set up to relay official correspondence or to provide fresh transport for messengers. Eventually, the systems were sufficiently refined so that officials on public business could be conveyed along with correspondence.

Examples of clay tablets dating back to the 19th century B.C. were discovered at the early Assyrian business community of Kanesh in Cappadocia (now Turkey). These tablets were enclosed in clay envelopes which apparently secured efficient and safe transport.

Other systems were introduced in Egypt after the introduction of papyrus in 2400 B.C. and of a somewhat later date in China and Persia. In China, post-stages — "I Chan" — were instituted during the Chou Dynasty, 1122-255 B.C. Ten thousand stations utilizing 200,000 horses were found by Marco Polo in the 14th century A.D. By the 20th century, during the Ch'ing Dynasty, 15,000 stations had been established for routing correspondence by foot couriers, and there were 1,600 horses and boats for priority mail.

One of the most efficient of the early posts was that of Persia in the fifth and sixth centuries B.C. with its outstanding road system and highly organized communications. The Greek and Roman Empires adapted the main features of their postal systems from the Persian counterparts — a common language to help simplify postal communications, maintenance of the facilities by the local communities, and restriction to official business. The postal systems grew as the empires grew, and became essential to successful administration.

## PRIVATE ORGANIZATIONS FOR COMMERCIAL AND PERSONAL MAIL

During the first few centuries A.D., individuals were becoming more and more mobile and less tied to their local communities. One result was the appearance of private organizations for commercial and personal mail. Despite the antiquity of the Chinese postal system as a whole, these private services — people's letter offices — did not appear until about the 15th century. Firms that needed transport for their own business affairs managed them and allowed others the use of the routes for a moderate fee. During this same period, Ming Emperor Yung Lo opened the imperial mails to private use.

## EUROPEAN POSTAL DEVELOPMENT

With the decline of the Roman empire and the accompanying decline in commerce and literacy, European postal development in general was retarded by the absence of real central authority. In the 11th century, the efforts of religious and educational institutions brought about changes. Papyrus was substantially replaced by parchment and paper — best suited of all for correspondence — made its appearance.

Italian cities evolved into centers of commercial development, establishing postal routes necessary for business documents. The 15th century system established in Venice by Amadeo Tasso became the Thurn and Taxis service for the Holy Roman Empire and remained in operation into the 19th century. It was a single-family operation with contributions from the government and fees from private users.

The 19th century revolutions established — at least temporarily — the absolute authority of the individual nation states, and the added responsibilities and expanded activities of the new administrations apparently necessitated government monopolies of the past.

Edmond Prideaux, a member of the English House of Commons, was appointed Master of the Post in 1644. He established a rather primitive weekly delivery of letters to all parts of the nation.

Around 1680, a letter collection and delivery system was set up in London by William Dockwra. The origination of the postmark indicating the date, time, and place of making is attributed to him. Eventually, the government took over this system and operated it relatively successfully.

With the advent of the Industrial Revolution, it became increasingly apparent that postal delivery was not keeping pace with the rest of the world. Fees for postal rates were regarded as a tax. As a result, postage rates were high. They were based on a complex system of computation by distance and the collection of fees from the recipient, who often was not disposed to pay them.

## THE FIRST POSTAGE STAMP

It was during the reign of Queen Victoria, in 1840, that Rowland Hill originated a plan to establish a low, uniform postal rate throughout Great Britain, and to have the government sell indicia indicating that postage had been paid. The indicia were the first adhesive postage stamps — the one-penny black and two-penny blue. Both depicted the head of the Sovereign, a design which appears to have been chosen because:

1. Authorities regarded the new stamps as paper coin, and since pre-Roman times, the head of the monarch had always appeared on coinage.

2. It was difficult to make forgeries with accuracy. Both were imperforate and had to be cut apart by scissors or other means. These first stamps were far from the little specimens of art that some of its descendants came to be. Nice, clean, well-centered copies would be phenomenal finds, and in all probability don't exist.

Hill also commissioned the design of the first stamped envelope by William Mulready of the Royal Academy of Art.

Both the adhesive stamps and the Mulready envelope were put into used in England on May 6, 1840. The two stamps were a tremendous success. The public bought them out of admiration and for their souvenir value as well as for postal use. The Mulready envelope, though of elaborate and artistic design, met with ridicule. It was caricatured in the press and leading periodicals, which resulted in the post office withdrawing and destroying most of the Mulready covers. It also resulted in two highly prized collectibles — the original covers and the caricatures.

## THE UNIVERSAL POSTAL UNION

Much discussion arose during the 1850s and 1860s for a cheaper and uniform worldwide postal rate. The International Postal Association was founded in 1851 as the first step toward uniform international postage. Contacts were made with the governments of every civilized country in the world. The Association eventually worked out a plan which became the principle adopted in 1875 by the General Postal Union (now the Universal Postal Union), which had been established in 1874 as an outgrowth of the agreement among the world's postal systems to regulate and facilitate mutually the exchange of mails and the collection of international postal revenues.

## THE FIRST POSTAL CARDS

Postal cards should not be confused with post cards. Post cards predate postal cards by

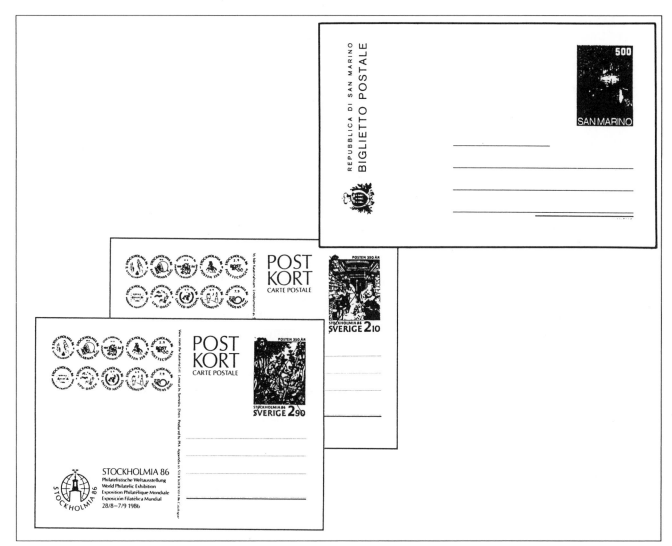

*Figure 18. Postal card issued by San Marino on May 6, 1986 to encourage the continued and increased use of this convenient and inexpensive means of correspondence and to increase tourism.*

*Figure 19. These two Swedish postal cards were issued in 1986 in conjunction with the Stockholmia 86 Postage Stamp Exhibition. The stamps depict postal workers. Special Exhibition cancels are depicted on the left side of the cards along with the Stockholmia 86 emblem.*

many years. They are an outgrowth of other paper items, imprinted with illustrations, whose primary use was by merchants to advertise their wares. (Chapter 7 deals with post cards.) Postal cards are government-issued cards with the postage stamp incorporated into the design and printed in the upper right corner (Fig. 18). Most early postal cards were rather plain, but some more recent ones feature commemorative themes, sometimes based on the design of the stamp (Fig. 19).

The first postal cards originated in Germany and Austria, not co-produced but coincidentally and concurrently in 1865. Both Heinrich von Stephen of the German Empire and Dr. Emmanuel Hermann of the Military Academy of Wiener-Neustadt in Austria submitted to the General Postal Conference held at Karlsruhe their proposals for postal cards — apparently independent of each other. Four years later the Director General of the Austrian Post accepted Dr. Hermann's idea, and the first government-produced correspondence card was issued on October 1, 1869.

England issued its first postal card in 1870, and the first United States postal card was issued on May 13, 1873. Postal cards proved to be such an overwhelming success that many other countries adopted the postal card system in rapid succession.

## THE BEGINNINGS OF THE UNITED STATES POSTAL SERVICE

The development of the United States postal service closely parallels the history of the United States itself. From humble beginnings both evolved into the present-day infra-structure of grandiose proportions.

The early European settlers in America tried to maintain communications with family and friends back on the continent as well as with persons in other colonies, but their efforts were fraught with uncertainty. The only real means of transportation being sailing vessels, the colonists were at the mercy of the ships' crews to transport the missives to their destinations or to places where more formal service was available.

Eventually, efforts were made to standardize and safeguard the treatment of postal items. Collection points were established for the dispatching and receiving of overseas correspondence. By the 1650s, local laws authorized the movement of letters overland from plantation to plantation and included specific penalties for lack of cooperation.

It was not until the 17th century that colonial officials sought to set up regular communication among the colonies. One such effort was that of New York Governor Francis Lovelace in 1673. Shortlived thought it was, it did set a precedent and served to open up communication during the Revolution.

British Master of the Mint, Thomas Neale, had been granted a monopoly on establishing a colonial post office. In 1693, Governor Andrew Hamilton of New Jersey opened a service as an agent for Mr. Neale, providing the first real project to link the colonies. In 1707, the Crown purchased the rights of patent holders when the system failed to pay its own way. However, this ambitious, colonies-side endeavor bought Andrew Hamilton the title "Father of the American Post." In 1710, an American postal structure was established by the Queen Anne Act and administered by a deputy postmaster general in New York, but it proved to be expensive, rather unreliable, and not very popular.

## ESTABLISHMENT OF THE UNITED STATES POSTAL SYSTEM

It was not until the middle of the 18th century that the American postal system began to come into its own under the innovative and energetic administration of Benjamin Franklin, deputy postmaster general. Eventually the service became a profit-making entity, but Franklin was removed from office in 1774 as a political undesirable.

The new revolutionary government took over the postal services on July 26, 1775 as an essential avenue of communication. Benjamin Franklin was appointed the first postmaster general but left that post soon after to go abroad as a diplomat. His son-in-law, Richard Bache, succeeded him. The postal service was placed under the authority of the federal government by the Constitution of 1789, and Samuel Osgood became postmaster general.

The 19th century ushered in a time of rapid expansion and development. Postal routes and offices moved westward with the country's boundaries and population. An improved transportation system brought mail by steamboat in 1813 and railroads in 1838.

## THE FIRST UNITED STATES POSTAGE STAMPS

The New York City Dispatch Post issues of 1842 and various Postmasters' Provisionals in 1845 were the first U.S. adhesives. Five-cent and ten-cent general issues were released in 1847. Over the next ten years, the U.S. adopted some of the 1840 British Penny Post reforms. Rates were reduced and calculated on weight rather than the number of sheets in the letter or the distance carried, and prepayment of postage became mandatory.

## POSTAGE STAMP PAPER

Paper used to print postage stamps is divided into two broad categories — "wove" and "laid." The surface of the frame onto which the pulp is fed determines the difference in the appearance of the papers.

Wove paper has a smooth and even surface, and the paper is of a uniform texture throughout, revealing no light and dark areas when held to the light. Paper pulp is fed on to a cloth-like screen of closely interwoven fine wires. When held to the light, little dots or points very close together can be seen.

Laid paper frames are composed of closely spaced parallel wires, with cross wires set at wider intervals. A greater thickness of the pulp will settle between the wires. The paper will reveal alternate light and dark lines when held to the light.

The paper is called "Batonne" (from the French word meaning staff) if the lines are spaced quite far apart and resemble the lines on ruled writing paper. This paper can be either wove or laid. In laid paper of this type, fine laid lines are visible between the batons. These laid lines are really a form of watermark and may appear as squares, diamonds, rectangles, wavy lines, or other geometric figures.

If the lines form little squares, the paper is called "Quadrille." If the lines form rectangles instead of squares, the paper is called "Oblong Quadrille."

Postage stamp paper is also classified by its thickness, thinness, softness, hardness, and by color, if dye was added during the production process. Color may be referred to as yellowish, greenish, bluish, reddish, or whatever.

A number of stamp-issuing countries have tried their own variations of the paper-making process in efforts to discourage counterfeiting. These include the incorporation of bits of colored thread or minute fibers of a variety of colors and lengths, chalk-like coating, two-ply paper in which any attempts to remove the cancellation would destroy the design, and printing the design on the gummed side. But even with all the efforts to counteract it, counterfeiting goes on. In some parts of the world, counterfeiting stamps is a thriving business. And some of those counterfeiters are very good at their trade.

Some stamp issues have been printed on more than one type of paper, and some of those paper varieties are on the scarce side. The paper can often make the difference in determining the value of a postage stamp.

## STAMP COLLECTING

Sir Rowland Hill could not have known that his brainchild would spawn what is probably the most popular avocation in the world. The first English stamps were hardly off the presses when the collecting rage began. Fashionable ladies of that day wanted them not to collect and mount but as accumulations to decorate screens, candy bowls, and other household items.

The story goes that the first stamp collector was a lady. She was not interested in stamp collecting as such but in securing enough of that first English issue to paper a wall of her house. Though the story never has been disproved–or proved–there still may be a wall of Penny Black stamps somewhere in London, perhaps under several layers of wallpaper and paint, waiting to be discovered.

One by one, other countries began issuing stamps, and by 1860, the number of stamp-issuing countries was more than twenty and growing. Children were encouraged to collect and mount stamps to assist in studying geography. Adults were caught up in the collecting clamor, and a new hobby was born.

A couple of years later, albums designed for organizing and mounting stamps were introduced, and small shopkeepers began carrying a line of philatelic supplies. The first stamp store was opened in London, and London remained the leading marketplace for stamps until World War II when the market shifted to New York where it remains.

## THE PRESERVATION OF POSTAL ITEMS

Perhaps more attention has been given to the preservation of postal items than other paper collectibles. Organization and protection are almost bare necessities in order to keep track of those little gummed squares and keep them in an orderly fashion. A variety of methods exist to do this, dependent on the contents of the collection and the whims of the collector, but most are meant to create an acid-free environment.

### Mounting Stamps

*Hinges.* The earliest and most common method for preserving stamps was and is to mount them in albums by means of peelable hinges. Stamp hinges were invented in the 1860s. They are small, oblong pieces of paper, gummed on one side. They are available in a variety of

sizes and must be moistened to adhere to the stamp and the album page. Some come folded and ready for use. They are quite adequate for the less expensive and more common stamps and used examples, however, they should be thoroughly dry before peeling or parts of the hinge may stick to the stamp or album. Most beginning collectors mount their first collections this way.

*Mylar mounts.* More valuable collections and mint examples require more advanced mounting techniques. Acid-free Mylar mounts are the norm for maximum protection from natural and manmade elements (Fig. 21). These mounts come in a variety of sizes including tubular shapes of varying widths that can be cut to size. They are either black or clear on the back side which is also gummed to adhere to the album page. A slight moistening in a few spots is enough to hold the mount in place. The stamp slips inside the mount and is visible through the clear topside. They also come in sizes to fit envelopes, postal cards, and other postal stationery, foreign and domestic.

*Stock pages.* Stamp collecting is one avocation in which it is almost impossible not to have duplication of many items. Of course, the collectors usually select the best specimens for their own collections. One of the most common ways to amass duplicates is the process of updating and replacing lesser specimens with better copies. These lesser items can eventually be disposed of if desired, but they must be preserved in some way in the meantime. The simplest method is to arrange them on stock pages. They are readily visible and available and can be arranged in any order desired.

These stock pages come in a variety of styles. The most common are made of a paper similar to that of manila folders with pockets arranged horizontally to hold the stamps in place (Fig. 22 & 23). These come with varying width pockets which will also accommodate envelopes (covers), postal cards, souvenir sheets, and other large postal items.

A more permanent stock page is made of a

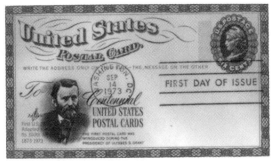

*Figure 20.  A selection of first-day covers. (Author's collection.)*

*Figure 21.   With Mylar mounts, stamps are held securely in position while permitting air to circulate freely around them. (Courtesy H. E. Harris Co., Inc.)*

heavier black stock with pockets covered by Mylar strips also arranged crosswise. The Mylar strips lift up on one edge for access.

Most stock pages are made to fit three-ring binders. Some are made into booklets.

*Glassine envelopes.* Another temporary means of storing stamps is in glassine envelopes. These are now available acid-free and are handy for transferring stamps or sorting out disposable items. They do have a tendency to tear and are not recommended for permanent storage. Some collectors insert specimens in glassine envelopes before storing in stock pages. Peelable labels can be attached to glassine envelopes to identify specimens, especially if they are items for sale or trade.

There are also glassine sheets for interweaving between pages, and in books to store full sheets of stamps.

*Albums.* Stamps should not be stored flat. The most imminent danger in storing stamps flat is that the stamps can stick together. Obviously, environmental conditions in the average home cannot be controlled like those in a museum. Over-dry and over-damp conditions can occur. Storing stamps upright and in albums also allows for air circulation.

Printed albums are available for a variety of countries and topics, but some collectors find albums assembled from blank pages more adaptable. Blank pages solve the problem of what to do with stamps that are not pictured in the album. Albums are also available for postal stationery-covers, postal cards, etc.-with acid-free Mylar slots of various sizes to hold the items without mounting. Some are the size of three-ring binders, and others are the approximate width and length of a cover. Each page of the cover-size album (Fig. 24) will hold two covers back-to-back and the album holds about fifty covers.

*Stamp tongs.* Like all other paper items, stamps should be handled as little as possible. Unlike most all other paper items, stamp collectors have a tool to aid in sorting and examining specimens without touching them too much — stamp tongs. These are king-size tweezers with rounded, blunt ends that come in a variety of styles and sizes. It is particularly advisable to use tongs when handling a dealer's stock or another person's collection. It is also easier to remove stamps from stock pages with tongs.

## POSTAL ITEMS AS COLLECTIBLES

The art of communication represents a major link in the chain of the history of mankind. Postal items are the culmination of man's skill in learning to communicate with each other and with other nations. Though the use of postage is a relatively new innovation within the postal system, it represents an important segment in the

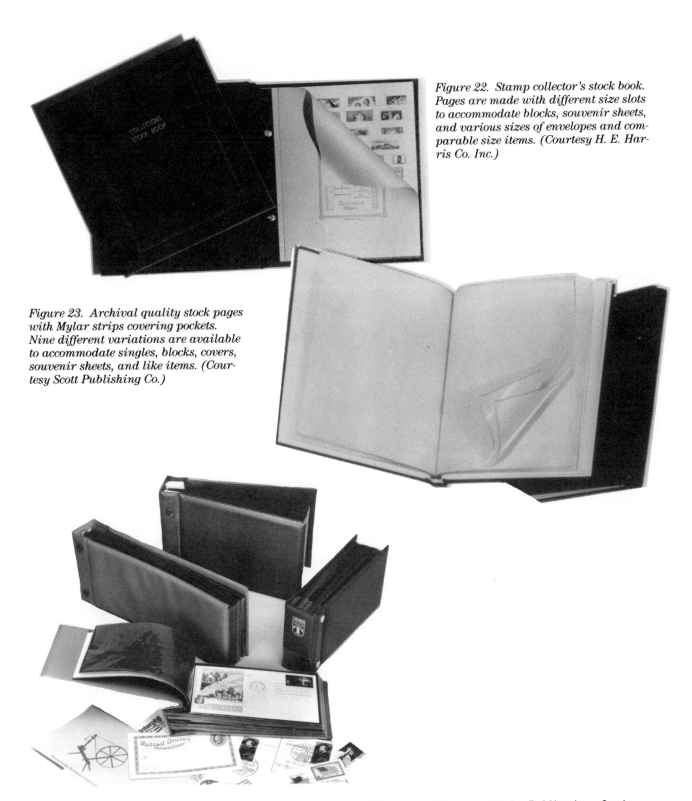

*Figure 22. Stamp collector's stock book. Pages are made with different size slots to accommodate blocks, souvenir sheets, and various sizes of envelopes and comparable size items. (Courtesy H. E. Harris Co. Inc.)*

*Figure 23. Archival quality stock pages with Mylar strips covering pockets. Nine different variations are available to accommodate singles, blocks, covers, souvenir sheets, and like items. (Courtesy Scott Publishing Co.)*

*Figure 24. Cover-sized album for postal cards, envelopes, and like items. (Courtesy Linder Publications, Inc.)*

documentation of man's communication efforts.

The postage stamp itself, one of the smallest of the paper collectibles, casts a large shadow. In addition to its postal purpose, it represents — in miniature — the arts and sciences, literature and history, commerce and world affairs. The crises, conflicts, cultures, upturns, and downfalls of the world are reflected in postage stamps.

Stamps do not necessarily have to be collected as stamps. They can be collected as pieces of history. They are an immediate reflection of the tenor of a country at the time of issue. They are documents, too. What better validation of its history than the postal issues of a country? The general climate of a country has a direct effect on the postal system.

Postage stamps can be fun, too. They are beautiful, stately, delightful, poignant, intriguing, sporty, and amusing. They are miniature works of art, tributes to the mighty and the fallen, remembrances of things past, projections into the future, and mirrors of the present.

Stamps can offer history and documentation to other collectibles. Many other collectibles — paper and otherwise — are emulated in postage stamps. Name almost any topic or category, and you'll find a corresponding group of postage stamps.

Postage stamps can stand on their own or add a special touch to any other collection.

# 6
# Prints I:
# Posters, Maps, and Photographs

**P**rints encompass such a wide range of variations that it seemed incumbent to divide them into two major sections and give each its own chapter in this book. The first part deals with prints as most of us think of them — artwork for display purposes that can be reproduced as many times as the artist desires. Sometimes the number of copies is so strictly controlled that each becomes a major work in itself. They are numbered and almost all are hand engraved by the artist in addition to the plate signature. Many prominent artists have reproduced their work this way, and these prints are much sought after.

Webster's Dictionary defines the word "print" three ways:

1. To make a copy by impressing paper against an inked printing surface.

2. To impress with a design or pattern.

3. To make a positive picture on a sensitized photographic surface from a negative.

All facets of print making fall under one of these definitions. What sets apart these two chapters is not how the prints are made but how they are used. Chapter 7 deals with prints in the form of cards.

## THE EVOLUTION OF THE PRINT

Man's need to communicate and his artistic aptitude seem to have developed along parallel paths. Words and pictures are a form of language, each at times speaking a language all its own. Pictures seem to have come first. Prehistoric man recorded his exploits on cave walls — man's propensity for decorating his surroundings. Man seems to have a natural inclination for wanting the place where he must spend a great deal of his time to look nice. Pictures of favorite persons, locales, and objects were an obvious and simple way to accomplish this.

Like most of man's achievements, prints evolved through many stages of development into a variety of styles and reproduction methods.

### Wood Blocks

Early prints were made from wood blocks of relatively thin wood. Pear, apple, lime, and other soft woods were the most commonly used. Later blocks were thicker in sections and made of boxwood. The life of a wood block was limited because it did not wear well. Limited, too, were the number of high quality impressions from a single block.

The early 16th century was the most popular period for the woodcut when it flourished, mainly in Germany. Albrecht Durer, that most celebrated painter and engraver, elevated the art of the woodcut from its relative crudity to an elegance which was rarely achieved by later engravers and designers. From 1630 to about 1770 wood blocks were overshadowed by metal, and wood engraving declined so that the art almost became nonexistent. Thomas Bewick (1753-1828) revived the art, and his work is comparable to the old masters. By the middle of the 19th century the wood block was no longer the medium of original designers. Its main use was by craftsmen engravers for book illustrations. Modern block makers provide much the same service for present day publishers.

### Etching

Etching, the process of producing lines on metal with acid, is thought to have originated in medieval times to decorate gold and for ornamentation on swords. It was in use in the 16th century, but the 17th century is looked upon as the heyday for etchings.

One should not mention etching without mentioning the most celebrated etcher of all time — Rembrandt. His etchings are estimated to number 300 plates. That's in addition to about 650 paintings and 2,000 drawings! Rembrandt was born in 1606 in Leyden and died in 1669. It should also be noted that many Rembrandt plates have been copied so well that it even defies the experts to tell the genuine article from the fake.

A notable step in the history of etching is marked by the work of the Spanish artist Goya, which bridged the 18th and 19th centuries. His etchings mirrored the happenings of his time.

In England, etching was not a popular mode of expression until well into the 19th century, though a brief interest was noted during the 1820s. At the same time, a revival of the art in France was well underway. Though the work was not considered to be of the highest quality, it paved the way for mid-19th century artists like Millet and Lalaune.

### The Lithograph and Other Later Techniques

Later engraving method incorporated more sophisticated techniques. Examples are:

*Line engraving.* A plate made by engraving lines into the plate to hold ink which is then transferred to paper. The origins of this method of producing prints cannot be accurately determined, but it is known that the process was used early in the 15th century and was originated in either Italy or Germany. Albrecht Durer was an early (and one of the finest) practitioner of this method.

*Lithography.* Drawing a design on a stone with a greasy crayon. Credit for developing the lithograph method goes to Alois Senefelder of Germany who discovered the process almost by accident in 1796. The French first saw the possibilities in this process, and it had already become an established art there by very early in the 19th century. It was first practiced in Britain sometime between 1818 and 1820.

*Aquatint.* Engraving by the use of acid on a resin ground. The aquatint process originated in France and dates from about 1760. Though it is nearly impossible to credit the origin to a single engraver, Jean Baptiste Le Prince's earliest plates date from 1768, and some sources credit him. At about the same time, two other gentlemen — one in the Netherlands and the other in Sweden — used similar techniques.

## POSTERS

Posters are still another step in the communication process of man. His first step was in communicating with his own family and nearest neighbors. Then it was tribe to tribe, government to government, and the more affluent communicating with each other and government officials. Finally, there was the need of the government, the more affluent, and eventually merchants and businesses to communicate with the masses, most of whom could not afford to buy newspapers and books. The answer: posters. Several posters in strategic locations could inform a whole community rather quickly.

### Broadsides

One of the first methods of advertising used by officials and merchants was the poster. In its earliest form, it was called a broadside or broad sheet, the size ranging from approximately 13″ by 16″ to over five feet in length. The exact size was determined by the dimensions of the printing press. Most broadsides were printed on one side of coarse white paper stock in black ink. They were tacked up on public bulletin boards and were a source of current news and general information to the masses.

The earliest form of these announcements in England was by William Caxton in 1477. During the 17th century, France instituted a ban on posting bills without permission. Examples in America date from the first use of the printing press circa 1639.

Among the most common broadsides are announcement broadsides: public sales, religious occurrences, scientific events, balloon flights, steamboat races. Most coveted are dated broadsides and those bearing the printer's name. Civil War broadsides are also much sought after, especially those from the South, and any from the West. Most elusive examples include a reward broadside, "For the Murder of President Lincoln," and a plea for recruits in the Confederacy, "To the People of Maryland." Some incorporated striking color additions.

Many broadsides were made to be used as posters. The terms are generally used interchangeably, although posters were most often reserved for advertising and usually printed in two or more colors. They were pictorial and decorative and for public display to offer services, goods, entertainment, and transportation. The posters might advertise new inventions, firearms and ammunition, or the preferred forms of transportation of the day. Posters from wild west shows are desirable, as is the "wanted" poster, though technically it is more of a broadside than a poster since its primary use is as a notice rather than an advertisement.

## Art Posters

Posters, with their connotation as communication media, sometimes are looked upon as stepchildren of the art world. Yet during the first hundred years of their existence, posters have also been rather curiously related to paintings. The form of the poster as we now know it has its roots in France. Early French examples include a 1715 advertisement for folding umbrellas and an 1800 illustration of young couples drinking at an inn, however, both items were only the size of a book page.

In 1848, Jules Cheret began producing color lithographic designs in Paris from his own press, and in 1869 published his first posters. By 1848, it was possible to print as many as 10,000 sheets per hour. During the same period, a small poster by Monet seemed indicative of the new, simpler patterns of design that later encompassed the essence of poster technique.

This simpler visual pattern-making technique was not so apparent in Cheret's work which seems more related to the traditional designs associated with European mural painting. Cheret himself confirmed this in an interview with English critic Charles Hiatt, when he maintained that in his opinion posters were not necessarily good advertising media, but they did make excellent murals. Cheret's reputation as the first name in posters is not because his designs are advertising masterpieces, but that his more than 1,000 posters are magnificent works of art (Fig. 25).

Cheret made his real contribution to the history of the poster after he returned to Paris following seven years in England. He began to produce posters from new English machinery based on the designs of Senefelder. He drew his designs directly onto the lithographic stone much as Goya and others had done at the beginning of the century. This reestablished lithography as a direct creative medium. For a number of years since the beginning of the century, lithography had been used more often as a means to reproduce other art. Despite this demotion of lithography, lithographed book illustrations were a tradition in France, and technically, the evolution of the poster can be traced through the printed page.

Several early French illustrators created designs, including advertisements, for periodicals

*Figure 25. Reproduction of Folies Bergere poster "La Loie Fuller" by Jules Cheret, 1893.*

dating from the French Revolution. Cheret's posters on the plain walls of this new city emerged as a new and vital art form. The material success of this public exhibition of fine art gave posters new recognition — the art gallery of the street. Cheret combined the technique of the lithograph book-illustrator with the scale and style of the masters and imbued it with the currency of popular language. His posters unite traditional technique with an appreciation of great mural art and the feel of the popular idiom. His expansion of decorated circus programs to the poster medium is an example.

Cheret influenced younger artists who saw in the poster a form of visual shorthand — ideas expressed simply and directly. His posters are ever recognized as the first steps in that direction.

By contrast, Henri de Toulouse-Lautrec (1864-1901), while intensifying Cheret's style, recorded the lifestyles of the street people. Toulouse-Lautrec could use elements in posters — caricature and simple, flat shapes and decorative lines — that he could not use within the conventions of paintings in his day. The quality of broad silhouette is more apparent in his posters than in his drawings and paintings of the same subjects. This same quality reappears in the work of many painters during the first half of the 20th century.

Toulouse-Lautrec's work was not altogether popular, but his posters are a major contribution to the history of posters even though he made only thirty-one during his brief lifetime of thirty-seven years (Fig. 26). Had he lived as long as Cheret — ninety-seven years — he would have lived until 1961. Indirectly, his contribution to the 20th century, reflected in all poster design, helped to establish the poster as an art form. Ironically, no poster artist of his caliber followed him in France.

The work of Spain's Pablo Picasso is an example of Toulouse-Lautrec's influence on painting. His painting of 1901, "The Blue Room," a portrait of his own room, incorporates Toulouse-Lautrec's poster, "May Milton," done in 1895. Picasso first went to Paris in 1900. He designed

and books. Guillaume Chevalier (1804-66) specialized in everyday themes for the periodical *Charivari*. Denis Auguste Raffet (1804-60) did two advertisements for Norvin's *History of Napoleon* which were actually a part of his illustrations for the book. Tony Johannot (1803-52) created 800 illustrations for the novel *Don Quixote* which included one advertisement. Although, like advertisements, these works were made up of words and pictures, they were too closely allied with the printed book to be considered posters. Plus, because of their small size, they were all but lost among the larger size advertising posters on public display.

The Paris of Cheret's day was redesigned into a new capitol city for Napoleon III by his architect Baron Haussmann. A city of great style and less ornate design replaced the old buildings material for this monumental task at the same time selling subscriptions for the finished project.

Audubon was forced to turn to English engravers to complete the prints when American counterparts deemed it too difficult a task. The complete work called *The Birds of America* comprised 435 plates which were originally sold for $1,000 a set. It is thought that fewer than 200 sets were actually bound into volumes. The number of loose prints varies because some of the original subscribers defaulted, and there were additional subscribers during its eleven years in the making. Figure 27 depicts print No. 171, "Barn Owl," which alone could fetch several times the original price of the complete work.

*Figure 26. Reproduction of "Avril Jardin" poster by Henri de Toulouse-Lautrec, 1893.*

several posters for a group of Barcelona expatriates in Paris, the styles of which were echoed in his later work. The simple, monumental forms that appear in Picasso's paintings as late as the 1930s seem to be a reflection of these early poster designs coupled with Toulouse-Lautrec's broad caricature.

Foremost among the mid-19th century print makers was John James Audubon, a name synonymous with bird pictures. He was born in Haiti, grew up in France, and came to America around 1803 to settle in Louisiana. Finding his niche was not in the business world, Audubon studied ornithology and turned his artistic talents to painting all the known birds of North America. He traveled through the United States and Canada between 1826 and 1842 gathering

*Figure 27. Audubon print, "Barn Owl," done in 1833. (Photograph courtesy the National Audubon Society.)*

*Figure 28. Reproduction of poster by Edward Penfield, 1897.*

### Art Nouveau

A new art movement interpreted the modern style of the turn of the 20th century and included poster design. It added decorative and ornamental values to linear patterns often derived from organic shapes. The style, partly an offshoot of the English Arts and Crafts movement, was developed by individual countries in Europe and in the United States. Britain and the United States called it "Art Nouveau"; Germany, "Jugendstil"; France, "Le Style Moderne"; Austria, "Secession"; Italy, "Stile Liberty": and Spain, "Modernista." The key element in each interpretation was "new." In decorative terms, it meant new social developments, new technology, and new expressions of the spirit.

Among the most significant elements of Art Nouveau design were the shapes derived from

Japanese prints. Some of these designs were taken from the wrapping paper of articles from the Far East. The Japanese print, which reflected daily life as well as more glamorous aspects of life, profoundly affected pictorial advertising. Most posters reflecting the Art Nouveau style also reflect a marked similarity in composition to what was the European version of the Japanese. While anticipating future developments, Art Nouveau also included elements of the past.

Characteristic of much Art Nouveau is a pronounced deviation from naturalism. One prominent feature of the general merging of styles and media was that one art form could and did affect the development of others, and the poster, after its artistic acceptance, was a part of this exchange. The work of Alphonse Mucha, who worked in Paris, is one of the most characteristic examples of Art Nouveau. His best known posters are of Sarah Bernhardt. Others of the period were Henri Meunier of Belgium, J. G. Van Caspel of the Netherlands, and Mataloni of Italy. In the United States, Will Bradley and Edward Penfield (Fig. 28) were in the forefront of the Art Nouveau style of poster design. Like many of the artists of that time, their work incorporated the Paris style coupled with their own individuality.

## MODERN ART MOVEMENTS

Art Nouveau came into disfavor in the 1920s, eclipsed by modern design which was in itself two-sided. Formal modern was a more functional design overshadowing the ornamental design so characteristic of the 19th century, and representing the future linking art with industry and the age of technology. Decorative modern was a reflection of the past and a product of affluent times, individualized and allied with painting. Cubism is an example of a formal art movement of the time. The works of Picasso and Braque are prime examples. It was at about this same time that Parisian designer, Cassandra (pseudonym of Jean Marie Moreau), a prime mover, applied the language of the formal art movements to the advertising poster.

The beginning of the end for Art Nouveau was proclaimed in 1900 at an exposition in Paris. The same was said of the Decorative Art Movements at the Exposition of Decorative Arts in Paris although the effects of decorative designs would echo through successive waves of imitation until the surging of innovative decoration from the United States introduced fresh elements of style in the 1940s.

### Art Deco

From 1910 to 1939 in Europe, decorative design seemed to have progressed in each country according to local custom and usage. The more angular shapes of Art Deco were incorporated in design.

### Emergence of the Graphic Designer

While the modern art movements brought stylistic changes to poster art design, another factor arose which was to affect the role of posters in advertising in general and their style as well — the importance of the graphic designer, a turn of the century outgrowth of the interchange between the fine and applied arts, a derivative of the original design movements of the 19th century.

### World War II and After

Posters produced during World War II added little to the already established achievements in poster design generally. Methods of mass communication had changed. Radio and motion pictures produced their own forms of advertising. Consumer advertising gave way to posters showing civilians on the home front how to grow food, conserve supplies, and guard the military secrets of their country. Since 1945, posters have reflected the rise of the anti-war movements.

Emerging in the 1940s and 1950s was a change in style in decorative arts. An amalgamation of formal and decorative styles developed in the Scandinavian countries met with less success in other European countries. A more flamboyant version of this same amalgamation was seen in the United States in the streamlined decoration of automobiles and in architecture.

## COLLECTING PRINTS

At the risk of sounding like a broken record, the first step in collecting prints, as in collecting anything else, is to learn about your (print) collectible of choice. The best source of information is often the print itself. Visit local galleries and museums and view prints. Brochures, color cards, and other illustrations may be available but, without seeing the print itself, it will be difficult to determine if the print is really to your liking. It is also necessary to study a variety of prints to determine which artist is painting the type of prints you would most enjoy — still life, wildlife, Americana, western, Indian.

To determine just how limited the editions are of your preferred artist, check two things:

1. The artist's past history, to learn whether his works sell out at distributor level when introduced or if they stay around a while.

2. Find out how often this artist releases a limited edition print and how many he or she does per year.

Collecting limited edition prints does require a larger outlay of money than most other collectibles. Like historical document collecting, it should be determined from the start how much the print collector wants to put into a collection.

A number of new artists continue to enter the limited edition field, and there is always the possibility of latching on to a comer. With the exception of very limited editions, who can say what will really appreciate in time. Collecting trends run in cycles, so it is important to be educated about one's chosen field and keep abreast of the market. Art can be a rewarding field to the knowledgeable collector.

## COLLECTING OLDER PRINTS

Older prints are not always as readily available. One source that is sometimes overlooked is old books, but not necessarily art books. Histories, geographies, travel and story books often contained very fine prints to illustrate the text. In very old books, on the verge of falling apart, the prints were sometimes removed and the book discarded. Often, some very well-known artists of their day made prints for book illustrations. As mentioned, some paper made in the last 150 years or so has not held up well. Apparently, the paper used for prints was a better grade because, in several books in my collection, the maps and other prints are in much better condition than the text paper. A word of caution: If the books are in good condition, the prints may be of more value left intact in the books. If the books are in bad shape and beyond any hope of repair, the only salvation for the prints may be to remove them carefully so they can be protected properly.

## MAPS

Maps are another form of prints; the process used to produce both being identical. What sets maps apart from other prints in the eyes of collectors is their purpose and use.

Maps are graphic statements incorporating direction and contour, and striving to give three-dimensional effects on two-dimensional paper. Early cartographers tried to make their work as accurate as possible, but they were hampered by crude and inadequate equipment and little background knowledge for reference. It was also not possible to establish longitude with any degree of accuracy, and there was no established unit of measurement.

Maps are one more extension of man's means of communication, an outgrowth of man's natural instincts for plotting the direction of his movements. The earliest explorers brought map-making tools and, if possible, their own map makers to chart their course and bring back records of where they had been. Of course,

each community had to have charts of land grants so each individual could stake out his own plot of ground within the proper boundaries. Artistic merits did not enter into it, and copies usually were not made for general consumption. Even peoples without written languages utilized map-like aids in their travels. Eskimos scratched crude maps on scraps of wood or ivory. In the Pacific Islands, Polynesians made charts of rattan to indicate prevailing winds and ocean currents.

### Ancient Maps

The oldest map known was found in Iraq (Babylonia) and dates from about 2300 B.C. It is a small clay tablet which appears to depict an estate in a mountain-lined valley. Egyptian map making can be traced back to as early as 1300 B.C. One of the few ancient Egyptian maps still in existence depicts the route from the Nile Valley to the gold mines of Nubia, part of ancient Ethiopia.

The Greeks made maps in the early 4th century B.C. of the inhabited world and were one of the first peoples to realize that the Earth is round. They were designers of the first projection and developed a longitude and latitude system. Regrettably, no ancient Greek maps are in existence today.

The Romans used maps for assessing taxes on land and as aids in military campaigns. They excelled at surveying and were among the first to make road maps, but few of their maps were preserved.

The most well-known ancient maps were the work of Claudius Ptolemy, a scholar who lived in Alexandria, Egypt circa 150 A.D. Included in his eight book *Geographia* is a map of the world as it was known at the time, and twenty-six regional maps of Europe, Africa, and Asia. Ptolemy's maps were known to very few scholars until the late 1400s when they were printed in an atlas.

### European Map Making

During the 1300s and 1400s, a sailor's chart

called a "portolano" came into common use. It was drawn on sheepskin and was developed to aid navigation along the coasts of the Mediterranean Sea. These maps showed the outline of coasts and harbors and marked shipping ports. The oldest examples of these charts date from about 1300, and judging from their fine workmanship, they were probably patterned after earlier maps.

Christopher Columbus, a map maker as well as navigator, used portolano charts. He was also a student of geography and quite familiar with the maps of scholars. Just one map made by Columbus, showing the northwest coast of Hispaniola, exists today.

The expansion of world knowledge can be traced in maps drawn to record discoveries. Almost every exploration voyage had a map maker to make sketch maps of coastlines, harbors, and islands plus a general map of each expedition. Scholars and cartographers would then add these new discoveries to their atlases and globes.

The earliest maps, dating from the 15th century, were primarily concerned with assisting travelers and recording land parcels. Though primarily for scientific value, they were sold to the public, and one must assume that their artistic value did not go unnoticed.

### Early Cartographical Techniques

The techniques of early cartography did not require all the printing techniques involving tonal gradations. Relief and engraved block prints were the usual forms of reproducing maps, and most of those of the 15th century and early 16th century were reproduced by these processes. The blocks served well because most early maps were produced in book form.

These early types were made with separate blocks of wood, with letters engraved in relief, which were assembled in the printer's form or frame along with the block carving of the map.

Copper plates were also in use at this time, but very few exceptional maps were produced by this technique during the 15th century. It was about the middle of the 16th century when the copper plate replaced the wood block. The quality of these early maps is dependent upon the same factors as any other prints. Obviously, the earlier impressions would be of higher quality than later ones.

The life of a wood block and copper plate were about the same. Though the wood block was of a softer material, less pressure was required to obtain an impression than with copper. The number of impressions that could be taken from a wood block or plate was dependent upon the quality of the original engraving and how careful the printer was in handling it. It is estimated that about 3,000 copies were possible from a new block or plate before it had to be reworked.

### Decoration on Early Maps

Decorations on these early maps of the 15th century were more or less restricted to the border. A whole host of decorative devices began to appear during the first half of the 16th century, including imitations of wood-carved scrolls, the compass indicator dividers, coats-of-arms, ships, cherubs with wind issuing from their mouths, and figures. From the mid-16th century to the 18th century, decorative cartography and technical achievement reached its zenith (Fig. 29). Usually, the older the map, the more embellishments it had.

### Coloring Maps

During this same period of excellence, maps were sold either plain or colored. Central European maps, produced from wood blocks, had color applied in flat washes sometimes quite thickly, while the Netherlands employed the craft of illuminating, which had become an established craft in that country before the middle of the century. Coloring maps was part of the illuminator's trade, and map engravers either employed illuminators in their own shops or placed the work with specialists in the art. As with any successful enterprise, unscrupulous ones often attempted to get into the act. Many experts, and some amateurs as well, have

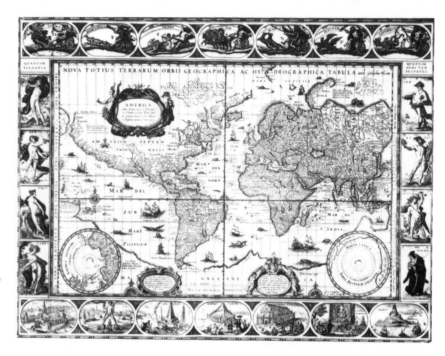

*Figure 29, Map of the World as known in 1638 with (roughly translated from Latin on map) "America as depicted by Christopher Columbus in 1492 and named for Americus Vespucius in 1499." (Photograph courtesy The Newberry Library, Chicago)*

attempted to color maps made in black and white because color generally demands higher prices than uncolored examples! Some collectors don't seem to mind, but it is something to consider.

## PROMINENT MAP MAKERS

Martin Behaim (1459?-1507), a German merchant-navigator, made the oldest existing representation of the Earth on a globe in 1492 in Nurnberg. It gives a fair indication of what European geographers knew of the outside world at that time. The Earth is not quite a true sphere, being more spheroidal in shape, but a globe is close to being an exact model of the Earth and has several cartographic advantages over flat maps. Longitude and latitude can be correctly drawn to chart locations. Scale over all the curved surfaces is true, and the shapes and areas of continents and seas are depicted accurately. Though a few globes are handmade, most

globes are made by a printing a world map on a number of tapering triangular forms called "gares" which are stretched and glued to a spherical shell.

A German map maker, Martin Waldseemuller (1470?-1518), made the first map to use the name "America" in 1507. The map was printed from a woodcut on twelve separate sheets measuring 18″ by 24″ each. The entire map measured 4½′ by 8′.

A Flemish geographer, Gerhard Kremer (1512-94), who adopted the Latinized name "Mercator," was one of the greatest map makers of the 1500s. Not only did he produce some of the best maps and globes of his day, but he also developed a map projection of much value to sailors. Abraham Ortelius (1527-98), another Flemish map maker, produced the first modern atlas in 1570. Johann Lambert, a German mathematician, was instrumental in contributing to the mathematical projection of maps.

# EARLY MAP MAKING IN AMERICA

Adventurer John Smith (1580-1631) made the first map when English settlers arrived at Jamestown. It was published in 1612 in England. The first English map of New England was also made by John Smith.

The American colonies did not have any professional map makers, but many maps of the area were produced by skilled amateurs. What is considered the best map produced by a colonist before the Revolutionary War, "A General Map of the Middle British Colonies in America," was produced by Lewis Evans of Philadelphia in 1755. Also in 1755, in England, John Mitchell produced "A Map of the British and French Dominions in America," a copy of which was used in 1783 to mark the boundaries of the newly established United States of America.

Newer and better maps were made by travelers and scholars following the movement to the West. An English map of North America, made by Aaron Arrowsmith, was used by Lewis and Clark to guide their westward explorations. They drew their own maps when they returned east. Zebulon Pike, Jedediah Smith, and John C. Fremont were other explorers of the West who provided newfound information for the map makers. Maps utilizing this information were used for immigration to Oregon during the 1800s and the California Gold Rush in 1849. The government later sent army engineers into the West to make railroad and geographical surveys. The maps (Fig. 30) illustrating the reports of these surveys were the foundation of the first accurate and fairly complete maps of the United States dating from about 1875. The United States Geological Survey, organized four years later in 1879, began to make large-scale, detailed topographical maps.

## Map Making in the 1900s

Road maps came into widespread use about 1910 with the advent of the automobile. With the introduction of air travel, many new kinds of

*Figure 30. Topographical and Railroad Map of the United States in 1869, including parts of British Possessions, West Indies, Mexico, and Central America. (Photograph courtesy The Newberry Library, Chicago.)*

maps and charts were necessary for pilots and passengers (Fig. 31). Air travel also made several important contributions to map making.

1. It gave map makers more accurate information about the Earth.

2. It aided the development of photogrammetry, the science of making maps from air photographs.

3. Map making could be speeded up by the use of vertical and oblique air photographs.

All of the United States has been photographed, and nearly all large-scale detailed maps rely on air photos.

Modern technology has also had its effect on map making. Computers are used to sort and arrange data for mapping and then to draw the map on film, paper, or television screen. Remote sensing devices, which include radar and infrared instruments, collect pertinent data about the Earth from airplanes and artificial satellites.

*Figure 31. Maps from airlines' packages for passengers which also may include post cards, catalogs, and the airline's magazine. (Author's collection.)*

## COLLECTING MAPS

No doubt, most rare, original antique maps are reposing in museums and other institutions around the world. The majority of older maps available to collectors will be in print form, but there may be rarities among them. Those of prominent map makers are very desirable. Some maps are very fine works of art though the artist may not necessarily be known. Maps are the ultimate in wall hangings. That¢s really the only way to read and really appreciate the larger ones. Maps of ancestral locales are very popular decorative items.

As with prints, old books can be very good sources for old maps, and also as with prints, it may be best to leave the maps intact unless the books are beyond redemption. History books were profusely illustrated with maps. Travel books and geographies are good sources, too. Caution must be used in examining these maps. Some of them are fold-out types, and after being folded in tight creases for so long, may tear when unfolded.

In my own collection is a book written in 1907 by a priest for the use of other priests traveling in Israel. It appears to have been very well made and not used very much. The text paper is the sheer tissue-type often seen in Bibles, and it is illustrated with many maps, some of which fold out. With the exception of one sheet of text which was torn loose, the text paper has held up well. Most of the folding maps have tears in them which may have been caused from being folded so long that the creases broke down the paper fibers rather than from excess use.

Of course, one can collect maps without ever acquiring any of the antique or older ones — originals or prints. Many other kinds of maps can make a collection or a specialized collection of just one type. Maps used to be among the giveaways by appropriate businesses and services, and some still may give them away — service stations, airlines, railroads, tourist bureaus and chambers of commerce, here and abroad. Service station maps are road guides to show you how to get to where you are going. Airlines and railroads (buses, too) depict their travel routes on their maps to tell you where you are going. Tourist maps picture all the exciting places to visit in a certain area to tell you what you can see when you get there. All large cities and some small ones have street guides (Fig. 32). Many cities offer guided walking tours with accompanying brochures and booklets laying out the route. Though these maps are more accurate than those early ones, they are not necessarily works of art. Most of them are really meant to be thrown away eventually, but they contribute one more facet to the lifestyle of an era.

## PHOTOGRAPHS

Unlike paper, painting, lithographs, printing, bookmaking, or other innumerable categories of paper items that are collectible, the category of photographs is a relative newcomer.

Man's fascination with the photographic art goes back to the Chinese who wrote in the fourth

*Figure 32. U.S. city maps and guides. (Author's collection.)*

century B.C. of a process in which an image of the scene outside could be projected inside onto a wall if a piece of paper containing a small hole was placed in the opposite window of a darkened room. Later, a first century A.D. Arab scholar, Alhazen; Roger Bacon in the 13th century; and Leonardo da Vinci in the 15th century commented on this same phenomenon. It was da Vinci who first used the phrase "camera obscura" meaning "darkened room" to describe the scientific experiment.

The camera obscura process was of great use to artists in copying nature with fine perspective by tracing the reflected images with brushes or pencils. By the beginning of the 19th century, three models of the camera obscura were available, the most sophisticated being a portable box that reflected the image onto paper made translucent by soaking in oil.

The next step was inevitable. Scientists realized the need for a method by which the image of the subject could be projected though the opening onto a material that would retain the image. The step was a big one and took centuries to come to fruition.

## THE BEGINNINGS OF MODERN PHOTOGRAPHY

The answer to the question, "Who invented photography?" is really multiple choice. Many minds contributed to the development of modern photographic methods. In 1727, J. H. Schultz made the first photographic copy of writing. In 1802, Thomas Wedgewood copied pictures by the action of light. In 1814, Joseph-Nicephore Niepce produced the first permanent pictures. In 1839, Louis Jacques Daguerre publicized his "daguerrotype" process of sensitizing a silver plate with iodine and developing, with vapors of mercury, the image produced on exposure. In 1840, Professor John W. Draper of New York University, made by this method the first photograph of a human face. In 1841, William H. F. Talbott presented his calotype process, which permitted many copies to be made from one paper negative. In 1851, Scott Archer introduced the process of producing sensitive silver salts in a film of collodion supported on a glass plate. In 1871, Dr. R. L. Maddox discovered the gelatin-silver bromide emulsion that is the basis of modern dry plates. In 1884, George Eastman patented a successful roll film of paper and, in 1887, Rev. Hannibal Goodwin applied for a patent on a transparent, sensitive, celluloid-like pellicle — the basis of the modern roll and cut film.

Both films and glass plates are coated with a creamy yellow emulsion of gelatin containing the bromide and iodine of silver.

Modern photographic apparatus is usually made up of a light-tight box (camera) equipped with a lens which, when the shutter is opened, focuses an image upon the sensitive surface of a plate or film. The exposed plate is developed by immersion in an alkaline, oxygen-absorbing solution of pyrogallol, metol, or similar reducing agent in which the plate gradually darkens and an image appears. The use of highly sensitive film will produce photographic results which far out-distance the capacity of the human eye. X-rays are a prime example.

## PHOTOGRAPHIC PAPER

The purity of paper has always been of major concern to manufacturers of photographic materials because there is a definite relationship between the purity of the paper base and the keeping properties of an emulsion coat on it. At one time almost all photographic paper base was manufactured from linen and cotton rags, but as the demand for paper of all kinds increased, the supply of suitable rags diminished. With the increased use of dyes, pigments, and other materials being used in the manufacture of cloth, much of the available rag stock did not meet the purity standards required for photographic use.

Over forty years ago, Eastman Kodak Company instituted a program of research and development into the possibility of making pure paper from wood pulp. Eventually this step and the efforts of pulp manufacturers themselves resulted in a product that proved to be as good or better than the best quality rag stock. Research is still going on.

Practically all photographic paper base today is made with purified wood pulp as the raw material. The quality of the paper currently used to make prints is not a factor in the deterioration of photographs. More deterioration of photographic prints is caused by the presence of residual processing chemicals more than any other single factor. Plus, deterioration due to exterior agents is always hastened by the presence of residual chemicals. These chemicals are sulfur-containing substances used for fixing, and silver compounds formed as a result of the fixing reaction. Some of these compounds react with the silver of the image to form silver sulfide, which turns the image a brownish yellow.

Residual silver compounds decompose and also form silver sulfide. The result is usually an overall yellowish stain on the print. An extremely small residue of silver compound is sufficient to cause a slight overall stain. The stain is much heavier if a relatively large residue is present, and the residue can affect the image as well.

## COLLECTING PHOTOGRAPHS

Photographs are also a relatively recent entry in the world of collectibles, but they have made rapid strides in achieving major collectible status. Early photographers often put together their own collections. They were proud to present deluxe books, personal albums, and limited-edition portfolios to friends and institutions. Photography was used initially as an adjunct to words, since it was thought of more as a scientific advancement than an artistic one. Libraries were especially happy recipients of works such as Peter Henry Emerson's *Life and Landscape on the Norfolk Broads* with text by naturalist Thomas Goodal, and William Henry Fox Talbot's *The Pencil of Nature*. The small size of these images coupled with their delicacy often required the security of the book pages to preserve them.

The British were especially fond of preserving photographs, especially those collected in their travels between 1850 and 1870. They are eagerly sought collectibles today. Others collect photographs not for their aesthetic quality but for their historic value. Unless it has been retouched, a photograph reflects and records a true image of a face, a structure, a location, or an event.

In the early 20th century, the greatest accumulations of photographs were those of booksellers. Some of the most discriminating private photographic collections today are indebted to these booksellers' often obsessive and indiscriminate salvaging and rescuing of photographs destined for the trash collector. Though the early efforts of these booksellers in buying and trading photographs were not really successful, their stock was eventually bought by astute collectors who realized that the photographs were preserved by the booksellers in their original state and often in complete sets. Examples of these 19th century photographs are not easy to find today.

Some of these early photographers collaborated in illustrating books but these illustrated books, dating from the middle to the end of the ninteenth century, were sometimes rather expensive.

The art of photography began to come into its own in the mid-1970s. Skyrocketing prices for paintings and prints in the late 1960s, coupled with an American economic downturn and less available income for luxuries, left the art marketplace with a sizeable void with less art available that would fit the traditional collector's budget. Photography filled the breach.

As with any other collectible, it is important to study before you buy. Know what you are buying. Collectors should know the criteria by which editors, publishers, scholars, and critics define "desirable" photographs. Only certain photographs have intrinsic value, and it is important to know how to discern, from the millions of photographs available, which ones are worth preserving. Photography books abound, and many are excellent and also quite collectible in themselves.

Some collectors may wish to consider a darkroom course. The best way to learn what constitutes a truly fine photographic print is to learn what is required to make one. Then you can judge the skills of a photographer from his skills as a darkroom technician.

Some of the same places where you find other collectibles may also yield photographs — bookstores, flea markets, antique shops, estate sales. And don't overlook the family attic. Vintage family photographs may fill a void in the family history as well.

Another aspect of photography that is growing in popularity is the collection of fashion photography and pre-World War II Hollywood photography. Also looked upon as one of the most exciting aspects of future photography collecting is commercial photography. Commercial photography long has been ignored by dealers and collectors because of its advertising and editorial connection. Real "artists" don't make work for hire, but collectors now are seeing this art form in a different light.

What then should a collector buy? Buy what is good, but also buy what you like. Photographs are taken to look at, and that should be the ultimate reason for a collector to buy them.

## PRESERVING PRINTS

Since posters and maps are variations of the same print-making technique, the methods for handling, preserving, storage, and display are the same. Photographs, being of different composition and media, require different preservation methods than other prints. That will be discussed following this section. In addition to observing the general preservation procedures in Chapter 3, several other considerations must be given to prints. Prints in general are more akin to works of art than most other paper items and are usually handled in that context.

Surprisingly enough, many fine prints have weathered several centuries in pristine condition. Unfortunately, many more have been damaged and lost because of neglect and careless treatment. Even today, irreplaceable prints — old and new — are destroyed by improper handling; faulty matting, mounting, and framing; unfavorable climatic conditions; overexposure to light; and well-intentioned but amateur attempts at restoration.

### Handling Prints

As with any other paper item, unframed prints should be handled as little as possible — and with clean hands. When lifting unmounted prints is necessary, hold with both hands near the edges. If a print is on rather thin or fragile paper, carry it laid flat on a sheet of acid-free, archival board.

### Tears in Prints

Accidental tears in prints should not be touched. Handling will soil the edges and hinder repairs. Lay the torn print between two sheets of acid-free, archival board until an expert can repair it. Damage can result from any amateur "first aid."

### Old Mats

Some prints may still have old mats intact. These old mats may be of historical interest or aesthetic value. They may contain notations or markets of famous collectors or be examples of decorative mats of the 18th or 19th century. If these mats appear to be in good condition with no sign of fungus infection, chances are they were made from good paper. It may be possible to reuse them after cleaning of surface dust, but since the components of these mats are not really known, it is safer to replace them with acid-free, archival mats. Any backing boards should also be replaced with archival quality, acid-free boards.

### Protecting the Surface of Prints

The delicate surfaces of prints can be damaged if allowed to rub against each other or any other non-archival quality surfaces. Acid-free, archival quality interleaving sheets can be used to separate the prints for storage or for stacking several together. Archival quality Mylar envelopes are also available to facilitate handling. These are made in several styles and sizes ranging from 5½″ by 8½″ up to 24″ by 35″ to accommodate large maps, prints, or broadsides. Acid-free storage and display folders with covers made of special archival polyesters are another option. Sizes run from 10″ by 12″ up to 36″ by 48″. Acid-free envelopes similar to large mailing envelopes are available in sizes from 6″ by 9″ to 11½″ by 15″.

### Preserving Oversize Prints

Oversize prints, 19th and 20th century posters for example, require special handling. Because of their awkward size, they are easily damaged. Sometimes they are not made from the best paper and can become brittle over the years even under the most favorable conditions. Deacidification may be a necessary first step followed by reinforcing with a strong, archival quality backing. Experts should be consulted for both purposes. Care in selecting backing materials is imperative because the backing materials are subject to aging and deterioration and may expand and contract at different ratios than the paper when exposed to atmospheric changes. The results can produce tensions between paper and backing, ultimately rippling and breaking the paper. Also, pressure applied during the mounting process may impress the texture of the backing right through the surface of the print. Mounted posters should be stored horizontally.

### Storage of Prints

Prints are usually stored horizontally to avoid warping. Small prints may be stored vertically if they are properly matted or encased in archival quality sleeves with archival boards for stiffness. This is so they will not slip out of place and become creased, bent, dog-eared, or possibly torn. Don't forget the interleaving sheets between the matted prints.

### Print Storage Boxes

Archival quality boxes made from acid-free board are available for the storage of prints. These are for horizontal storage and have drop fronts so that stored items can be removed without removing the boxes from shelves. They are available in sizes from 8½″ by 11″ to 28″ by 22″. Lignin-free drop front boxes with a calcium carbonate buffer are also available. Under proper conditions, these lignin-free boxes can remain durable for 500 years. Both types of boxes will accommodate the Mylar sleeves and the acid-free envelopes.

## PRESERVING PHOTOGRAPHIC PRINTS

### Black-and-White Photographs

Since some photographic materials are alkaline-sensitive, neutral pH storage materials as opposed to buffered storage materials should be used. Both are acid-free, and most photographic materials are safe in buffered enclosures, but it may be difficult to identify those that aren't.

### Categories of Black-and-White Photographic Prints

There are many kinds of photographic prints which are distinguished from each other according to format, image tone, surface gloss, and texture. Most museums, art galleries, and archives have photographic print collections. The concerns in the context of preservable prints are those in which the image-forming substance consists of microscopic particles of silver. With the exception of pictures dating from the beginning of photography (the so-called salted paper prints from the late 1830s to the mid-1860s), the image silver is embedded in a thin layer that may consist of albumen, collodion, or gelatin, the latter being used almost exclusively for the past hundred years.

Photographic prints usually fall into three categories, according to the nature of the support material:

1. Salted paper prints on a paper base not specifically formulated for photographic purposes. They have no distinct image layer in a binding medium.

2. Fiber-based prints, made by a handful of manufacturers from the 1860s to the present.

3. Contemporary resin-coated prints (RC papers) introduced in the late 1960s.

Collectively, all of these categories of photographs are often referred to as silver prints.

Very little is known about the properties of the early salted paper prints. These have proven to be more sensitive to factors causing deterioration than have the later prints.

Fiber-based prints are made on a paper base that ranks among the highest in quality and permanence. But like all photographic records containing elemental silver, the image, though on stable support, is susceptible to discoloration resulting from attack by aggressive chemical reagents.

To compound the issue, fiber-based prints are subdivided into printing-out papers (P.O.P.) and developed-out papers (D.O.P.), dependent on their manufacture and processing, which results in differences in the size and shape of the silver particles in the image. Images on printing-out papers, which include salted paper prints, albumen prints, collodiochloride papers, and certain silver gelatin prints, are more susceptible to image deterioration caused by chemical attack than are photographs on developed-out papers.

Though RC prints are developed-out, they do possess special properties arising from a plastic coating on either side of the paper base which enables them to be processed in a few minutes into dry, flat prints. However, they are considered less suitable for preserving images over extended periods of time (i.e., hundreds of years) than are conventional fiber-based papers.

### Handling Black-and-White Photographic Prints

Photographic prints often are used heavily for study and research. Ideally, they should be handled only with protective lintless nylon or cotton gloves. Prints should be mounted to prevent damage to corners and edges.

The appearance and integrity of the surface of a photographic print are principal factors in its aesthetic value. Surface properties are described in such terms as gloss, matt, luster, and texture. In combination with the image tone, they are inherent characteristics of a photographic print. Disturbing or destroying these delicate surface qualities changes the aesthetic value of the print.

Notations written in ink are likely to fade when photographs are displayed, and will invariably bleed and become illegible if they accidentally come in contact with water. If something must be written on photographs to identify them, it should be written on the back, as close to the edge as possible, with a soft lead pencil. A better method is to place the photographs in Mylar sleeves first and then into acid-free paper envelopes on which can be written all necessary documentation. Do not staple or paper clip other documents to photographs. Do not bend, fold, or roll photographs.

## Preservation and Storage of Black-and-White Photographs

Key requirements for long-term preservation of photographic black-and-white prints are uniform, low relative humidity (RH), a constant temperature, and the absence of reactive pollutants in the atmosphere. Excessively dry conditions will cause photographs to curl up tightly. Exposure to high relative humidity will relax the photos and uncurl them again. Properly processed prints on fiber-based paper are relatively stable when exposed to dry heat alone. However, because of the possible presence of aggressive chemicals — hydrogen sulfide, peroxides, ozone, and sulfur dioxide — conditions of dry heat are best avoided. The combination of many of these chemicals with either high relative humidity or high temperature almost always results in a discoloration of the image. Recommendations published by the American National Standards Institute (ANSI) are "RH for the storage of photographic prints may fall between 30% and 50%, but should never exceed 60%. However, recent investigations show that RH of 30% to 35% is optimum. Storage temperature may range from 15-25 degrees Celsius, but must never exceed 30 degrees Celsius. Daily fluctuations of more than 4 degrees must be avoided. Cold-storage conditions, even below the freezing point of water, are beneficial to the longevity of photographic prints."

Exposure to light is not a problem in the preservation of photographic prints since they are usually kept in the dark for long-term storage (i.e., in envelopes, boxes, or albums).

As with other prints, photographs should not be stored in contact with one another or in contact with the backs of the boards on which other prints are mounted. Archival quality individual Mylar photograph sleeves are available in several sizes. Sleeves offer high optical clarity that allows visual inspection without removal from the sleeve. Frosted extended tabs provide space to write indexing information. Several types of archival quality acid-free storage boxes are available in sizes compatible with the Mylar sleeves. One type of sturdy paper board resembles a shoe box. Another type, also of paper board, has a drop front. Several types of kits are available containing everything one may need for proper storage of photographic prints. Archival quality, acid-free albums and archival safe polypropylene pages with slip-in pockets are also available. The page pockets come in a variety of sizes. Mylar sheet protectors with pockets to fit a variety of print sizes are also available.

Photographic prints should not be stored for long periods in wooden boxes or wooden filing cabinets. Cabinets and other containers made from wood or wood pulp contain non-cellulose materials such as lignins, waxes, and resins that oxidize or break down in time and produce acids and other substances that migrate to any material in their immediate vicinity. In addition, peroxides released by the bleached wood often used for storage cabinets, as well as residual solvents from varnishes, can cause substantial damage to photographic prints. Steel with baked-on synthetic enamel coating, anodized aluminum, and stainless steel are recommended for shelves, filing cabinets, and storage boxes.

## Color Photographs

Unlike black-and-white photographs, which are made up of metallic silver densities, color images are made up of dyes, and like all other dyes, these can change with time, with resultant changes in density or color or both. Fortunately, the rapidly advancing technology of color photography has resulted in more stable dyes than were previously available.

Color photography as it is known today was introduced in 1935 when Eastman Kodak Company introduced Kodachrome film. The following year Agfa Company introduced Agfacolor film. The popularity of color film has grown steadily since then, and it has increased so rapidly in the past two decades that black-and-white prints are now both rare and more expensive than color prints.

**The Principal Processes of Color Photography**

Prior to 1935, color photographs — mostly in the form of lantern slides — were made by additive processes of color formation. Their principal characteristic was the presence of a silver gelatin layer and a layer consisting of blue, green, and red filter elements containing organic dyes. While some of these photographs, dating from the 1920s to 1930s, were on plastic films, the majority were on glass plates. Among them were commercial products such as Lumiere Autochrome Transparency Plates, Agfa Color Plates, Finlay Color Plates, Dufay Color Plates, and Duplex, Thames, and Paget Color Plates. Little is known about the permanence characteristics of these materials, but the recommendations given under "Permanence Characteristics" for other types of color photographs apply to these as well.

Most color photographic processes introduced after 1935 were made by the subtractive systems of color formation. Color photographs made by any of these processes, descriptions of which follow, have a complex physical structure. There are at least three distinct gelatin layers, into which are embedded the subtractive yellow, cyan, and magenta dyes. Some contemporary color films have twelve or more layers.

1. Chromogenic Development Process. The most common and the most important color photographic processes employ the principle of chromogenic development, in which the dyes that form the final image are chemically synthesized during development from colorless precursors initially present in the film layers. This process is used to make the majority of color slides, prints, motion picture films, and all color negatives. All major manufacturers in the world have produced color prints generally on a resin-coated (RC) base for the past decade or so.

2. Dye Imbibition Process. Dye imbibition is a second color photographic process in which preformed dyes are successively built up in a gelatin mordant layer from a printing matrix film to produce dye imbibition prints. Eastman Kodak's Dye Transfer Process is the only process of this type in use in North America. The now

defunct Technicolor motion picture process worked on this same dye imbibition principle.

3. Silver Dye Bleach Process. The silver dye bleach process incorporated into the emulsion during manufacture preformed dyes which are catalytically destroyed image-wise during processing. It is a material of low sensitivity but is used for identification photographs, in color microfilm, and is suitable for preparation of color prints and positive color transparencies.

4. Dye Diffusion Transfer Processes. Dye diffusion transfer processes are the technical name for instant color photographic processes which include, among others, Polacolor 1, SX-70, and Polacolor 2 by Polaroid, the discontinued PR-10 system by Eastman Kodak, plus similar products marketed in Europe and Japan.

5. Pigment Processes. Since the late 19th century, color prints have been made by printing processes that use pigments not unlike those found in oil paintings, and they are still made by these processes today. These pigment prints — tricolor carbro prints, gumbichromate prints, and Fresson Quadri-chromie prints — are highly stable, even upon prolonged exposure to light.

**Permanence Characteristics of Color Photographs**

All other conditions being equal, the stability of color photographs is determined by their inherent properties. These recommendations apply to all color photographs. Storage and display are major factors in the permanence of color photographs. Qualitative changes in the stability of color photographs vary according to whether storage conditions are under light or in darkness. The terms "dark storage" and "dark storage stability" specifically refer to color photographic materials. Dyes in color photographs appear to be the only materials in a visual art medium that fade appreciably in the dark. A possible exception are the varnish layers on oil paintings, which respond differently to dark conditions than to exposure to light. Color photographs may also build up stain when stored in the dark. As an example, a white area may become yellow.

When exposed to light, dyes in color photographs can fade just like textiles, watercolors, and printing inks. Add to this, a build-up of stains can occur in other components of the photograph. As a result, the photographic industry monitors the stability of its products under dark storage conditions and under light-fading conditions as well. Destruction of organic dyes through chemical reactions — oxidation or hydrolysis, for example — is considered irreversible. At present, it is not believed possible to restore faded color photographs by chemical means. Therefore, prevention of dye fading is essential.

### Preservation and Storage

Color photographic materials are more sensitive to high relative humidity (RH) and high temperature than black-and-white photographs. Recommendations of the American National Standards Institute (ANSI) are an RH of 25% +/- 5%. RH must never exceed 60% and should not be allowed to fluctuate. Currently, cold storage is recognized as the most effective preservation measure for large collections of color photographic materials. Storage at temperatures below the freezing point of water (0 degrees Celsius) will extend the longevity of all color films and prints considerably if the relative humidity is kept at 25% +/- 5%.

### Handling Color Photographic Prints

Like black-and-white photographic materials, color photographic materials undergo much use for study and research. Lintless nylon or cotton gloves should be worn at all times when handling any of these materials. The appearance and integrity of the surface of a photographic print are major factors in its aesthetic value. Surface properties are described as gloss, matt, luster, and texture. In combination with the image tone, they are inherent characteristics of a photographic print. Disturbing or destroying these delicate surface qualities changes the aes-

thetic value of the print. Mounting color prints can avoid damage to the corners and edges in handling. Color photographs should not be bent, folded, rolled up, left unprotected, stapled, or attached to other documents with paper clips. If identifying information must be written on the photograph, it should be done on the back with a soft lead pencil, and as close to the edge as possible.

## MATTING AND FRAMING PRINTS

There are many reasons for matting prints other than the most obvious one of framing them.

1. A mat provides support and protection from damage during handling.

2. Mats facilitate storage and protect against wrinkling and buckling.

3. A window mat creates an air space to protect the image of a work, when framed, from direct contact with the picture glass.

4. Accession numbers, title, and other information can be written on a mat rather than on the print itself.

5. A mat adds to the aesthetic quality of the presentation of a print.

Since paper is extremely sensitive to contamination by poor-quality materials, the use of archival quality, acid-free boards, papers, and adhesives is essential. The best boards are made of 100% rag fiber. White or buff boards are recommended. The matting techniques described here are the simplest and the most commonly used. Paper items requiring special techniques are best left to qualified experts.

### Mat Sizes

The size of the mat may be dictated by the size of an existing frame. Barring an existing frame, mats are best cut to a standard size for convenience and economy in storage and display. Frames can be made or purchased to fit when and if display is desired. Mats and frames are available in a number of pre-cut sizes from 8" by 10" up to 28" by 36". Mat size should give a balanced appearance to the print as well as provide adequate protection during handling. The window opening should be large enough to expose the image, platemark, signature, title, and any other signature notations. Normally, the top and side margins are the same width, while the bottom margin is slightly larger. This creates a balanced optical effect.

Do not under any circumstances trim a paper item to fit an existing frame or fold any edges under for the same purpose. Some of our ancestors did just that. Fine prints and other works of art — even oil paintings — were cut to fit odd-shaped frames — round, oval, etc., or smaller sized ones. Alterations of this type can destroy the original intent of the artist as well as damage a fine work.

## Preparing the Mat

The following techniques are recommended by the Canadian Conservation Institute for preparing the mat (Fig. 33):

### Materials for one mat:

2 pieces of acid-free matboard

1 strip of gummed linen tape, cut to the length of the longest mat edge

mat cutter

weights

paste brush

release paper (coated with silicone so that glue will not stick)

blotting paper

Japanese paper for hinges

wheat starch paste

1. Cutting the Window. Place the print on one of the pieces of matboard and measure the margins. Using a pencil, lightly mark the window on the board. Cut the window out with a mat cutter, ensuring that the edges will overlap the edges of the print by at least 2-4mm in order to hold it down. Windows are usually cut with a 45 degree bevel to enhance their appearance, reduce shadows, and minimize the possibility of pressure marks left by a straight cut. Because a slight burr is created when the board is cut, the back of the beveled edges should be lightly rubbed down using fine sandpaper.

2. Joining Front and Back Boards. Join front and back boards together along one edge using gummed linen tape. The tape provides maximum support if placed on the longest edge — on the top, if the print is horizontal, and on the left edge if the print is vertical. Use weights on both boards to prevent slipping. Moisten the tape with a sponge and center it over the join. Cover with release paper, blotting paper, and weights. Leave to dry for several hours.

3. Hinging. Hinging is the best way to attach works on paper to their mats. Hinging provides secure attachment while permitting some movement of the paper in response to changes in climatic conditions. Suspending by hinges also permits easy examination of the reverse of the work. In addition, removal from the mat, if necessary, is simple and straightforward.

Although commercially available gummed and pressure-sensitive tapes are convenient to use, they are often made of inappropriate materials with poor aging properties. Eventually they will cause staining and damage and may be difficult to remove. One hundred percent bast fiber Japanese mulberry paper, which is made from long fibers, is strong and therefore suited to hinging. The choice of hinging paper depends on the size and weight of the print. Hinges should not be heavier or stronger than the print itself, yet must provide adequate support.

The T-hinge is the strongest and most versatile hinge for standard matting. Most works on paper require two hinges. Additional hinges may be required to support larger works. A T-hinge is made from two rectangular pieces of the selected paper. One (the stem tab) is attached to the top reverse edge of the work. For additional strength, the other (cross) tab is placed at right angles across the stem tab on the support board.

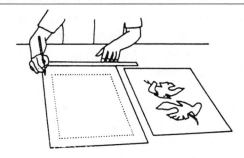

A. *Marking the window on the board.*

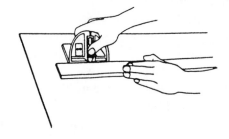

B. *Cutting the window out with a mat cutter.*

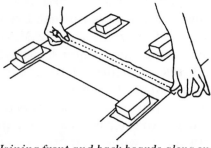

C. *Joining front and back boards along one edge using gummed linen tape.*

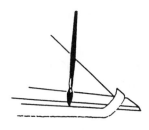

D. *Feathering the edges of the tabs.*

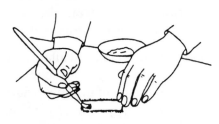

E. *Brushing paste onto the stem tab.*

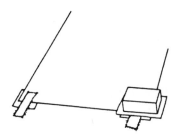

F. *Attaching the hinge.*

G. *Attaching the crosspiece tab.*

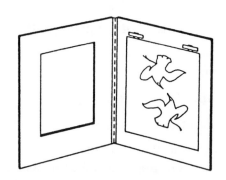

H. *Repeating process on second hinge.*

*Figure 33. Matting a print. (Matting techniques courtesy Canadian Conservation Institute.)*

Feathering the edges of the tabs (tearing rather than cutting them from the hinged paper) provides better adhesion and avoids formation of ridges which might result from cut edges. To make a feathered tab, dip a small pointed brush or a ruling pen in water. Draw a line on the hinge paper as long as the desired hinge. Tear a strip off against the edge of a ruler. Use the same technique to divide the strips into appropriate lengths to make the tabs. The width of the tabs will depend on the size of the work but should not be narrower than 1.5 cm.

Wheat starch paste is the best paste for hinging. A superior smooth wheat paste adhesive can be made by very carefully cooking purified, uncooked food-grade wheat starch. However, there is now available a new precooked, crystallized wheat paste from which you can create real museum quality wheat paste with no cooking. Just add water slowly. Dry crystals make it possible to mix very small quantities of paste at a time.

Brush paste onto one centimeter of the stem tab. Attach the hinge to the reverse of the work on the top edge near, but not at, the corners. Place release paper on both sides of the pasted area to prevent sticking to other surfaces. Add blotting paper and a weight and leave to dry for several hours. Repeat the procedure for the second hinge.

When the tabs are dry, position the work on the mat, using a small weight to prevent it slipping. Place a clean piece of white paper between the weight and the artifact. With scissors, trim off the feathered edge from one long side of the crosspiece tab. Brush paste onto the tab and put in place across the stem tab on the back support board. To permit free lifting of the matted work, leave a narrow space corresponding to the thickness of the paper between the top edge of the object and the cut edge of the crosspiece tab. Place release paper and a weight over the crosspiece tab and leave to dry for several hours. Repeat the procedure for the second hinge.

### Glazing Materials for Framing Prints

Glass has been the traditional glazing material for framed works on paper. However, in recent years sheet plastic products suitable for glazing have become available. When selecting glazing materials for the works on paper, it is important to be familiar with the properties of glass and sheet plastic and their appropriateness as glazing materials.

### Advantages of Plastic

1. Weight. Plastic is lightweight and ideal glazing for large works, and if a work must be transported to another location, the light weight facilitates moving.

2. Breakage. Plastic is less breakable than glass. Broken plastic fragments are not as hazardous to the work or to individuals involved with them.

3. Ultraviolet Absorbers. Plastic is available with ultraviolet (UV) absorbers which eliminate or significantly reduce the amount of ultraviolet light transmitted to a work. If windows and lights where the work is housed do not have UV filters it is essential to use sheet plastic with a UV filter for glazing light-sensitive artifacts.

4. Types of Sheet Plastic. Plexiglas, an acrylic, is the sheet plastic most commonly used for picture glazing. It is available with or without UV absorbers. Acrylite and Lucite, produced by other manufacturers, are the same as Plexiglas. Lucite SAR is the same acrylic as Plexiglas but has been treated with a coating which resists marring.

Lexan 9034, a polycarbon plastic, is much stronger than acrylics such as Plexiglas and Lucite SAR. It is advertised as unbreakable. Lexan Margard MR-5000 is similar to Lexan 9034, but is coated for superior resistance to abrasion. When used on pictures or in windows, Lexan 9034 and Lexan Margard MR-5000 are a safeguard against vandalism. Both types incorporate UV absorbers.

**Disadvantages of Plastic**

1. Electrostatic Charge. Plastic glazing readily picks up and holds an electrostatic charge. Excessively dry atmospheres and rubbing of plastics in the cleaning process aggravate this tendency. A charged sheet of plastic attracts and holds dust on the outside surface. On the inside of the frame, it can attract and hold flaking paint, or lift particles from the image of loosely bound media like charcoal, pastel, chalk, and conte crayon.

Obviously, plastic material is not recommended for glazing works with images done with loosely bound media or those with cracked or flaking paint.

2. Abrasion. Uncoated plastic glazing materials are susceptible to scratching and must be handled carefully. Lexan and Lucite SAR are recommended over other products since they are treated to resist abrasion.

3. Bowing. Plastic materials are less rigid than glass and have a tendency to bow when used to glaze large works. A thicker plastic will help avoid bowing in large works, but the thicker plastic will not always fit into the average frame, which is designed to accommodate the thin plastic.

4. Glare. Sheet plastic cannot be coated to reduce glare. If adjusting lighting does not reduce the glare, coated glass is an alternative.

**Advantages of Glass**

1. Electrostatic Charge. Glass picks up very little electrostatic charge.

2. Abrasion. Glass is more resistant to scratching than plastic.

3. Rigidity. Glass is rigid. A glass of the thickness normally accommodated by most frames will remain rigid even when used for large works.

4. Glare Reduction. Glass can be treated to reduce reflected glare. Standard non-glare glass is etched on one side to create a finely blurred surface which scatters light, in turn reducing glare. This glass has a hazy appearance, and the only way to reduce it is to place the glass in di-

rect contact with the work. Since proper preservation methods dictate that a space should be between the work and the glazing, this type of non-glare glass is not recommended.

Denglas, sheet glass treated with a coating, significantly reduces glare without losing transparency. It is used in the same manner as uncoated glass. Denglas is the preference when non-glare glazing is required. Because of its coating, Denglas does tend to smudge easily and requires a special cleaning fluid.

**Disadvantages of Glass**

1. Weight. Glass is heavy. When large sheets are used, sturdy frames and adequate hanging systems are a must. Thin, lightweight aluminum frames may not be strong enough for large works. Heavier, more traditional frames may be more suitable and necessary. Hooks and wire must be strong enough to carry the weight of the mat, frame, and glazing.

2. Ultraviolet Filtering. Glass is not available with ultraviolet absorbers, with the exception of heavy laminated glass. Ultraviolet light must be filtered by other means if glass is used for glazing.

3. Brittleness. Glass is sharp, breaks easily, and is hazardous when being cut, installed, or shipped. Masking tape should be applied in a grid pattern over the glass before shipping so that, in the event of breakage, splinters are less likely to fall onto or damage the work.

**Care of Glass and Plastic**

Glass may be dusted periodically with a soft brush or lint-free cloth. Both glass and plastic materials should be removed from the frame before being cleaned with liquid cleaners of any kind.

**Framing Prints**

When framing a print, care should be taken to ensure that there is sufficient space between the glass and the print. Changes in temperature may result in condensation of moisture on the inside of the glass. Besides water stains, it will increase vulnerability to microbiological and photochemical harm if the print is allowed to touch the glass. Also, once the moisture has dried, the print may stick firmly to the glass which can severely damage its surface.

A properly matted print should not touch the glass, but some prints are not meant to be matted — some modern and early American ones. To compensate for the lack of a mat, a ragboard, acid-free strip or fillet can be inserted between glass and print all around the frame.

The board used to close the back of the frame should also be archival quality and acid-free. Thin wooden boards were often used on early American frames, but they are harmful because of the acid and resinous contents of the wood which will penetrate to the print and in time stain and damage it.

To prevent dust penetration, the frame should be sealed at the back with archival quality paper framing tape.

## PRINTS AS COLLECTIBLES

Prints often are collected for their aesthetic quality more than for monetary value, although many collectors seek out the best that is available. The true artistic quality that enhances the aesthetic value may be lacking in inferior prints. Unlike most other paper items which are preserved primarily for their historical value or nostalgic character and may possess little or no aesthetic quality, print collectors almost always look upon their acquisitions in context and must like them as art before they consider purchasing.

Though it might be possible to assemble a print collection that represents a small history of print making, collectors are usually more interested in the work of particular artists or school of artists or a favorite subject. Prints represent the artistic side of paper memorabilia, and that intrinsic artistic quality may be the best reason for collecting them.

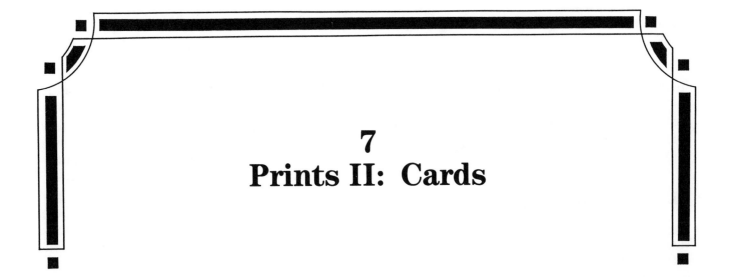

# 7
# Prints II: Cards

Humans have always needed some means of communication with others, first within their own tribe and small sphere of the world, then gradually expanding their communication skills as their world expanded. Even the most primitive communication methods were reserved for government officials and the well-to-do to deliver messages and keep tabs on other tribes. With the advent of paper and the Industrial Revolution came mass communication and the means to relay news and happenings between and among families, communities, and nations.

Prints, Part II explores several popular means of printed communication that in their heyday exposed a whole new world to the masses. No longer was postal communication limited to the government hierarchy and the affluent. It was also the era of the printed word as the primary means of communication.

The term "card" spans a wide spectrum, and the introduction of this form of communication coincides with the onset of the use of paper by and for the masses, as well as with the invention of the printing press and the development of modern printing methods and the incorporation of color into the printing process. Cards are classified as "prints" since any reproduced design or picture falls into that category.

For collectors' purposes and ease of cataloging, cards usually fall into three major divisions: advertising cards, insert cards, and souvenir cards.

Advertising cards were given away or used solely for advertising purposes. They were not sold or paid for in any fashion. There were two major types of these cards. The first type is referred to as "Trade Cards." They were handed to customers by the retail tradesmen and store-keepers and include most of the smaller varieties. The second type is referred to as "Store Cards." They were used as in-store advertising as hangers, counter cards, banners, etc., and ranged up to several feet in length. Though intended only for store use, many have been preserved, and all are now highly prized collectibles.

Insert cards were packed or inserted with a product, and sold to a customer that way. The only way to get them was with some product like cigarettes, coffee, or candy, and they are commonly referred to as "Cigarette Cards," "Gum Cards," etc., depending on their origin. They were intended to be collected and have remained popular with collectors. Sometimes they were given in exchange for coupons included with the product and those may be in the form of albums or large size items. Many were made of cloth or metal instead of cardboard. Their first use was in the late 1870s. Baseball cards are a prime example.

Generally, souvenir cards were made to be sold because of their own intrinsic interest. All of them were meant for a practical use or purpose, but their primary appeal to collectors is the subject matter of the illustration or design and the artistic elements, as well as the historical aspects. Some of them have an advertising or gift connotation while retaining their essential souvenir quality. The most popular forms of souvenir cards are picture post cards and greeting cards.

## ADVERTISING CARDS

The businessman's first advertising was in the form of a board above the entrance to his establishment painted with a word or two announcing his line of goods or services — SHOE REPAIRS, TOBACCO, GENERAL MERCHANDISE. After printing became readily available to the masses, it did not take Mr. Businessman long to realize the value of handing out small printed cards with the name of his business and its location. If the printer was so equipped, the cards were decorated with borders and ornaments, or if the businessman's budget allowed, a small illustration made for that particular business.

These cards were not colored and probably not considered attractive, so were not of much interest as collectors' items. Probably the most famous card of this type is that of Paul Revere which advertised his silversmith business.

Few of these cards are dated, and sometimes the most intensive research will not reveal the period of use. A listing of about 150 United States advertising cards has been adjudged to be pre-1810, and practically all are in various older eastern museums and libraries. Cards from the 1810-50 period are more numerous, but not plentiful, and few have been found by collectors. Types of the "pre-1850" style were still in common use in the 1870s, and the style is still being used for personal business and calling cards.

Early cards can sometimes be recognized by the typefaces and the absence of brand names since they tended to advertise businesses rather than products. Clothier, tailor, hatter, builder, printer, gunsmith, and similar occupations may be found. Some were embossed in color. Many were printed on the highly glazed cards popular at that time. The earliest ones may be on heavy paper or very light card stock without color, glazing, or embossing.

These early advertising types were gradually replaced by colored cards personalized for individual businesses. Businessmen were quick to note that the more ornate of these cards were attractive to collectors, which in turn meant a long-range medium for the promotion of their products and services.

The use of colored cards increased yearly with improved and less costly printing techniques. By the 1880s, making scrap albums of these cards was a nationwide hobby. This boon in the card-making industry lasted over ten years. The demand was so great that just about every business, large or small, was obliged to give out cards of one kind or another. The common name for them is "Trade Cards" (Figs. 34 & 35) since they were distributed by tradesmen to customers either by hand, laid on the counter, or wrapped with a purchase. Others were distributed by salesmen and agents or sent through the mail. Most of these cards were about 3″ by 5″ although some were as long as 7″ and 8″ or even longer.

## INSERT CARDS

Once the popularity of advertising cards was established, the next inevitable step was the development of the idea of distributing them by packing one with a manufacturer's product. Some evidence indicates that this first occurred in the 1870s, but the practice did not become widespread until 1885 when tobacco companies picked up on the idea and used it extensively. From there, it spread to other packaged products — coffee and other food products, chewing gum and other items. The practice is still widely used to create demand and goodwill. Since an insert must be obtained by purchase of the product, technically, it is not a giveaway.

## TOBACCO CARDS

The tobacco industry in 1880 did not consider cigarettes of great importance, especially the paper-wrapped kind. The tobacco leaf wrapped kind, then called cigarettes but now

Figure 34. Reproduction of a 19th century trade card advertising Scott's Emulsion.

Figure 35. Reproduction of a 19th century trade card advertising Clark's Thread.

called little cigars, were more popular and widely used. Several manufacturers thought otherwise and sought to enhance their appeal. Cigarettes were at first rolled by hand and wrapped in neat bundles of twenty, mostly by girls. The small shell and slide box containing ten cigarettes for five cents was introduced about 1885. A small picture card was packed in each box, and sales spiraled. From 1885 to 1892, almost every manufacturer included the cards, at least briefly. Cigarettes became such a big business, the demand was too much for the hand-rollers, and they were replaced by fast automatic machines.

The 1890s marked the beginning of the end for that era of cigarette cards. With the indomitable Duke of Durham holding sway over the industry, competition was stifled, and the need for cards ceased.

Turkish tobaccos dominated the market from roughly 1910-15. Old brands were all but crowded out of the market to be replaced by Turkish names, completely foreign to an industry which has its roots in American soil. Small, independent manufacturers were responsible for the change, mostly Greeks, who used imported leaf from Asia Minor to give their product a slightly different taste. They revived the card inserts as a part of their advertising, and collecting was off and running again. A few cards were issued in 1909, the Hudson-Fulton Series, for example, and a few in 1916 such as World War I pictures. Several sets resembling later 20th century issues were issued from 1898 to 1902. These were mostly issued with packaged cigars.

## COFFEE AND OTHER CARDS

For a brief time around 1890, a number of card sets were distributed in packages of coffee. Other cards were also issued as coffee advertising, and it is sometimes difficult to distinguish them from the inserts. Cards were issued with other food and grocery items for brief periods. Among these were baking soda, bakery items, ice cream and other dairy products, meat products, beverages, paper napkins, tissues, soap.

## PERIODICAL INSERTS

Newspapers and magazines also offered removable insert items, including other forms like photos of prominent people, gallery art, paper dolls, flag sets, and historical events, as well as cards. They were usually distributed as supplements to the paper, in exchange for coupons clipped from the papers, or as premiums for new subscriptions.

Supplements are not attached to the paper, and they were once a common feature of Sunday newspapers and many magazines. Most of them are of the "print" type, and very few are seen today. Several sets in card format were given in exchange for coupons. The new subscription method was not extensively used.

Supplements may be one of the earliest types of inserts known. They date back to at least the late 1870s. Many card collectors have not actively sought the large-sized print types because of their size and difficulty in mounting. Sports and historical events are possible exceptions.

## U.S. CANDY AND GUM CARDS

Cards were also issued in packages of candy — caramels, Cracker Jacks, candy cigarettes — and bubblegum. These cards were issued from about the turn of the 20th century into the early 1930s, and featured military scenes, flags, animals, movie stars, and other topics as well as sports figures, primarily baseball players. They were originally meant for children, but over the years have attracted a large adult following. The sizes of these early ones varied from 2″ by 3″ to 3″ by 5″, with some slightly smaller and others a bit larger.

## BASEBALL CARDS

The first baseball cards were issued in the 1880s, some twenty years before the American League was organized in 1901. The early baseball cards were included with cigarettes, and they dominated the trading card field through the early part of the 20th century.

By today's standards, the photographs and action on the cards were crude. The photos were taken in an artist's studio with the action simulated to appear like actual game conditions. Ball players were depicted catching or hitting a baseball suspended on a string or sliding into a base set on a wooden floor. These pictures were printed on paper with a sepia tone.

Bubblegum came on the market in 1933, and with it came a new type of picture card of heavy cardboard and averaging 2½″ by 3″. These were quite popular until their production was halted by World War II.

### Topps Bubblegum Cards

Topps entered the baseball card field in the post World War II period with its first series in 1951. The series consisted of two individual series of fifty-two cards each.

The baseball cards that have become the prototype for all subsequent Topps cards were introduced in 1952. They were larger cards that included statistics, personal information, team emblems, and color pictures of the players.

Topps has also produced a long line of non-sports cards, from Elvis Presley and Davey Crockett in the 1950s, to Michael Jackson and Roger Rabbit in the 1980s.

Topps photographers take pictures of baseball players at the spring training camps of the Major League teams and at the baseball stadiums during the season. Several different types of photos are taken of each ball player. Action pictures are taken, as well as posed portraits. Pictures are taken from different angles, with and without caps.

The staff of the Topps Sports Department compiles the statistics listed on the back of each player's card from the official league records. Millions of youngsters over the years have used baseball cards as their major source of statistical information. The sports staff also is responsible for creating the facts and highlights on the backs of the cards.

### Valuing Baseball Cards

The value of an average card ranges from a few cents to a dollar, depending on the age of the card and the demand for the individual player. Rookie cards of the leading stars of the game have become highly prized by collectors. Also, when a player enters the Hall of Fame, his card become more valuable.

The most valuable baseball card in existence is a 1910 Honus Wagner issued by the Sweet Caporal Tobacco Company. Wagner, a non-smoker, objected to the cigarette company's use of his name and picture. The card was removed from circulation and few are known to be in existence today. Wagner's card has been sold for as much as $25,000.

The most valuable Topps card is the 1952 Mickey Mantle card. Mantle's card has been sold for over $6,000 and is now valued at approximately $8,000.

## SOUVENIR CARDS

While advertising cards and insert cards offered the means for officials and businessmen to communicate with the masses through the written word, souvenir cards offered the means for the masses to communicate with each other on a personal and one-to-one basis through the written word. The best known and most popular forms of souvenir cards are greeting cards and picture post cards. Each has developed into a burgeoning industry all its own, but often are interchangeable. The post card form is often used in creating greeting cards. Greeting cards often serve the same purpose as post cards.

## GREETING CARDS

### New Year's Cards

The tradition of exchanging greetings predates the advent of Christianity. Today's greeting cards can trace their ancestry much further back than most of the human race. Born of man's need for emotional expression and shared experience, the greeting card first took concrete form in the celebration of the New Year. Early Egyptians and Romans looked on the New Year as the time of nature's awakening and celebrated by exchanging small tokens. These often were symbols of goodwill or friendship — fruits, olive branches, flowers, feathers, lucky copper pennies, etc. Later these symbols were pictured on terra cotta tablets and other objects and were accompanied by inscriptions such as "A Happy and Prosperous New Year to Me." The hope was that the intended recipient would look upon it as a token of friendship.

Two copies exist of such medals addressed to the Emperor Hadrian who reigned from 117 to 138 A.D. These medals bore a portrait of the Emperor on the front and carried the following message on the back in a somewhat abbreviated form: "The Senate and People of Rome wish a Happy and Prosperous New Year to Hadrianus Augustus, the father of the country." It is presumed this was a mass-produced "greeting card" to be bought by those who wished to remember their Emperor on this all-important first day of the new year.

No doubt there were many more forms of greetings down through the years descended from those early Greek and Roman examples. We can assume the artistic Egyptians of a later age inscribed their messages of greeting in hieroglyphics and drawings on papyrus scrolls. The learned Greeks, too, inscribed their greetings on scrolls, terra cotta, or metal. The Assyrians and the Jews probably did as well. Regrettably, none were preserved so a wide gap exists in their recorded history. The trail doesn't pick up again until about 1450 in Germany with the appearance of ready-made New Year's cards.

After 1450 and up to about the 16th century, New Year's cards done in woodcut appeared in abundance. A typical one is a woodcut depicting the Christ Child with His cart loaded with bags of good wishes. Traveling with the Christ Child and in the background is St. Christopher. "Who is at the gate?" inquires the gate-keeper. "It is I," replies the Christ Child, "Bringing a good year." Cards of this type may have been used for holiday decoration as well as for sending.

These crude woodcuts evolved into more refined works, and the messages and greetings came closer to the ones we send today. Another German woodcut of the 16th century is a good example. Freely translated, it reads: "I, Christ, am new, a child born of a pure virgin. May this New Year — new and pure like myself — be auspicious to thee, O Man."

The trail was lost again for a brief time to be picked up again in Vienna. During these lost years, another big step was taken in the progress of the greeting card. Dating from 1770 until well into the 19th century, a big business evolved among engravers and printers in supplying most of continental Europe with New Year's cards with numbers available to fit almost anyone, from sweetheart to mother-in-law. Strangely enough, English-speaking countries appear not to have favored this practice. Perhaps another claim to the romantic nature of continental Europe!

The New Year's holiday in modern times has become, in conjunction with the rise in popularity of the custom of celebrating Christmas, a part of the holiday season. As such, these two days have evolved almost into a unit in the greeting card world.

## Mother's Day Cards

Mother's Day greetings are not so recent an innovation either. One Sunday each year, 17th century apprentices went a-mothering unless they were too far from home. Then they sent greeting letters — the first Mother's Day cards. The origins of other card-sending occasions are rooted in times almost as ancient.

## Valentine's Day Cards

The second oldest branch of the greeting card family and second to Christmas cards in popularity are Valentines. Historians claim that the true origin of the day we call St. Valentine's dates back to the pagan days of ancient Rome to an annual lottery called Lupercalia which was always held in February. In honor of their god Pan and goddess Juno, young people of Rome would draw the name from an urn or bowl of the one who was to be their beloved of the year. This lottery survived for centuries.

One offshoot of Christianity was the naming of February 14 in honor of several saints named Valentine. Historians contend that the Lupercalia lotteries eventually were held on that same day. From that arose the association of Valentine's Day with the avowal of one's love. The logical conclusion of these historians is that nothing is revealed in the lives of any of the Saints Valentine to indicate why that most romantic of days should have been named after any of them!

Of course, handmade cards existed long before the superior artistically printed ones. It was not until after 1840 that printed valentines were sent on a wide scale. Illustrations were fashioned to suit the sender, often also the maker and the capabilities of the maker. Little pictures were pasted on. Aside from Dan Cupid and his bow and arrow, one of the earliest and most popular of all pictures depicted a loving couple seated beneath a bower of flowers. In the background was a church hinting of happy times to come. It was to become a standard picture in the era of lace valentines.

The earliest known valentine dates to 1415 and was sent by Charles, Duke of Orleans, a prisoner in the Tower of London, to his wife. John Lydgate, the 15th century English poet, spoke of the "custome of Seynte Valentine" as a "religion."

This suggests that the custom may date back to the medieval code of Courtly Love. St. Valentine's Day was well-established by the mid-17th century.

As with many products, one creation often spurs the necessity for by-products. Those early valentines were no exception. An early offshoot was books of verses written by the more gifted, to be sold to those less poetically inclined, to transcribe to their valentines. One such book appeared in England in 1797, *The Young Man's Valentine Writer*. Sentiments of all kinds in verse or rhyme were contained therein. As late as 1876, *The Quiver of Love* was published by Marcus Ward and Co. of London. It was filled with verses for the do-it-yourselfer.

Closer predecessors to the modern valentine date back to pre-Revolutionary America. They were the handmade cutouts and "pinpricks" — delicate, elaborate, and sometimes intricately folded cards — exchanged as love tokens, not just on St. Valentine's Day, but throughout the year.

The earliest known commercially printed valentine, a copperplate, dates from 1819. The filmy, lacy styles, which to many minds were the idea of what a Valentine should be, were first published during this time, but the inventor remains lost in obscurity. These lacy styles reached their zenith during the Victorian era.

Commercial Victorian valentines evolved into an elaborate product in keeping with an elaborate era. Lace paper, machine-woven tapestries, satin pillows, parchment, and many other fancies were incorporated into the designs. In the 1890s, the Germans introduced mechanical cards. These were usually three-dimensional pull-outs incorporating a series of sets lined up one behind another — a typical manifestation of the ornate Victorian age.

*Figure 36. Jonathan King valentine circa 1860–80. (Photograph courtesy Hallmark Cards, Inc.)*

*Figure 37. Esther Howland valentine circa 1849–81. (Photograph courtesy Hallmark Cards, Inc.)*

Figure 36 pictures a valentine from the collection of Mr. Jonathan King, a noted greeting card collector of the mid 19th century and the foremost authority of his day. His collection reached monumental proportions — 700 volumes, weighing collectively between six and seven tons, and including about 163,000 varieties. It offered nearly a completely illustrated history from 1862-94. The collection was ultimately broken up and sold piecemeal to interested parties.

Another offshoot of the valentine, also of obscure origins, were the "comics" — eventually called "penny dreadfuls" or "vinegar" valentines. All through the Victorian age, they rivaled the sentimental valentines in popularity. Cheaply printed on newsprint or similar paper in several colors, they were a disgrace to the buyer and an insult to the receiver.

America's first valentine publisher was a young Mt. Holyoke College graduate of the 1840s named Esther A. Howland. Her inspiration was a valentine sent from England to her father in Worcester, Massachusetts. She aspired to sell $5.00 worth but, with her brother's help, sold $5,000 worth of valentines her first year in a business which grew and prospered. Figure 37 pictures one of her creations.

### Christmas Cards

The inspiration behind sending Christmas cards is attributed to Henry Cole. In 1843, Henry Cole commissioned his friend Calcott Horsley of the Royal Academy, to design a Christmas card for Cole to send friends whom he owed Christmas letters. They were lithographed and printed by Jobbins of Warwick Court, Holborn, and colored by hand. Only one thousand were struck, each marked with, "Published at Summerly's Home Treasury Office, 12 Old Bond Street, London." It was much later, in 1881, that Christmas cards were produced in abundance by the De LaRue Company, one of several early English publishing houses, using the chromo-lithographic process. The next known Christmas card, executed by W. M. Egley, dates from 1848.

An established publisher of playing cards, Goodall & Sons, is credited with the first large edition of Christmas cards in 1862. Soon after other publishers, most prominently Marcus Ward Co., the aforementioned De LaRue Company, and Raphael Tuck and Co. with their beautifully printed or engraved work, followed suit. The excellence of the artwork is characteristic of all publishers of early Christmas cards. Many of the foremost artists of that era lent their talents to designing cards. Often the designs were first used as cards, and then sold to magazines and picture houses for other purposes.

Raphael Tuck and Co. is still in operation today. They are the official designers of cards for the British Royal Family. Needless to say, anyone who makes any of the Royal Christmas card lists is not likely to turn loose such a prized keepsake!

Also in the 1860s, "the father of the American Christmas card," Louis Prang, a German immigrant, fostered the production of Christmas cards in the United States. In 1856, he founded a small lithographic business in Roxbury, a Boston suburb, and in 1866 he perfected the lithographic process of multicolor printing which he called "Chromos." Today we look upon the chromo as a poor reproduction of an original picture, but none of Prang's work ever deteriorated. Age only improved and refined it. His reproductions of oil paintings were so perfect that often only an expert could differentiate the print from the painting. He was critically acclaimed on both sides of the Atlantic for his outstanding lithography and uncompromising quality.

Prang concentrated on Christmas cards, and his first publications were sold in England in 1874. The next year he placed them in the American market. He continued publishing these cards for several years until cheap German imports began to hurt his sales, and he found other interests to take his time. He had given up the greeting card business entirely by 1890. Later, he turned his attention to producing illustrations of the famous collection of Oriental ceramic art owned by Messrs. Walters, father and son, of Baltimore. Prang had a reputation for superior craftsmanship. Even artists and art experts were hard pressed to believe that printing could be done with such minuteness of detail and color.

Coupled with the decline of the English-made Christmas card in 1890 was the fall from popularity of the Christmas card custom. Though no real break in the making of Christmas cards in America occurred between 1890 and 1906, the huge quantities of cheap and tawdry foreign imports, which were far removed from the original concept of the Christmas card, were a complete turnoff to the buying public. The non-buying resistance to the cards continued until World War I closed the foreign supply entirely and opened the market to quality production. Illustrated post cards for Christmas made their appearance as well as cards for Valentine's Day and Easter. Coupled with a cheaper postal rate of one cent, they made inroads into what buying market was left and further alienated a public demand for quality. By 1906, the modern era of the Christmas card had begun, and present day names like Rust and Gibson entered the greeting card publishing field.

### The Modern Era of Greeting Cards

During the last half of the 19th century and the early part of the 20th, greeting cards grew to modern proportions. Easter cards are attributed to those innovative Germans. They began to surface in England and America in the 1880s, but it was 1908 before Easter cards made their appearance as we know them. Also in the early part of the century, "everyday" cards commemorating birthdays, weddings, friendships, illness, memorials, and other occasions were issued in volume.

## PICTURE POST CARDS

The evolution of the picture post card is rooted in other paper memorabilia, and it is doubtful that any researcher could pinpoint an exact date when an individual or firm first conceived the idea of reproducing a picture on a piece of cardboard for mailing purposes. In England in 1843, Sir Henry Cole commissioned for his personal use a Christmas greeting printed on one side of a piece of cardboard which was inserted into an envelope. However, this is perhaps more a forerunner to the modern greeting cards than to picture post cards.

### Visitors Cards (Cartes de Visite)

A more lineal ancestor to our conception of the picture post card may be the cartes de visite which were a popular Victorian formality from the 1860s to the 1880s. On appropriate occasions, but most in particularly on New Year's Day, those very proper members of Victorian high, and perhaps not so high, society would scurry from the home of one acquaintance to another leaving their calling cards, which were accepted on a silver tray by the recipients' maids. The cards bore the caller's name and were perhaps embellished with a lithographed scene. Like most of the innovative ideas of the 18th century, pictorial print was reserved for the fads and fashions of the rich and privileged who could indulge themselves in whatever novelty caught their fancy. Later the embellishment was a photograph.

These items were not only beyond the means of "ordinary folks," but usually did not appeal to their taste or fit into their lifestyle. Visiting cards, of any design or ilk, were part of the conceit of those who considered formal introductions part of the social graces. Also to be taken into consideration: the number of people who could neither read nor write which eliminated the necessity of fancy stationery.

### The First Picture Post Cards

The creation of the penny post by the United Kingdom in 1840 made the large-scale exchange of cards possible. The first pictorial post cards to be generally recognized were published in 1870 by a French stationer, M. Leon Besnardeau, in a little village near Le Mans, France. He produced special post cards for the use of the troops stationed in a nearby village during the Franco-

Prussian War. The illustrations were of military and patriotic designs. It wasn't until forty years later that M. Besnardeau staked his official claim as the originator of the first picture post cards. He chose the occasion of his eightieth birthday, in 1910, to address a card to Madame G. Caymens, the editor of the magazines, *The Interesting Cartophile* and *The Free Exchange*, at Lierneux, Belgium to officially record this distinction.

In conjunction with the Paris Exhibition in June 1889, in France, the first public opening of the Eiffel Tower was memorialized with a pictorial vignette of this magnificent 984-foot high edifice on the message side of a post card. These cards could be bought, stamped, and posted from the top of the tower.

Britain followed two years later with a drawing of the Eddystone lighthouse on the reverse side of an official post card for the Royal Naval Exhibition. A year later, Germany introduced her remarkable photo-litho printing techniques producing beautifully designed and printed picture post cards that were great attractions to the export markets.

The debut of the first American picture post cards was chosen to coincide with the opening of the World's Columbian Exposition in Chicago on May 1, 1893. The public could purchase ten different views of the Exposition in packets of two each from strategically placed vending machines for five cents a packet.

Prior to this, the United States had already staked another claim to fame in the post card field. In 1861, John Charlton of Philadelphia created the idea for the first private mailing cards. He later transferred the copyright to another Philadelphian, H. Lipman. "Lipman Postal Cards" were intended for brief messages since their sole adornment was the inscription and discreetly decorative borders.

Before 1910, only a few American printers were equipped to handle post card orders in volume, but a small number blazed the trail in this country, producing some of the finest and most collectible views and greetings.

The golden era of picture post cards was

from 1907 to 1915. They were a great fad during that time. Billions of cards poured from the presses. First were European issues for U.S. distribution. Raphael Tuck and Sons, Valentine and Sons, Salmon, and other British publishers and printers supplied post cards by the thousands, featuring local views and holiday greetings to the English-speaking world. Modern printing methods were developed in Germany and German craftsmanship created thousands of designs for worldwide distribution including the United States.

## COLLECTING CARDS

Advertising, insert, and souvenir cards all have their aficionados, and each in its own right is high on the list of collectibles. There are so many subdivisions within those three main sections that collectors must make serious decisions as to exactly where their collecting interests lie. Post cards alone offer a multitude of options in topics, styles, artwork, views, novelties, time frames, etc. However, unlike postal items which have been accurately cataloged, no complete listings or catalogs exist for the various types of cards, with the possible exception of baseball cards.

### Advertising Cards

Advertising cards, one of the earliest card forms, may be the hardest to come by. Consideration must be given to the fact that they were not meant to be saved and, indeed, many of the early cards were not so attractive as to generate much collector interest. Though the cards originally cost nothing, the scarcer items can be of high value. Their charm is in their depiction of life as it once was, and they may also be a source of the origins of many of today's commonplace items.

Collecting advertising cards also may be difficult, not because of scarcity, but because it is difficult to appraise and value them. Much experience and study is necessary to affix a value that reflects the actual worth. The average dealer just doesn't have time to make a complete study of these cards and learn what characteristics are involved in assessing value, especially if he deals in other more valuable, not necessarily paper, items. Many dealers sell them as found, and include a nominal profit for themselves, which may be over or under the figure an expert might put on them.

Dealers are probably the best source for advertising cards. Given their eclectic nature, almost anything can show up at a flea market, so it can't hurt to keep an eye out at them. There are also numerous paper memorabilia shows and exhibitions; some specialize in one type or group of paper collectibles while others feature a bit of almost everything. Estate sales may offer cards from time to time, too. Books are available that give some of the history of advertising cards and pinpoint some of the better known ones.

### Insert Cards

Insert cards may be a little easier to come by, at least some of them. Certain of them were issued in abundance, and new ones continue to be issued. Though most insert cards are relatively inexpensive, the earlier, scarcer ones may run in to some money. The later issues seem to have evolved into inserts in candy and gum, and some of those early issues — circa 1933-42 — are becoming scarce. Though present-day issues are primarily baseball-oriented cards, these earlier ones were of a variety of subjects. Military, airplanes, comic book characters, Boy Scouts, animals, automobiles, and other sports are examples. Present day cards also include celebrity issues.

Baseball cards are by far the most prolific of the insert cards and the easiest to find, though some elusive and expensive specimens do exist and are quite coveted. Baseball card shows are the most likely places to find the hard to find, and there seem to be many of them across the country. Dealers have discovered the flea markets, too, and some of them have the rarer items to offer.

Baseball cards, too, offer a number of options to the collector, primarily in subject matter — favorite team, favorite players, favorite position, special eras, rarities, etc. With a set of cards for every team every year for fifty years, that can add up to an awesome stack of cards. That's from just one company, but add to them similar issues from several competing companies, and the number of cards available is staggering. One almost has to set collecting limitations. Books and magazines are available to aid the collector in keeping abreast of the hobby and up to date on prices.

### Souvenir Cards

Souvenir cards are high on the list of collectibles. Though not initially meant to be among long-term collectibles, souvenir cards were an almost immediate attraction to collectors. Most of them, especially the early ones, were very attractive and often miniature works of art. They were just too pretty to throw away. They were meant to attract the buyer to a means of brief and quick correspondence. Others were issued to attract the collectors' eyes. Among the types of souvenir cards are special sets, various subject matter cards, issues on special occasions such as The Columbian Exposition. Some, of course, had sentimental value to the recipient. Various types of publications relating to the different types of cards are available for the benefit of the collector. A variety of organizations exist for collectors of many of the card types.

## GREETING CARDS

Greeting cards were meant to be sent on special occasions to special people, and they perhaps possess more sentimental value than any of the other cards. They, too, are not very well documented so there is some difficulty in knowing exactly what is available. Some of these may also be classed as works of art. Many types and varieties exist with the early ones the most coveted.

Antique dealers and exhibitions are probably the most likely prospects for early and rare examples. Estate sales may yield some from time to time. Paper items are sometimes a bit lost among all the furnishings, bric-a-brac, china, and crystal that are expected to bring much better prices than anything on paper. But it can pay to keep your eyes open. Don't overlook grandma's attic either or other ancestral premises. During those times of yore when people weren't so inclined to changed their residence, they also weren't so inclined to throw things out. Anything not currently in use went into storage, including treasured keepsakes. Check your mail, too, especially at those special card sending times. Some very fine examples are of recent origin. A case in point: A few years ago, a 1932 Walt Disney Christmas card, the first Christmas card ever issued by Walt Disney Studios, brought $1,100 after some feverish bidding around the world. The Studio started what has now become a tradition, when it created a Christmas card for its several hundred employees to keep the warm Christmas tradition going during those dark Depression years. Disney employees now number in the neighborhood of 70,000 with all the Disney enterprises around the globe, but a Christmas card still goes out to one and all.

## PICTURE POST CARDS

Picture post cards are among the most popular of collectibles, and the antique varieties are the most sought after, with pre-World War I given the highest priority. It did not take publishers long to realize the attraction of cards as collectors' items, in addition to mementos of happy times. They began to issue sets of cards, numbered to whet the collector's interest in completing the sets. Since no accurate listings are available, it is not always known just what or how many comprise a set. Sometimes an extra card — similar to a title card — is included in a set with details about the set, but it is not always known if there is this extra card with a particular set.

Pioneer post cards bear two distinguishing marks.

1. The words "postcard" or "postal card" do not appear on the card. The address side of the cards bears the description "mail card," "souvenir card," etc.

2. A pre-May 19, 1898 cancellation and a two-cent stamp (five-cent for international mail) indicate a true pioneer card.

Post cards can be collected a number of ways. Some of the most sought after are those by publishers such as Raphael Tuck. A comprehensive collection could run up to more than 500.

One of the most fascinating approaches to collecting post cards can be by artist. Often the signature of the artist-designer of the card was printed on both the greetings and the views. Of course, the artist didn't sign each card, but the print from which the card was produced. More than 10,000 artist signed their cards, and some had thousands of designs. Others had only a few. Prominent among the artists drawing the attention of collectors are Ellen H. Clapsaddle, Frances Boundage, C. Klein, and Twelvetrees.

Probably the most obvious way to collect post cards is by geographical area. It is also one of the most popular ways. The variety of ways to collect geographically is almost endless: views from around the world; one town or one state or parts thereof with the emphasis on life there at the turn of the century. Included in the collection might be street scenes with trolleys, old cars, city squares, old buildings no longer standing, firehouses, etc.

Another popular way to collect is by subject, and the variety of subjects appearing on post cards is almost infinite: trains, lighthouses, dolls, stamps, coins, currency, notable personages — artists, actors, kings, queens, Presidents. Every historical event, World's Fair, exhibition, and shooting match since the turn of the century rated its share of picture post cards to send to the folks back home.

Still another approach to the hobby is assembling cards of various types of manufacture. The interest here is on how the card was made or of what materials. Leather and metals of various kinds have been used to make cards. Cards have also been made with a variety of attached objects, and with hidden pictures, moving parts, etc.

Though some aficionados think the early cards are the only ones, a very presentable collection can be assembled of cards issued from about 1930 to the present. A variety of topics is available, many in sets. Among them are railroads, World's Fairs, comics, airlines, collections of all the states in several varieties, also in sets, which make very attractive collections.

From the early 1930s to the 1950s, linen post cards dominated the American post card market. Linens are those pretty and often colorful cards with a textured finish resembling linen cloth. They also bear a resemblance to oil paintings. Linens are growing in popularity and may be the sleepers among collectible post cards. They represent the only post card format that is pure Americana. The major producer of linen cards was Curt Teich Company.

The World War II era spawned a whole raft of varieties, mostly with patriotic themes. Some foreign cards sent to "the girl back home" were still a bit Victorian in concept and design. France issued fancy embroidered ones.

The top-selling post card in the United States today is Mickey Mouse, created by H.S. Crocker Co., Inc. for Walt Disney World (pictured in color section). Disney memorabilia in general is a very popular collectible, and no doubt that includes post cards.

## PRESERVING CARDS

The general rules for preserving paper items discussed in Chapter 3 apply to any paper items mentioned in this book. For each of the general categories mentioned in the various chapters, there are some specifics that apply to that particular category of paper items.

Cards can be treated much like the postal items discussed in Chapter 5, and some of the same supplies may be used. The difference is that it may be desirable to see both sides of the cards. While this is true of some postal items, they are not usually mounted that way. Albums are available for both postal items and cards with sheets of acetate pockets in a variety of sizes, making it possible to see both sides of an item. Individual pockets are also available for storing cards in special acid-free boxes. Care should be taken not to pack cards too snugly in these boxes. Some air should flow through them, and there should be no difficulty removing one or two at a time for viewing.

If cards are to be exhibited, acetate (acid-free) mounts should be used on acid-free paper as with stamps noted in Chapter 5. Paper is usually in 9″ by 12″ sheets, and these sheets should be slipped into individual acetate sheet protectors, once the cards have been mounted, for ease of handling. Take care when inserting in storage albums, sleeves, or mounting not to completely seal the card in. That is an ideal setup for moisture accumulation.

Special care should also be used in mounting cards for framing. Cards should be treated as prints, and detailed instructions for the mounting of prints can be found in Chapter 6.

There are also albums with slots to accommodate the four corners of a card. Baseball card albums of this type are seen frequently, but care should be taken to ascertain that the paper is acid-free. It may also be advisable to insert the cards in acid-free sleeves before mounting in this way. These sleeves are stiff enough that the cards should not bend when mounted in this manner.

A word of caution in dealing with post cards. Those that have been postally used can reveal much through the postal markings — cancellations and date stamps — and the type of stamp and its value. Markings and notations by the sender also may be revealing, even if they are written on the picture side of the card. Do not under any circumstances try to remove any of these markings.

Anyone who goes to the trouble of assembling a worthwhile collection of any sort, owes to that collection and to posterity to treat it properly. Often the most damage is done to a near-mint collection after it comes into the hands of an aficionado. Collecting is only half of it. Taking proper care of the collection is the other half.

## CARDS AS COLLECTIBLE

Cards are the fun collectible. They are available in a variety of sizes and shapes, and even the earlier ones are relatively inexpensive. Abundant supplies of picture post cards offer the collector many options for assembling a collection governed by his own wits and whims. Greeting cards also abound; because of their fragile nature, earlier ones may be a little more difficult to come by. Earlier trade cards may be even harder to come by. Considering that many of them were giveaways and ultimately throwaways, that is not difficult to understand. The most prolific offshoot of the insert cards is sports and baseball cards which, despite several ups and downs and stops and starts, remain extremely popular collectibles. Later entries proliferate. Cards are easy to store, pleasant to look at, and often gems of miniature art. Overall, they offer picture portraits of lifestyles of bygone eras.

# 8
# Commercial Paper

"Commercial Paper" is the term used by collectors to designate business and financial items — correspondence, letterhead, billheads, ledgers, stocks and bonds, checks, etc. Why bother with such items? They were not exactly throwaway items, but most of them were not meant to be kept permanently. Space limitations usually dictated just how long most of these items were kept. Active accounts were kept as long as they were active, but once relegated to inactive status and the storeroom, their fate was suspended. Eventually much of it ended up on the trash heap.

They represent another step in man's need for recordkeeping — keeping track of business: buying, selling, inventory, customers, bookkeeping. Still, there is the question of what is so appealing to a collector about these things. The monetary value of most of it is small. Ah, but the historic value! It is largely through relics of this nature that the history of trade, commerce, manufacturing, and related industries can be traced — those day-to-day happenings that don't get recorded in the history books. Much antique commercial paper from as far back as the 1700s, the 1600s, and some even earlier than that, of great historical significance, is still in existence.

## CORRESPONDENCE

### Early Correspondence

Some early business letters were often handwritten and appear, at first glance, to look more like personal correspondence. The letters were written on a sheet of paper folded double and were usually brief and to the point, discussing a purchase order or business transaction.

These early letters were written before the introduction of the postage stamp, and collectors call them "stampless covers". Envelopes were not always used, since that would add weight which in turn would up the postage. The letter was folded to about the size of a 3″ by 5″ card, but sometimes smaller, incorporating a narrow flap on one edge, and sealed with a wax seal. The remnants of the wax seal are apparent when these letters are opened.

### Printed Correspondence

The billhead has played a large part in everyday life for two or three centuries. It is a direct descendant of the trade card and the forerunner of the letterhead.

Early billheads were distinguished from trade cards primarily by the provision for space for the name of the recipient, the date, and the words "bought of," "to," or "purchased by." Also like early trade cards, color was confined to the use of tinted paper. It further resembled the trade card in that it served formal notice of the business's existence.

More revealing is the role of the billhead as a financial instrument. It is the validated evidence of an outstanding debt. In addition, it is a record of commodities and services supplied, their quantity, quality, and prices, which may be more revealing than the printed heading at the top. During the 19th century, the billhead developed into a minor means of publicity. Illustrations of the business were incorporated into the heading.

As the trade card did, the billhead went through its own evolution, attaining its final form during the mid-19th century. By the end of the that century, it had evolved into the letterhead, without the rule columns and wording of the billheads. This was a bow to the oncoming wave of correspondence brought about by the invention of the typewriter. The propensity for buildings as illustrations on letterheads continued in popularity until well into the 1930s, especially in the United States.

The 1920s and 1930s were marked by the introduction of the general graphic designer, in addition to the commercial engraver, to create letterheads. The letterhead become part of the recognized output of the publicity design studio. Many of today's letterheads reflect the touch of the graphic designer.

Printed letterheads are collected for several different reasons. Many of the illustrations are fine engravings. Besides the aforementioned buildings, there were a variety of other illustrations which were in essence miniature pictorial histories of the times. Scenes of the day and business-related items were popular themes. There were regional preferences, too. Out west, ships — either sailing or steam — and miners panning for gold were popular illustrations. In the east, historical and patriotic motifs were preferred.

Letterheads are also collected for the company, date, or signature of the writer. Letterheads from well-known people or places, the White House for example, are much sought after. Of course, a personal letter or signature is an even better find. There is a word of caution about this type of correspondence. Many letters of celebrities were and are written by staff personnel, and facsimile signatures are not uncommon, especially from the 20th century to the present.

## Collecting Correspondence

Collecting stampless covers is a facet of stamp collecting, and most dealers have some, at least part of the time. Stamp exhibitions are good places to look for them, too. Exhibitions offer the opportunity to come in contact with dealers from all parts of the country, thereby multiplying the chances of finding good examples. They are also offered at auctions and mail sales, and ads for both can be found in most stamp publications.

Many collectors of stampless covers specialize in one section of the country, one state, or even one city. The ones shown in this book are all from Savannah, Georgia. Stampless covers are usually valued higher than most philatelic items, which is understandable considering that they pre-date stamps by many years. They are also harder to find than most philatelic items. Depending upon what is wanted in respect to location, postal markings, and contents, prices may run higher on some than others that seem similar.

Paper memorabilia dealers and shows are probably the best sources for billheads and letterheads, most especially the earlier ones. However, it may be possible to secure specimens from companies that have recently gone out of business, or that have been closed for some time but have yet to vacate the premises. Often sales and auctions are held to dispose of the contents, and who can tell what might turn up? Items have been found in old desks and other furnishings that no one bothered to empty before they were sold.

For frequent travelers, hotel and motel stationery is there for the taking, if that facet of commercial paper piques your interest. World travelers could amass quite a large and varied collection.

Writing to prominent personages may yield authentic stationery, if not authentic signature, especially if you are writing for a purpose other than the hopes of securing a sheet of stationery. Legitimate business letters usually yield a reply on letterhead, even if the original addressee didn't write it.

York Times

LATE CITY EDITION

Weather: Rain, warm today; clear tonight. Sunny, pleasant tomorrow. Temp. range: today 80-66; Sunday 71-66. Temp.-Hum. Index yesterday 69. Complete U.S. report on P. 50.

K, MONDAY, JULY 21, 1969

10 CENTS

# K ON MOON

# AND PLAIN;
# T FLAG

## Powdery Surface
## Closely Explored

By JOHN NOBLE WILFORD
Special to The New York Times

Monday, July 21—Men have landed

astronaut
dule safely
day at 4:17:40
M., Eastern day-
38-year-old
civilian commander,
control room here:
ase here. The Eagle has landed."
the moon—Mr. Armstrong and
drin Jr. of the Air Force—
evel, rock-strewn plain
d Sea of Tranquility
r, Mr. Armstrong opened
slowly down the ladder
human foot print on
one giant

MPLE
Color

ntesi

Dolly Dingle
Learns to Paint

DOLLY'S
COSTUME

Check your mail, particularly your business mail. All kinds of things are written in the name of business, often from the most unlikely sources. Stamp dealers may also have some from time to time. There is often a philatelic connection, either because of the contents or the postal markings. Estate sales may offer some commercial paper, too.

## BUSINESS CARDS

The development of the business card overlaps somewhat with that of the calling card and the trade card. According to a Victorian etiquette book, the purpose of the business card was, in addition to being an introduction to business acquaintances, a valuable form of advertising. They were originally the size of a calling card, approximately 1½″ by 2½″, a bit small by today's standards of approximately 2″ by 3½″. Some were increased in size so they would resemble trade cards. As a general rule, the reverse side of the business card was blank.

The 18th century business card and some early engraved cards were a cross between a business and a trade card. An example of this type is Paul Revere and Sons' business card with a patriotic illustration and a brief text referring to their wares. The address reads simply: "At their Bell and Cannon Foundry, at the North part of Boston." The reverse was blank, and the card measured approximately 2½″ by 4″.

Some of the first pictorial business cards were printed on colored stock in sheet form, and then divided into separate cards. The designs were stock illustrations that did not necessarily pertain to the advertised business. Customers could select from a variety of designs — birds, animals, flowers, comics, etc. — and have their name and business address printed above the illustration. Another type used a pictorial representation of a business — a harness for a saddlery, a tray of type for a printer — with the business name above the illustration. Limited advertising was sometimes included — coming events, products, etc.

Later, colored lithograph cards with blank spaces for advertising were enlarged, becoming more like a trade card than business card. Subsequently, some business cards evolved into advertising or trade cards. Others developed into the standard business cards as we know them today.

### Collecting Business Cards

There are a variety of ways to obtain business cards. Antique shops or dealers are one of the best sources for the early business cards. Ask for calling cards and/or trade cards. Estate sales, flea markets, and garage sales are also good sources, and you might even come upon a reasonable deal on some.

Companies that go out of business or change their names offer an opportunity to secure a large number of cards. Ask the owners of these businesses for their leftover cards.

Serious collectors often trade with other business card collectors to secure particular types of cards. This is usually done by mail. There are also organizations for collectors which enable them to get in touch with other collectors. One organization is the American Business Card Club.

Modern cards are the easiest to get. Business cards seem to be everywhere. In addition to almost any business, cards can be found at all kinds of shows and exhibitions, shopping malls, grand openings, conventions and business meetings, and other business-related functions.

Collectors usually try to get several cards of the same kind so they can keep one and swap the rest. They also insist that black-and-white cards are boring, and most collectors don't want them. Collectors want only mint cards to trade with other collectors. Dirty, smudged, ink and pencil marked, torn, bent, or worn cards with writing, staple, pin, or thumbtack holes, are not tradeable. Paper clip marks are also unacceptable.

## CHECKS

Checks are a multi-faceted collectible.

Numismatists like them because they are so much like paper money. Some early checks were printed by the American Bank-Note Company, a firm which also printed money for the United States and foreign governments.

Print collectors like them because the beautifully engraved vignettes on the checks represent a variation of limited edition art prints. The number and variety of vignettes on checks is almost endless. These detailed vignettes served as deterrents to counterfeiting. Vignettes depicted goddesses, the eagle, animals, locomotives, and buildings, as well as personifications of liberty, agriculture, industry, peace, and education. Most buildings appearing on checks are banks.

Stamp collectors are interested in old checks because revenue stamps are sometimes found attached to them. During the Civil War, the federal government needed money, and in 1862 levied a tax on many types of financial documents. The tax rate on checks was two cents, which at the time was a sizable amount to most people. This tax lasted until 1881, and was reinstated from 1898 to 1901 to help pay for the Spanish-American War. Some revenue stamps were adhesive while others were pre-printed.

Checks are also helpful for genealogical purposes. A number of checks from one community can often aid in confirming the names of residents or businessmen of the area.

Checks are also ideal sources for autograph collectors. Strangely enough, checks rarely appear in the catalogs of autograph dealers, considering the billions that have been written during the past 400 years that people have been writing checks.

### Collecting Checks

Old checks can be found in a variety of places, the most obvious, of course, are the paper memorabilia dealers. Postage stamp dealers may also have some. Antique dealers sometimes have them. Often, they will be included with an old desk or other furnishings. Closed businesses may yield some checks along with other commercial paper. Checks from defunct banks, ghost towns, and celebrities can be intriguing finds. A check from the first United States chartered bank, the Bank of North America of Philadelphia, founded in 1781, would be a rare prize. Checks in unusual amounts — small or large — are also desirable.

Check collecting is a relatively new avocation, so untouched hoards of old checks may still be found. Individuals as well as businesses wrote checks so the collector should consider that possibility, too, when seeking out examples.

The vignette can be a deciding factor in determining the value of a check since it is the attraction for most collectors. Supply and demand are also factors. A less ornate specimen may bring a better price because fewer of them exist. Most post-1900 checks, with the exception of those bearing a famous signature, sell for nominal prices — less than a dollar. Because of the newness of the hobby, prices have been on the low side, but as the hobby grows in popularity, prices will probably go up.

## STOCKS AND BONDS

Stocks and bonds are part of a group of documents produced by security printing, a method of printing incorporating special protective measures. Currency and revenue and postage stamps are also produced by this method. A secondary field requiring these methods is fast growing. Included are licenses, passports, permits, money orders, traveler's checks, visitors' passes, season tickets, and cash and credit cards.

Special papers containing watermarks, metal threads, embedded lint and other materials, soluble inks to deter tampering by would-be artists and craftsmen, and special printing methods are some of the security devices. One of the earliest devices, which dates from the early 1800s and is still widely used, is the complex pattern produced by a geometric lathe as an engraved image. The multiple micro pattern of tiny lettering combined with color merging is also popular. In 1820, an early effort to defy the forger was the invention of compound plate printing in which two separate plates were interlocked like a jigsaw puzzle, separately inked, and printed two colors in one impression. Modern technology cannot duplicate the accuracy of the fit of the finished image.

### Collecting Stocks and Bonds

To most people, corporate stocks and bonds conjure up images of big business, big money, wheeling and dealing on an international scale. People who own stocks value them for their investment potential. They own a piece of the action, and can at least feel they are in the same league with the wheeler dealers.

Though collectible stocks and bonds may have been worth thousands of dollars at the time of issue, many of these documents were rendered worthless when the issuing corporations went bankrupt during the depressions of the 1890s and 1930s (Fig. 38). For decades, these worthless certificates were stored away in bank vaults, safe deposit boxes, and old chests.

Collectors began to take an interest in these once valuable pieces of paper about twenty years ago. Like old checks, there are multiple reasons for seeking out old stocks and bonds, and most collectors have their specialties.

Also like checks, stocks and bonds represent an art form — limited edition engraved prints. Like checks, the engravings (vignettes) were finely detailed to prevent counterfeiting, and like checks, the subject matter of the vignettes is similar.

Some collect stocks and bonds by industries — railroads, mining companies, automobiles, etc. Automobile certificates are not usually as ornate, and few carried illustrations of automobiles because the changing styles would date the certificates. Trademarks and assembly plants were usually pictured. Others collect them geographically — those issued in a certain state or city.

Stocks and bonds are also an ideal source of local and business history. These certificates usually bear the name of two high-level company officers and the name of an investor. Historical analysis of these certificates can reveal the

*Figure 38.  Three defunct stocks: Crown Zellerbach Corp., 1965; Magna Copper Company, 1931; Gulf, Mobile and Ohio Railroad, 1955. (Author's collection.)*

names of major owners, profits and losses by major investors, and how much the investment capital was. Since the names on the certificates were probably those of prominent citizens, insights can be obtained into both business and personal history. These certificates may be the only sources for this information, if a firm's old records were destroyed for any reason. The vignette may also be a form of history — a picture of a founder or the old company building.

The value of these certificates is determined by many factors.

1. The rarity of the certificate — a small firm may have issued only twenty-five or thirty certificates while a large one issued hundreds of thousands.

2. The quality of the engraved picture.

3. The importance of the names on the certificates — the existence of a famous name is one aspect that is most likely to drive the price up.

4. The degree of interest by business and local historians.

5. The original value of the certificate.

6. The industry in which the firm was involved — railroads, automobiles, gold and silver

mining, petroleum, and motion pictures are high on the list of popularity and apt to sell for more than other types.

The most likely sources for stocks and bonds are dealers. Some dealers specialize in stocks and bonds and like items only, while others carry a variety of paper memorabilia. Specialized dealers will provide lists of their offerings, sometimes for a small fee, and probably accept want lists from good customers. Antique shops may also have some. Being of an eclectic nature, antique shops often acquire odd lots of materials while seeking out the larger, more lucrative items. Paper memorabilia can be among such lots.

Recently formed societies for collectors of stocks and bonds offer their expertise to aid members in determining the value, if any, of their finds. No doubt, swapping and trading goes on among the members as well.

## ADVERTISING ON ENVELOPES

Beginning in the 1870s, advertising on envelopes and their contents was extensive and continues to the present day. Businesses used pictorial envelopes to match their letterheads. The designs might depict the place of business, the product sold or produced, a map of the area, an emblem of a school, institution, or association. Sometimes the envelope was turned into a billboard by enterprising businessmen who pooled their assets and divided the back of the envelope into rectangles with each containing a different local advertisement. In recent times, some businesses joined into the spirit of the Bicentennial celebration.

## PRESERVING COMMERCIAL PAPER ITEMS

Commercial paper should be treated much like historical documents and prints. Though very few commercial paper items fit the "one-of-a-kind" classification or resemble standard prints, there are similarities. The paper, the inks, and the printing processes may be similar. Some specimens may be as delicate as an old document. The same repair and restoration processes may be required. (See Chapter 4.) The paper of other commercial items may resemble that of a fine print. Framing techniques suggested for fine prints apply, if framing is desired.

A substantial portion of commercial paper was created for advertising purposes and not meant to be saved for any length of time, but much of it did survive. It may not always be found in the best condition, because often it was printed on the poorest of paper. Careful handling is essential to avoid further damage. Some of it was meant to be folded, so unfolding could result in tears if none are yet apparent. Insertion in Mylar sleeves may be the quickest and best remedy.

Encapsulation is suggested by some authorities, but that is something best left to experts. The drawback is that a piece of paper that is completely sealed in Mylar sheets, acid-free though they may be, is a prime setup for the accumulation of moisture. The only exception may be the framing of an item by experts, in which the item is encapsulated before framing to keep it dust-free.

Acid-free folders and containers of various sizes are available for filing purposes. Commercial paper can be stored much as it is in an office, taking care to file each item in an acid-free sleeve or folder to separate it from the others. A variety of paper types was used for commercial paper items, including letterhead. That which looks good may turn out to be not so good, and damage its neighbor if allowed to touch it.

Business cards are handled the same as the other cards discussed in Chapter 7. The acid-free albums and pages with different size pockets can be adapted for business cards. Some collectors like to use baseball card sleeves (acid-free) which are nearly the same size as a business card. Several types of acid-free boxes are available to hold the cards. Do not use rubber bands or paper clips on the cards. They could damage them. File odd-sized cards separately. They could be damaged if left mixed in with the others.

## COMMERCIAL PAPER AS COLLECTIBLE

Commercial paper may well be a major link in the chain of our heritage. Historians chart the cultural progress of man through his efforts to provide shelter and sustenance for himself and his family. Whatever course he took to achieve this end evolved into his business. From the caveman stalking his prey with a spear to the pioneers scratching a living out of the soil to the age of mass production spawned by the Industrial Revolution, business has grown and prospered, and the use of commercial paper has grown right along with it. Businesses came and went as others sprung up with new and better ideas to accommodate the changing needs of man.

Commercial paper is the documentation of this evolution — on a day-to-day basis. History books can tell you only what happened. Commercial paper documents the what as well as the who, when, where, why, and how — names, dates, places, reasons for being, and the means of being. It is the written proof of the happening as it happened. The bits and pieces come together to form the basis for our cultural existence and in turn our lifestyles.

# 9
# Paper Currency

Concurrent with man's efforts to perfect his means of communication were his efforts to develop a means to barter with something he had for something he wanted. Rocks, shells, pieces of wood, skins, bones, and other items were all used by ancient man as items of trade. Sometimes these items were fashioned into crude art objects to make them more desirable. As man's monetary skills developed, and the demand grew, simple monetary systems were devised; metal coinage first and then paper money were created.

## THE WORLD'S FIRST BANKERS

References abound in the Bible and the literature of ancient times to bankers and others dealing in currency. The Babylonians, Egyptians, Greeks, and Romans all had their own elaborate banking systems in which goldsmiths and rich merchants lent money to businessmen or kept money in trust for others. The Igibi Bank in Mesopotamia is known to have been transacting business — lending money and receiving deposits — in the middle of the sixth century B.C., possibly earlier than that. Accounts of life in Roman times frequently refer to banking transactions.

## THE FIRST PAPER MONEY

Paper money began, where else but where paper began — in China. The earliest form of paper money known dates from the T'ang Dynasty, somewhere between 650 and 800 A.D. Coins used in China at the time were made of bronze, and large quantities of these coins were needed for even the smallest business transaction. Besides being inconvenient and impractical, it was a bit unsafe. The unwieldy wagons, needed to transport these coins from one part of the country to another, were subject to ambush by bandits. In an attempt to foil these highwaymen, the Chinese merchants devised "fei-ch'ien" which literally translates as "flying money." These were paper drafts negotiable in bronze currency, and were not authorized paper money or the modern equivalent of paper money as we know it. No doubt, they did pave the way for the paper money issued about 1000 A.D. by the Sung Dynasty. Redeemable in coin, these Sung notes quickly gained public acceptance.

Even back then, smart operators were quick to latch on to what appeared to be a "sure thing." Banks sprung up rapidly and were more than willing to issue more and more notes without funds or assets to back them. The people weren't long in spurning these notes, called "chiao-tzu" or "exchange money," and the government stepped in and began to issue "kuan-tzu" or "citadel money." Unfortunately, the government didn't learn from the mistakes of private enterprise and it, too, over-issued its currency. This was one of the contributing factors to the downfall of the Sung Dynasty in 1278.

The Yuan Dynasty (1270-1368) that succeeded the Sung also failed to heed the mistakes of their ancestors, and over-issued paper currency, too. So much so that before the end of the Mongol occupation of China, this paper money was rendered utterly worthless. A few examples of these bills-very large and imposing — survive today.

More plentiful are the notes of the Ming Dynasty (1368-1644). They were made from mulberry tree bark and printed from wooden blocks in vast amounts. The collapse of the Ming Dynasty in 1644 marked an end to the use of paper money in China for two centuries.

The T'ai-ping Rebellion of 1853-64 brought on an economic crisis, and the Imperial Government found that the easiest way out of its financial difficulties was to resurrect paper money. From that time on, China topped the world in issuing paper currency, which ultimately had disastrous effects on the country's economy and political stability.

Often the designs of these early Chinese notes were very elaborate and usually depicted something of religious significance. The seal marks called "chops", added in vermilion ink to authenticate the notes, were inscribed with such phrases as "to circulate cast" or "to circulate under the heavens" printed in Chinese characters. On some notes, coins equivalent to the value of the notes were inscribed so there would be no doubts as to their value.

## EARLY EUROPEAN PROMISSORY NOTES

The rich merchants in medieval Europe in the Italian cities of Milan, Venice, and Genoa, the Hanseatic ports of Hamburg and Lubeck, and the international towns of Antwerp, Bruges, and Geneva acted as bankers. They lent and received vast sums of money. Many of these transactions were in the form of promissory notes made of paper or parchment. As an example: A merchant might give a note to a banker promising to pay him a certain sum of money when his ship brought back cargo from the East. The banker

might in turn use that same note to pay a goldsmith for a quantity of his wares. The goldsmith might use the note to pay a farmer for a supply of corn. Lastly, the farmer might present the note to that original merchant on the date the payment was due in exchange for the value of the note in coins. Eventually, these promissory notes were accepted in much the same way paper money is today.

The earliest promissory notes are thought to have been made of vellum, parchment, or some other kind of animal skin. Paper was all but unknown outside of China until the middle of the 12th century when it made its way to Europe via Arabia and North Africa. Paper remained a scarce commodity in Europe for hundreds of years thereafter.

## FIRST EUROPEAN PAPER MONEY

The first European paper money was issued in 1661 in Sweden. Copper currency was rapidly losing its value and to replace it the Stockholm Bank of Sweden issued credit notes. These first bank notes, which were forerunners of the modern type, were the brainchild of a Dutch resident of Latvia (then a dependency of Sweden), John Palmstruch. Unlike the previous receipts issued by goldsmiths, these notes were current in the hands of the bearer. Also, they did not earn interest as the promissory notes sometimes did.

None of that first issue of 1661 has survived, and the few specimens — less than a dozen — of the 1662 and 1663 issues now in existence are all in various museum collections. Much more plentiful is the issue of 1666, the last issue to appear. Swedish businessmen seem to have readily accepted these notes since they were much more convenient to carry than the bulky copper-plate money. Unfortunately, the Stockholm Bank succumbed to the same temptations as those early Chinese bankers and over-issued this paper currency. Even as early as 1663, the bank could not redeem its notes, and two years later the Swedish government decided to do away with them. Since copper went out of circulation in 1665-6, the last issue was redeemable in silver thalers.

## EARLY ENGLISH PAPER NOTES

The earliest kinds of paper money in England were notes issued by goldsmiths as receipts for valuables deposited in their vaults by merchants. These receipts could be used as securities for loans, and like promissory notes, were quite widely circulated as a form of currency. Following an Exchequer Order made by the authority of King Charles II in 1665, these receipts and promissory notes were accepted as legal tender. Another thirty years passed before paper money, as we understand it today, was issued in Great Britain.

## FIRST ENGLISH AND SCOTTISH BANKS

It was through the efforts of two Scotsmen that paper money achieved popularity in England and France. In 1694, William Paterson founded the Bank of England, and the following year, the Bank of Scotland. In 1716, his fellow countryman, John Law, founded the first French bank — the Banque Generale. They both realized the convenience and advantages of paper money and issued the first bank notes on both sides of the English Channel.

## FRENCH REVOLUTION CURRENCY

John Law was a speculator, and though several of his theories proved profitable for a time, he was discredited in 1720 leaving a legacy behind him that caused both misery and financial chaos to his country. One of his propositions adopted by the French government, then on the verge of bankruptcy, precipitated the Revolution of 1789-92.

Paper money called "assignats" was issued in 1789. Its value was backed by land confiscated from the Church at the start of the Revolution. These were interest-bearing notes valued at 100 livres each. The first issue alone circulated 4,000 million livres; each issue grew larger and larger and the output faster and faster, and the value of the "assignat" fell rapidly.

When the worth of "assignats" sank to virtually nothing, the French government turned to territorial money orders called "mandats," but these notes were no more trusted than the "assignats." In 1797, the Directoire finally quit experimenting with paper money and called in "assignats" and "mandats" in exchange for coin in a ratio of one livre coin for every 3,000 livres paper money. Examples of these remnants of the French Revolution are plentiful and still available at nominal prices, but numerous counterfeits and bogus notes also exist.

## AMERICAN PAPER CURRENCY

The political and economic history of the countries that make up the American continents is traceable through its paper money. Latin America's colorful notes reflect the upheavals of that part of the world. Governments toppled, banks crashed, and paper money was rendered worthless.

At opposite ends is the paper money issued under United States authority since 1861, all of which is still legal tender at its face value. Of course, some United States notes are worth more than face value either because they bear interest or because of their popularity with collectors.

The United States is unique in that it is the only country in the world that has never called in or demonitized obsolete authorized, government-issue paper money. United States notes are protected against changing fashions in collecting, and the collector can always redeem a collection at face value.

### Early United States Paper Currency

Long before the United States was compelled by the Civil War to issue paper money in 1861, various types of non-metallic currency existed in what now constitutes the United States. The original thirteen colonies used paper money, some dating as far back as the late 17th century. The Massachusetts Bay Colony produced the earliest examples of paper money in

December 1690, primarily for payment of troops recruited for the expedition against the Jacobites in Canada. In the 18th century, gold and silver Spanish coins, mostly from Central and South America, circulated in the British Colonies, but paper money was used from time to time for payment of troops in colonial wars and campaigns. The governors of the British colonies were under strict instructions to limit the issue of paper money to times of military emergency, and these early examples are extremely scarce.

Colonial notes issued during the Revolutionary War (1776-83) are more common. The Continental Congress met at Philadelphia in 1775 and authorized an issue of paper money inscribed "The United Colonies." This "continental currency" was renamed by a Congressional resolution in April 1778 and the inscription changed to "The United States." To make the colonists more receptive to the notes, they were actually signed by leading political personalities of the day, including those who signed the Declaration of Independence, the Articles of Confederation, and the United States Constitution. Despite the turbulent times, these notes were often well made and quite artistic. Among the artists who designed and engraved these notes was Paul Revere.

The individual colonies and later the states issued their own paper money from 1775 onward. Paul Revere designed and engraved notes for New Hampshire and Massachusetts. As the Revolutionary War progressed, metallic currency became scarce, and vast quantities of paper money were issued, in particular for payment of George Washington's troops.

### State-Issued Paper Currency

Following the Revolutionary War and the founding of the United States, economic progress was rapid. Though the United States did not feel compelled to issue paper money until 1861, the individual states did. Since there weren't enough gold and silver coins to fill their needs, the states authorized banks to issue paper money to breach the gaps. Theoretically, these paper notes were to be backed by the amount of gold and silver on deposit in the bank. Regrettably, these banks began to churn out paper money at record rates.

Any financial crisis brought a rush on the banks and the withdrawals of the gold and silver forced foreclosure and broke the banks. The paper notes became worthless and were at one time quite common. Usually artistically designed and beautifully printed, they provide a fascinating illustration of American pioneer life.

### Confederate Currency

Shortages of gold, silver, and copper coins plagued both sides during the Civil War, and inevitably both sides were forced to turn to paper money. Union paper money retained its value as it does to this day, but mounting inflation forced the Confederacy to issue more and more paper money which in turn plunged in value as the War went on. By 1865, when the Confederacy surrendered, their paper money had no value.

The first Confederate currency was authorized in March 1861, at Montgomery, Alabama. These were interest-bearing notes to be redeemed twelve months after issue. Face value ranged from fifty cents to $1,000. Savings banks, individual state banks, and local chambers of commerce also continued to issue notes in even greater quantities than before. Maturity dates on the Confederate notes were extended to two years, as the War dragged on, and after the Ratification of a Treaty of Peace between the two sides. Since the Confederacy lost, the notes were never redeemed, and the United States refused to honor them.

An interesting sidelight to the private issues of the Confederacy was the one dollar note issued in 1862 by the Cherokee Nation at Tahlequah, its capital.

# PAPER CURRENCY IN THE CIVIL WAR ERA

On July 17, 1861, Congress passed an act authorizing the Treasury Department to issue paper money. Several times previously, the United States had adopted similar measures. Promissory notes were issued by the Treasury during the War of 1846, the hard times of 1837-43, the great bank panic of 1857, and the shaky economic period of 1860 prior to the outbreak of the Civil War. These promissory notes were a temporary measure and not intended for wide circulation as bank notes usually were. They were interest bearing, and the government redeemed them as soon as the emergency passed.

### Demand Notes — Greenbacks

Following the outbreak of the Civil War, the United States government suspended payments in silver, gold, and even copper coins and coinage was not long in disappearing from commerce. Sixty million dollars in paper money was authorized. The first issue was referred to by collectors as "demand notes" because the inscription on the notes included the words "promise to pay...on demand." They were the original "greenbacks," named for the predominance of green coloring on the back.

In 1862, these demand notes were followed by "legal tender notes," a name also taken from the inscription: "This note is a legal tender for all debt..." Between 1862 and 1923, five issues of legal tender notes with several sub-varieties were released.

### Compound Interest Treasury Notes

From 1863-64, when the Civil War was not going well and the federal government was all but bankrupt, "compound interest treasury notes," the second rarest category of United States paper money, were issued. They were to earn 6% interest, compounded twice a year, for a period of three years. "Interest bearing notes" are the rarest form of United States paper money, so much so that even the most persistent collector may never see one. They were another wartime emergency measure, issued with attached coupons giving the rates of interest due. In 1879, "refunding certificates," in ten dollar denominations and earning 4% interest, were in-

troduced. It was meant for holders to hang on to these certificated indefinitely, but Congress terminated the interest due on them in 1907.

## SILVER CERTIFICATES

"Silver certificates" first appeared in 1878 in denominations from ten dollars to $1,000. They continued until 1923 and were to be redeemed in silver dollars. There were a total of five issues with the second and all subsequent issues including lower denominations of one, two, and five dollars. Silver certificates were discontinued in the mid-1950s.

## TREASURY OR COIN NOTES

The Legal Tender Act of 1890 authorized the Treasury to issue "treasury" or "coin notes," which were backed by silver bullion set aside for that purpose. Even today, anyone redeeming one of these notes must be paid in silver dollars, though their rarity makes them worth many times their face value to a collector.

## NATIONAL BANK NOTES

"National bank notes" are the largest and most popular category of United States paper money. They were issued between 1863 and 1929 as a result of the National Banking Act of 1863 which regulated the note-issuing activities of state banks. It permitted the banks to issue paper money up to 90% of the value of the United States government bonds deposited by the banks with the government as security. The basic designs were the same as treasury notes.

## FEDERAL RESERVE NOTES

A financial crisis in 1907, which precipitated a run on the banks, revealed a number of weaknesses in the national banking system. This led to the establishment of the Federal Reserve Act of 1913 and the introduction of a new kind of currency, "federal reserve bank notes" and "federal reserve notes." Federal reserve notes were to be redeemed by the government, not the banks.

## SMALL-SIZED NOTES

In 1929, economic measures necessitated the reduction in size of paper money. Notes issued since that date are referred to by collectors as "small-sized notes," and include some previously issued categories of bills.

## GOLD CERTIFICATES

There are also "gold certificates" which first appeared at the end of the Civil War and were quite strikingly printed in bright orange to simulate gold. Once redeemable in gold coin, payment is now made in silver or paper money since the United States is no longer on the gold standard.

## COLLECTING PAPER CURRENCY

Most coin and postage stamp dealers also deal in paper currency, and chances are that if they don't have what you want, they can put you on a want list and keep an eye out for it. There are also several organizations available to paper money collectors to aid them in developing their collections. Some are concerned only with paper currency while others deal also with coins, stamps, checks, stocks and bonds, and other related items. Several periodicals are available on the subject, usually including coins as well. Catalogs are available for some types of currency. Political upheavals in some parts of the world may preclude complete and authorized listings of all the currency issues of some countries. Catalogs are issued regularly for United States currency. A number of books are available giving an overall picture of the history of paper currency worldwide. Some books concentrate on a specific area — early paper money, World War II issues, etc.

Like many other paper collectibles, currency doesn't have to be old to be collectible. The monetary systems of many countries have their ups and downs along with wars, political upheavals, and depressions, yet never seem to learn from these experiences and the cycle keeps repeating itself. Currency from some of these times is plentiful since so much of it was necessary to compensate for the inflated monetary unit of a country. At other times when money was scarce, emergency money was printed to fill the breach. World War II spawned a variety of issues, on both sides.

Paper currency, too, has its artistic value, much like that of stocks and bonds and checks. The illustrations on early specimens are similar though sometimes much more ornate and colorful. They, too, reflect the activities of their times.

## PRESERVING PAPER CURRENCY

Currency, by its very nature, goes through much handling. Early examples probably will not be found in mint condition. It is also folded a lot. Even what are now considered small-sized bills won't fit into pocket or pocketbook without folding at least once. And who hasn't secreted a bill or two in some small, hidden recess?

Paper money was made in all sizes. Some bills are impossibly large. Others are small enough to be carried without folding. A variety of paper grades and types have been used to print paper money. Almost every currency-issuing country did it their way. Add to this the local issues — scrip or emergency — printed to accommodate short supplies. Some of the paper was quite good and the money resembled little works of art. Some of it was printed on whatever paper was available and printed rather crudely.

Very early specimens of paper money probably will not be found in mint condition, and just might be suspect unless they reside in a museum or national archives somewhere.

Considering all this, it seems prudent to encase each specimen in see-thru archival Mylar currency envelopes. Several types of acid-free storage boxes are available in which these envelopes can be stored upright. A more convenient method for some collectors might be in pages of Mylar pockets punched to fit three-ring binders.

Albums are available specifically for paper money with the acid-free pages of pockets. Those used for postal items and photographs are readily adaptable for currency, too, and the pockets are available in a variety of sizes which should accommodate most currency sizes.

## PAPER CURRENCY AS COLLECTIBLE

Paper currency, like postage stamps, reflects the temper of a government — the good times and the bad, prosperity and adversity, war and peace. Often paper currency was established as a bridge over troubled times, and more often than not, the bridge collapsed without achieving its purpose.

Since records exist of the monetary systems of most governments, even if no specimens have survived, accurate depictions of the times can be determined through a study of the issues of paper currency. Studies of the actual currency can be even more revealing, while offering proof positive of their existence. Paper currency is the documentation of a monetary system.

# 10
# The Performing Arts

Even before man learned to make primitive drawings and markings to record his deeds and exploits, he could pantomime his thoughts and ideas and act out his deeds and exploits to his compatriots. Crude as they were, they were the beginnings of drama — acting out stories, eventually incorporating a stage to set the players apart from the audience. Dramas acted out on the stage date back to early festivals, when legends connected with the god or patron of a feast were represented with music, dancing, and recitation. In all countries, the history of the stage and the drama reveals, more or less, an intimate connection with the service of religion as well as man's love of entertainment.

The performing arts comprise a complex variety of forms that fall roughly into three major areas — theater, motion pictures, and broadcasting — the last two of which stem from the first. Each is an industry within itself, and each has its variations and offshoots, yet each often overlaps with another. The difference really lies in the media involved in the producing and staging of an entertainment.

Theater came first in its many guises — drama, musical, revue, concert, dance, mime, acrobatic, circus, vaudeville, burlesque, ad infinitum, almost. The invention of the camera spawned the motion picture industry, which has, in its time, captured all the theatrical variations on film. Broadcasting brought all the variations of the theater and motion pictures into the home.

Each has generated a sizable amount of paper memorabilia in all its many forms which are sometimes interrelated. Much of this paper horde was and is intended for advertising and promotional purposes: fliers, posters, playbills, programs, calendars, playing cards, post cards, paper dolls, photographs, and sheet music. Other paper items are and were used by the performers themselves: scripts, correspondence, greeting cards, musical scores, checks, diaries, and it goes on. It may be well to keep in mind that up to the advent of motion pictures and radio, paper was the prime means of conveying information; this includes newspapers. Once the machinery was in place to produce paper items for the masses, the variety of paper items produced seemed boundless.

With such a conglomeration of items, there can't help but be a spillover of forms discussed in other chapters. Most of the items touched on in this book have been adapted for use in the performing arts: prints, cards, magazines, books, games, puzzles, newspapers, matchbooks, stationery, whatever. Obviously, we can't cover all aspects, but we can look at some of the major offshoots.

## THEATER

### Early History

The exact roots of theater arts are lost in obscurity. Even scholars can't trace its lineage back through time to a definite starting point.

One theory is that theater arose from man's natural instincts for mimicry combined with an emphasis on ritual. Performances were geared towards rituals marking the changes of the seasons or the gathering of food. Ceremonies enacted the passing of winter, the coming of spring, or a ritual dance portraying a hunt. Costumes and masks of particular cults depicted the non-human character of these presentations. Sometimes the audience would participate in these presentations. For instance, the dance ceremonies of the Plains Indians making offerings to the gods would use the entire tribe more or less as a chorus. The primitive ritual of these ceremonies was associated with a sacred performing area. Regrettably, the links connecting these ceremonies with the fully developed theatrical forms that appear in Europe and the Orient cannot be clearly established.

### Greek Theater

The first evidence of a fully formed theater is found in Greece although evidence exists that a rudimentary passion play was enacted at Abydox in Egypt as early as the 19th century B.C. In 534 B.C. in Athens, the tyrant Pisistratus established, as part of the principal celebration for the god of wine, Dionysus, an annual contest for tragedy. Called the *Great Dionysia*, the celebration was held in late March or early April to commemorate the introduction of the Dionysian cult into Attica, and lasted for five or six days. It consisted of a procession which re-enacted the entry of Dionysus into Athens, a day or two of impassioned hymn singing contests, and three days of theatrical performance. With religious and political overtones, the Great Dionysia was the most significant celebration of the year.

The greatness of Athenian theater coincided with the expansion of the Athenian empire under Pericles in the middle of the fifth century B.C. In a remarkable tribute to longevity, the three tragic dramatists Aeschylus (515?-456 B.C.), Sophocles (c. 496-406 B.C.), and Euripides (484?-406 B.C.) spanned the century, providing a sequence of major works from about 472 to 406 B.C.

Athens also celebrated two other festivals that featured dramatic performances, in addition to the Great Dionysia. Lenaea, held in January, was the more important. Comedies were featured at Lenaea, though tragedies were also presented and were emphasized at the Great Dionysia. These comic contests of the Lenaea dealt with local matters. The only extant examples of this comic genre are the eleven plays of Aristophanes (c. 450-c.385 B.C.) which concentrate on political, social, and cultural issues in a caustic and farcical manner.

Performances were given in the Dionysian theater in Athens, located along the southeast slope of the Acropolis where the sides of the hill formed a natural unroofed amphitheater. Initially, it was a modest structure which was successively embellished. The surviving fragments of seats and stage are of Roman origin. The performers, professional or amateur, were all male.

### Roman Theater

Roman theater was derived from the Greek in forms and objects, but Roman theater was never the center of Roman life as it was in Greek life. Though fragments of Roman tragedies do exist, the only complete tragedies — the ten works of Seneca — were not products of the popular theater and may never have been performed in their own day. By contrast, comedy was the forte of an active Roman theater. Plays were performed on civic and religious holidays as in Greece, but unlike Greece the civic rather than the religious element predominated. New holidays were always being added to the calendar, so that by the fourth century A.D., more than 100 were devoted to theatrical performances.

Performances were at first presented in temporary wooden theaters built in streets and squares. It was 55 B.C. before the Roman Senate allowed a permanent stone theater to be erected in the city. Roman theaters were modifications of the Greek, although the Romans built their theaters on flat ground instead of against the sides of hills. The Romans did retain the amphitheater arrangement with the sides of the amphitheater joining the scene house which entirely enclosed the building.

## Medieval Theater

The classical tradition in theater all but disappeared with the fall of Rome in the fifth century A.D. Signs of an independent drama had begun to appear by the 10th century. Mostly in France, but elsewhere in Europe as well, brief theatrical scenes (tropes) were introduced into the Christian liturgy. Scholars are in debate as to how these first steps, crude though they were, evolved into full-blown theatrical presentations. It was once thought to be gradual but steady progression, but now it is clear that the history of medieval drama is more complicated and more elusive than first suspected. There are some certainties. The dramatization of Biblical materials and the presentation of religious drama expanded considerably throughout Europe from the 10th century to the 14th century, and by the 15th century play production was both ambitious and widespread.

Theater remained a joint clerical and civic undertaking throughout the medieval period. It was opened to all and participated in by most townspeople. The performers were initially members of the clergy, but as the number of productions grew and entire communities became involved, laymen became performers and in later years, some became professional actors.

Staging methods involved either a series of platforms constructed around the perimeter of the town square or "mansions" representing the various locales in the story arranged in a row. Either type of simultaneous staging allowed the actors to move from place to place as the action demanded.

## Renaissance Theater

There is no clear date to mark the end of the medieval theater and the beginning of the Renaissance theater. The yielding of liturgical drama to secular neoclassical drama occurred at different times in different countries. Consequently, the last vestiges of the cycles can be found in England at the same time that Greek plays were first being revived in Italy. Nevertheless, the character of European drama underwent a major change between the 15th and 17th centuries. On one hand, artistic impulses generated by the rich and widespread medieval theater — without the religious purpose — blossomed in the theater of England. Conversely, the newly rediscovered and appreciated Greek and Roman theatrical tradition pointed to lines of development that excited the imagination and stimulated fresh artistic effort.

The essentially religious in character communal audience slowly disappeared. In its place appeared two types of audience — the general public made up of artisans and burghers who found the theater an attraction and diversion, and a select aristocracy that cultivated the theater for their own glory, learning, and pleasure. In some countries, these two audience types overlapped, but for the most part, each type of theater audience developed in its own way.

In Italy, two kinds of theater emerged during the late 15th century: the theater of the fairs and the streets — "commedia dell'arte," and the theater of the academy and the court — "commedia erudita" and "intermezzi." The commedia dell'arte was a product of wandering troupes often appearing in the open wherever an audience could be assembled, but sometimes playing at ducal courts along the Italian peninsula. Initially, the stage was usually a bare platform backed by a drape to provide entrances for the performers. In later years, when they became more acceptable in court, the scenic stage was adopted.

As the same time as the development of the commedia dell'arte, a tradition of theatrical production developed among the Italian nobility when aristocrats and scholars were stimulated to revive the ancient Greek and Latin plays and pen imitations in Italian. Performances were presented in court or for academies organized to renew classical culture.

The Italian theater was a considerable influence throughout Europe because of its "commedia dell'arte" and its innovations in theater design. This influence began to be felt in both France and England in the early 17th century, but by then England had nearly finished a period of literary greatness and France had just embarked upon one. Both countries developed along similar lines, but the historical results were quite different.

### English Theater

In spite of its exposure to the influences that altered the Italian theater, the English theater retained its popular character for many years. School plays in Latin and English were early examples of classically oriented drama, but examples that were not followed. With the encouragement of the crown, English actors established a native repertory and permanent playhouses, and became the first Europeans to operate a successful commercial theater.

Under the nominal patronage of leading noblemen, acting troupes composed of men and boys wandered through England, appearing in town halls, country or city inns, or wherever they were tolerated until 1572. Appearances in London, though more frequent, were temporary, but in 1572 players were granted permission to perform daily in London. In 1576, James Burbage, an actor and carpenter, built the first building intended solely as a playhouse. It was an open-air structure named "theatre." Within the next forty years, seven playhouses were constructed, each seating about 2,500 persons. The most notable of these was the Globe Playhouse built in 1599, housing the company to which Shakespeare belonged and for which he wrote.

### French Theater

Since France was in the throes of civil war late in the 16th century, theater flourished there later than in England. During the first thirty years of the 17th century, France faced the same conflicts between native medieval methods and the newer classical revival as England had. The court played a more decisive role in France, and under the leadership of Cardinal Richelieu, imposed classical directions on the theater.

The reception of Pierre Corneille's *Le Cid* in 1636 was the final struggle, which critics said violated the structure and decorum of the classical theater. Richelieu invited the condemnation of *Le Cid* and set French theater on a neoclassical path when he referred the issue to the newly organized French Academy. All aspects of performing were guided by royal command. The king directly granted permission to perform in Paris, designating the place of performance and the number of weekly performances permitted. The troupes, composed of both male and female performers, played in comedies and tragedies.

### Middle-Class Theater of the 18th and 19th Centuries

The court taste for elaborate scenery was adopted by professional theater, but to achieve these effects, complicated machinery and extensive space were necessary. Control of the theater passed from the actors to the manager, who might or might not also be an actor, but whose authority stemmed from his position as head of a theatrical house. During the 18th century, London playhouses became larger, and by the early 19th century, theaters like Drury Lane and Covent Garden accommodated as many as 3,200 persons. These large structures continued to thrive throughout the 19th century, but more intimate theaters not intended for the general public began to appear. Every new theater movement tends to represent a force for social criticism, however, in the last quarter of the 19th century, the first to proclaim social criticism as their reason for being were the "free theaters."

### 20th Century Theater

With the 20th century came a time of invigorating but chaotic experimentation and change. A major part of the theater continues to be a commercial enterprise dominated by managers or producers purveying entertainment to the public. American "show business" is the ultimate expression of this style. Many "free theaters" have contributed to these commercial theaters, and in some instances, merged with them. Of the English-speaking theater, George Bernard Shaw and Eugene O'Neill created major dramatic works within the confines of a "little theater" movement that turned commercial.

Commercial theater did develop a significant art form with musical comedy, but being dominated by business managers, commercial theaters have suffered from a lack of artistic continuity, a lack that manifested itself in the 1920s. As long as it offered an interesting product at a reasonable cost, theater could succeed. The competitive position of commercial theater was seriously challenged by the advent of motion pictures, in particular sound movies in 1928. Though the theater continues to function, primarily in New York and London, it is operating under increasingly difficult circumstances.

### Oriental Theater

Considering their diversity in history and style, India, China, Japan, and other parts of Asia share a number of common features that distinguish Oriental from Occidental theater. In each of these countries, theater origin stems from religious observance, but these origins are so closely associated with mythical and legendary sources that it is difficult to distinguish tradition from fact.

The supposition is that Braham himself founded the Indian theater. Sacred plays were reportedly produced in China during the first millennium B.C. The Japanese Noh theater arose from a variety of priestly dances, the common source of which was the pantomimic dance used in Shinto worship. By the time theater was fully developed in these countries, whatever its origins, it was reserved for the ruling class, and like the Noh drama, an exclusive diversion of the court. Oriental countries also share common staging techniques — lengthy narratives composed of short plays, and a program which might consist of one continuous narrative or parts from several narratives.

Actors needed to be highly trained, though they occupied a rather low position in society. Women as well as men could perform in India, but in China and Japan — from the 18th to the mid-20th century, anyway — only men could perform.

## COLLECTING THEATRICAL MEMORABILIA

At first thought, anything connected with the performing arts sounds a bit frivolous, but when one considers theatrical history — as much of it as is known — there is no doubt that it is rooted in quite serious ground. Performing arts comprised a major portion of the lifestyles of those primitive generations. From a rather simple means of worship, it has evolved into a multi-faceted enterprise encompassing drama, music, and dance in infinite variety. Collecting theatrical memorabilia is one means of preserving the lifestyles of these past generations and paper memorabilia represents the documentation.

Regrettably, early theatrical paper memorabilia was not in great abundance or meant for the general public. Most of that which still survives is housed in museums and archives.

The most propitious opportunities for assembling theatrical paper no doubt lie with that which has been generated since the turn of the 20th century, though some Victorian era paper is still available. Flyers, posters, playbills, and programs are the most obvious items, but scripts and musical scores are also coveted. Opening night and autographed items are the most collectible.

Sources for the early and/or rare items will most likely be paper memorabilia dealers and antique dealers. Paper memorabilia and antique shows and exhibitions are likely sources, too. Flea markets and estate sales may yield some later items. And, don't overlook the old homestead or ancestral estate, if your family is fortunate enough to retain them. Some theatrical items are the stuff of which scrapbooks are made — those mementos of happy times.

## MUSIC

Man also learned to make music early on. His first instrument was his voice. The foremost musical fact in these early, primitive civilizations is the predominance of singing, though it is far removed from today's melodic styles. Primitive singing either took on a chant-like form of psalmodic, unemotional recitation of poetry incorporating two or three notes, or an outburst of emotional, passionate shouting with the voice jumping up to its high register and toppling helter-skelter down to its lowest sound.

Instruments were of much later origin. The most primitive civilizations known had no instruments at all, but most of them accompanied themselves by stamping their feet, clapping their hands, or slapping their chest, abdomen, or buttocks in even beats. Later, they intensified these beats by stamping their feet on a board, or striking the ground with bamboo tubes, or striking two sticks together or against another wooden object. The shapes and sounds of these early instruments evolved into an intricate network of magic ideas, some representing the masculine solar, and some the feminine lunar principle. Masculine solar instruments have an elongated shape and a shrill, terrifying sound, while feminine lunar instruments have a hollow and rounded shape and a hollow, muffled tone.

The earliest instruments are called idiophones, instruments made of solid sounding materials — wood, bamboo, fruit shells, and later metal — among which were rattles, clappers, and stamping tubes. These were followed by aerophones, instruments in which the air vibrates — propeller-like bullroarers, trumpets of branches or conch shells, and whistles of bone or reed. Conch shells were first used as megaphones. Third to appear were membraneophones — drums. Last to appear were chordophones or stringed instruments, which in the primitive world, were very primitive indeed.

In the higher civilizations of the East, stringed instruments were more predominant — the harp, lyre, lute, and zither. The harp was the chief instrument of ancient Egypt, Mesopotamia, and India. The lyre found a home in Southwest Asia. The lute was and still is common to all the East from Morocco to Japan, but has its roots in ancient Persia or Sumer. The zither is still the essential classical instrument of the Far East, China, and Japan.

Stringed instruments required two things that those primitive instruments didn't: 1) tuning the open strings; and 2) finding consistent stopping places on the strings of the lute family. The Orient provided orderly scales and systems based on arithmetic ratio — a systematic foundation for the composition of music. An Eastern music scale often means much more than it does in the modern West. Instead of a dry sequence of steps, it is a living flexible pattern which gives each note a function of its own, requires a certain tempo and a well-defined mood. It even has characteristic turns and formulas of melody. These patterns must not be violated, and the composer is bound to follow one of the traditional patterns. This standardization even embraces rhythm. Indian and Near Eastern composers select a ready-made metrical pattern for a piece — sometimes a very complicated one — and repeat it again and again to the end of the composition.

### Music of the Middle Ages

Since the Church was the seat of most organized knowledge during the Middle Ages, it also created its own music, and a large amount of this secular music has been lost, and attempts to reconstruct most of it from the few manuscripts available are open to supposition. A free exchange did exist between the musical resources of the church and the laity.

The French troubadours of the Southeast and their northern counterparts, the trouveres, along with the German minnesingers and meistersingers and strolling players as well were all instrumental in the development of music during this period.

The Baroque period dates from about 1600 to 1750 — from the beginnings of opera to the death of Johann Sebastian Bach. It produced a new musical style characterized by emphasis on a single melody supported by chords, brought to the fore an all important combination of music and drama — the opera — and saw the creation of a host of new instrumental forms. In short, it formed the basis of much of today's music.

Toward the end of the 16th century, a group of Florentine musicians discussing Greek drama opined that it had been sung in a declamatory manner, and theorized that music could be used to heighten the expressiveness of speech — a "song speech" called "recitative." They set out to prove their theory, and the result was the first "opera." The musical accompaniment — a few stringed instruments and a keyboard instrument — could, with the proper choice of arrangement, add emphasis to the recitative.

Opera experienced a phenomenally rapid growth in Italy, and a public opera theater opened in Venice in 1637. With cheap admission, the public flocked to this new entertainment. But the rise in paid admissions spawned a decline in dramatic values. The music, which had initially held an auxiliary role to the drama, soon became the thing in itself — the means became the end. With emphasis on solo song and pure melody, the dramatic factor receded into the background. Elaborate stage effects, complicated machines, and exotic costumes were incorporated into the production. The art of music received major impetus through the development of the solo song and the rapid recognition of the band of instruments located near the stage — the "orchestra," so named for its position in the theater. Eventually, this was to become the prime method of musical expression.

Classic masters of this era and on into the 19th century were, in addition to Bach, George Frederick Handel, Joseph Haydn, Wolfgang Amadeus Mozart, and Ludwig van Beethoven.

### The Romantic Era in Music

The romantic era in music, which began in the early 19th century, was concurrent with the same period in other arts and literature. Revolts by the masses, which eventually led to the central Europe uprisings of 1848, encouraged artists, writers, and musicians to make their work a more personal expression, to voice their own thoughts as opposed to those of their patrons and protectors. The classic forms were not abandoned, but they became more flexible. Composers of this period, following Beethoven's lead, made those forms more sensitive and more adaptable to the ideas they tried to express. There was also a closer alliance between music and literature. Harmonic combinations were bolder and richer, and there was a freer use of dissonances which had not been tolerated in 18th century music. Quite naturally, there was some initial resistance, much as the more advanced dissonances of the 20th century received slow acceptance.

### 19th Century Opera

Music lovers looked to Italy for their favorite operas for some time during the 19th century. Melodramatic plots were set to scores containing easily remembered melodies and effective arias, which developed the "bel canto" style of singing. In turn, singers were produced with the vocal capabilities expected in the opera house. Guiseppe Verdi, Giacomo Puccini, George Bizet, and Richard Wagner were but a few of the musical luminaries of this era.

### Post-Romantic Music

The Romantic movement continued after the middle of the 19th century with some composers writing both absolute and program music and carrying romantic ideals almost to decadence. Romanticism verged on the over-sentimental or neurotic. Others, like Richard Strauss, applied more advanced harmonies and instrumental techniques to writing descriptive or program music. Contemporaries of Strauss were Anton Rubinstein, Peter Ilyitch Tchaikovsky, Jean Sibelius, and Sergei Rachmaninov.

### 20th Century Musical Innovations

Nineteenth century academic and romantic

traditions of music were overthrown along with the social and political conventions of the time. Music was freer and expressed more vividly the complexities of human existence, the advances in science and invention, and the turmoil of political and social upheavals. What in the 20th century is considered modern music began with the Impressionist movement which was started in France at the end of the 19th century. Generally acknowledged as the founder of the Impressionist school in music is Claude Debussy who was influenced by Monet, Manet, Degas, and Renoir, painters of the Impressionist school, and by Mallarme and other symbolic poets. Debussy's music reflected the Impressionist style with its shimmering beauty incorporating vague, filmy atmospheric effects touched with delicate shading rather than solid tonal strokes. Also of the impressionist school of music were Maurice Ravel, Arnold Schoenberg, and Paul Hindemith.

## American Music

The earliest documented music of European settlers on the North American continent is the Psalm singing of the New England Puritans and Pilgrims. From 1620, it was practically the only musical activity of the colonists during the 17th century. Existing records indicate the presence of a few musical instruments in the Colonies near the end of the century, but it was the 1700s before the use of secular music achieved any prominence.

Both the Pilgrims in Plymouth and the Puritans in Massachusetts brought Psalter with them from Europe. The Pilgrims brought the *Ainsworth Psalter* and the Puritans the *Sternhold and Hopkins* collection. The Boston Puritans published a Psalter of their own in 1640, popularly called the *Bay Psalm Book*. The early editions contained no music, and for a full half century the melodies were sung from memory. A new edition of the book was issued in 1698 containing the music for thirteen selections. The more progressive churchmen of the early 18th century spurred on the congregations to learn to sing by note, and despite the opposition of reac-

tionaries, advocates of improved singing published instruction books. This eventually led to "singing schools" and subsequently to the formation of church choirs.

*The Urania* by James Lyon, published in 1761, and a series of six books compiled by William Billings with the first issued in 1770, were the earliest of the printed music collections to contain original compositions by American composers. Frances Hopkinson, a signer of the Declaration of Independence and a Judge of the Admiralty, was the first known native-born composer of music. The manuscript of his first known song, *My Days Have Been So Wondrous Free*, is dated 1759. He played with a group of amateur musicians who met at each others' homes and with professional musicians to give concerts.

Foreign musicians flocked to America in great numbers following the Revolutionary War. Better trained than their American counterparts, they became the nation's principal concert artists and teachers, and for many years monopolized the musical scene. By the early 19th century, these alien artists had become American citizens themselves, and the native-born musicians began to gravitate back to musical activities. Lowell Mason was the most widely known of the American-born composers during this period. He composed hymn-tunes and was an early advocate of music education.

While early formal concert music was slowly evolving from its European models, some American composers were eager to write music more expressive of American life than the more ambitious attempts of the "serious" composers. Several musicians did write some things, which appeared at the time to be little more than passing fancies, but did capture some of the homegrown lifestyle of the time. Many of these songs were written by white men for minstrel shows, a type of entertainment popular in the 1830s and 1840s, which emulated the singing, dancing, and humor of the Negro. The songs were influenced somewhat by Negro music but were also shaped by Scottish and English popular songs.

*Figure 39. Sigmund Romberg concert program from his Transcontinental Tour, 1947. (Author's collection.)*

In 1848, the Revolution in central Europe brought another major influx of foreigners, this time mostly German, who settled inland as well as on the coast. In nearly every American community, they became the principal musicians and teachers, saturating the country with German ideas and idioms so that most American composers modeled their work after German music.

During the latter half of the 19th century, an increasing number of American composers were successful in writing in this larger vein. John Knowles Paine was among the first, with his first symphony performed in 1876. Others were Dudley Buck, George W. Chadwick, Edgar Stillman Kelley, and Edward A. MacDowell.

Older composers of the 20th century include John Alden Carpenter, Charles Wakefield Cadman, and Deems Taylor. A somewhat younger group who were successful in adopting a contemporary viewpoint without venturing into radical departures from accepted tradition included Roy Harris, Howard Hanson, and Aaron Copland. An even younger group, encompassing those born since 1900 and expressing the typical 20th century point of view, include William Schuman, Gian Carlo Menotti, Leonard Bernstein, and Morton Gould.

A major contribution by the United States to world music is in the field of light music. The compositions of 19th century composer Stephen Foster received worldwide recognition, and his songs still may be heard in many countries around the globe. Others were John Philip Sousa with his stirring marches, and in the tradition of operetta, Victor Herbert, Jerome Kern, Sigmund Romberg (Fig. 39), and Irving Berlin.

"Ragtime" made its mark in the 1890s when popular music writers began incorporating rhythms from Black music. From these beginnings came 20th century "jazz" and later "swing" music. The Black rhythms of New Orleans are generally accepted as the roots of jazz, which began in 1915 and spread at a rapid pace throughout the nation. At first, it was mostly extemporaneous and of the variety "hot." Then a "sweet," mellower variety of jazz was introduced by bandleaders like Paul Whiteman and composer-arrangers like Ferde Grofe. The 1930s saw a resurgence in the popularity of hot jazz with the popularity of bandleaders like Louis Armstrong and Benny Goodman. "Jazz" was then rechristened "swing."

Serious music also felt the influence of jazz both in America and Europe. The most notable American exponent of this form was George Gershwin with his most recognized works, "Rhapsody in Blue" and "Porgy and Bess." European composers who experimented with this idiom included Igor Stravinsky, Arthur Honegger, and Maurice Ravel.

### Folk Music

In contrast to the structured forms of art music, folk music is a product of the communities and peoples and often of anonymous origins. The songs may be developed by one person or a whole group. Folk music and primitive music are not synonymous. Folk music originated and was sung by civilized, though rural, peoples and was influenced somewhat by art music.

Primitive music was spanned by races having no tradition or background in art music. Almost every race and every nation worldwide has its folk songs which generally tell of native characteristics. It is interesting to note that similar melodies can be found among widely separated peoples, indicating migratory patterns and the intermingling of nations.

United States folk music is generally divided into two main classifications — that of European origin and that developed by the Black Africans who brought it to American as slaves. Each had its effects on the various types of American folk songs — cowboy songs, frontier ballads, etc. Anglo-American folk music encompasses many Scottish, Irish, and English ballads that the early settlers brought to this country. Some versions close to the originals have been retained while others have been tailored to suit various groups around the country with the result that countless versions of these same songs exist today.

## COLLECTING MUSIC MEMORABILIA

Until the turn of the 20th century, autographs of the great composers were plentiful, but interest in collecting them was almost nil. One reason for the lack of interest was that great music was not accessible to the masses. Only the wealthy could afford the price of a ticket and the expense of dressing for the occasion, and only a large city could support a symphony orchestra or opera company. Manuscripts of great masters were available at nominal prices.

The invention of the phonograph and radio marked the advent of mass media where a flick of a switch could bring forth any type of music desired. This also increased the demand for the autographs of musicians, and by the 1950s they were no longer going for nominal prices. The limited number of great masters of music coupled with the limited number of their original manuscripts now in existence precludes ownership by an average collector. Bach, Beethoven, Schubert,

Mozart, Handel, and others of their league are among the rarest and dearest. The prices for the three Strausses, Stravinsky, Massenet, Grieg, Prokofiev, and others of their rank are escalating but not yet unattainable.

A great number of "modern" composers who have yet to achieve their potential in the collectible realm are available. These include Cole Porter, Duke Ellington, Kurt Weill, Hoagy Carmichael, Eubie Blake, Richard Rodgers, and Aaron Copland.

Musicians as well as composers are collectible. Conductors, big band leaders, jazz performers, and rock stars are also collectible.

Other musical mementos in paper besides manuscripts make nice additions to a collection. A fine letter in the composer's or musician's hand or an autographed photograph could do much to enhance a collection.

As with other collectibles, some selectivity is necessary since collecting everything would be an impossibility. Much of the more recent — from about World War I on — musical paper memorabilia is still available. Some very worthwhile collections can be put together for minimal costs.

Recording companies at one time issued catalogs of their popular disks of the moment. These are collectible, too, and can offer a wealth of information about what and who was popular when and even some that weren't so popular.

### Collecting Musical Scores and Sheet Music

Much of our musical heritage has been written down, and much of it is still attainable though some of the very early and scarce manuscripts now reside in museums and archives. What is of more interest to the average collector is the sheet music from about the turn of the century to the present. At one time, sheet music was just about the only way to hear and/or learn new music. With no records, radios, televisions, or sound movies, if you didn't sing it or play it on some instrument, you might never hear it. The musically inclined were hired by sheet music

Saony print of Jenny Lind to a comical 1923 cartoon of Barney Google and Spark Plug. Subjects ranged from the Civil War, minstrels, the Spanish-American War, and World War I, to opera stars, silent-film stars, and numerous others. Some of the most spectacular are the artist-signed covers and art nouveau illustrations of the early 1900s.

Sheet music was also used as a form of advertisement and promoted every item from Bromo Seltzer to the Peerless automobile! It is one more indication — and a good one — of the lifestyles of certain eras. Besides picturing prominent personalities of the time, they also depict clothing styles, vehicles, activities, furnishings, and architecture. The music itself mirrors the emotional climate of the time.

## DANCE

Although it is not documented, the early history of dance can be traced back to the days before the Greek Golden Age. Undoubtedly, the peoples of those ages were quick to relate the rhythms of the dance to music. Greek drama and pageantry achieved great heights with its chorus, dancers, and musicians. In later years, actors, musicians, and dancers were condemned by the Church for their "evil doings," but dancing continued and eventually was incorporated into the medieval miracle plays. Musicians also participated in the plays.

In the 16th century, the term "ballet" came into widespread use because professionally trained dancers were necessary to the performances. The center of the early 16th century ballet was Paris. The ballet became a part of the ceremonial spectacles for the courts, which also included singing, dancing, declamation, pantomime, and other entertainment forms.

Popular and classical dances have been part of the lifestyle of every country, but the country of most influence in the development of the ballet has been France. By order of Louis XIV in 1661, the world's first dance academy was organized, and the dancing masters of Paris were world famous. Ballet was always interspersed

*Figure 40. Sheet music, left to right: "Sweet and Gentle" recorded by Alan Dale, "Shuffle Off to Buffalo" from* Forty-Second Street, *and "Black Moonlight" from* Too Much Harmony *featuring Bing Crosby. (Author's collection.)*

dealers to sing or play new selections as an aid to selling them.

Several groups of hobbyists collect sheet music. Music lovers want it for the intrinsic value of the music (Fig. 40). Topical collectors want it as an adjunct to whatever their topic is. Collectors of railroadiana might look for railroad songs. Collectors of circus memorabilia might want circus tunes. Others might want certain types of music like ragtime or polkas. Still others might be more interested in the artwork on the covers. Collectors call it decorative sheet music. Many of these covers were designed by noted artists and could conceivably be called original prints though they were not issued in limited editions. It is one paper item that is now relatively inexpensive, but expectations are that it will more than double its value in the near future.

Cover designs of decorative sheet music span the artistic gamut from a delicate 1851 with the arias, interludes, and verses of Early French Opera.

Some years passed before ballet achieved a form all its own. Classic dance forms — minuets, gavottes, musettes, etc. — were used for early ballet before attempts to unite dancing with acting and appropriate music were successful. Jean-George Noverre collaborated with opera reformer Christopher Willibald Gluck late in the 18th century in arranging music to fit the planned dance action.

In the 19th century period of romanticism, the dances of the people — the polonaise, the mazurka, the waltz, and the polka — influenced the ballet. Though many ballets were written during this period, very few survived to be worthy of performance today. *Swan Lake, Sleeping Beauty*, and *The Nutcracker Suite* by Tchaikovsky and *Coppelia* by Delibes are some of the outstanding examples that are still popular today.

By the early 20th century, the art of the dance was in danger of losing its popularity because technique was beginning to overshadow expressiveness as ballerinas vied to show off their technical excellence. Isadora Duncan was instrumental in reviving the popularity of ballet. She took to Europe her ideas for a new type of dancing which abandoned the conventional dances of the day and turned for inspiration to the ancient Greek dances as they were depicted in art and to the rhythmic motions of wind and wave and the flights of birds and bees.

Also instrumental in the revival of the ballet were master choreographers Fokine and Diaghilev; dancers Pavlova, Nijinsky, and Massine; and composers Stravinsky, Ravel, Prokofiev, Auric, and Milhaud among others.

Many ballet theaters and companies still successfully continue the tradition of the ballet. The Bolshoi Ballet, the Ballet Russe, the Royal Ballet of England, and the American Ballet are but a few of the most prominent.

Some of the more modern dance innovations incorporate ballet movements. Broadway musicals have been instrumental in incorporating the dance in its many forms into popular culture. Ballet, modern dance, tap in all its variations, ballroom, and other dance forms have all had a place in the modern musical idiom.

### Collecting Dance Memorabilia

The most obvious of the paper memorabilia related to the dance are programs from the various dance companies. Some early ones featuring the premier dancers of their era may still be available. Autographed photographs, posters, and publicity stills are other possibilities. Scripts and dance layouts may also be found.

Because, with the exception of the programs, these are not among the more common paper collectibles, the most likely sources for finding them are paper memorabilia dealers and antique dealers. Flea markets and estate sales are always possible sources for paper items, but it is usually the more common items like post cards, baseball cards, and stamps that are seen.

## MOTION PICTURES

Motion pictures are really an optical illusion — a series of separate pictures projected so rapidly on a screen that to the eye they appear to be in continuous motion; an effect caused by a physical property of the human eye which retains an image in the line of sight for about one-fifth of a second after it has actually disappeared. The technical term is "persistence of vision."

Following the invention and development of photography, many scientific-minded individuals experimented with the problem of picturing motion. Using methods devised by John D. Isaacs, circa 1872-73, Edward Muybridge set up a row of twenty-four cameras to study the movements of a trotting horse. Each camera was exposed in turn as the horse trotted in front of them. The photographs were then projected so that they would simulate movement. But, since he had only glassplates, his apparatus was clumsy. A substitute for the glass in the form of a light, flexible, continuous film was invented by Goodwin and produced by Eastman.

Thomas Edison marketed in 1894 his kinetoscope which was successful in depicting motion by means of photographs printed on an endless strip of celluloid film. The only drawback was that the pictures could be viewed by only one person at a time! The first person to produce motion pictures by modern methods was Thomas Armat of Washington in 1895. The major improvement by Armat was a way to move the film intermittently with periods of rest and illumination greater than the periods of movement from image to image. In 1896, other projectors were made and exhibited. The following nine years, from 1897 to 1907, saw a violent upheaval in the industry because of litigation over patents.

Edison built the first studio for making motion pictures — a little black paper-covered shanty located near his factory in New Jersey. During the heyday of the motion picture industry, the 1930s to the 1950s, Hollywood was the undisputed movie-making capital of the world. And nearly every movie and movie star spawned a conglomeration of memorabilia — paper and otherwise. Photographs, programs, posters, movie stills, paper dolls, books, matchbooks, sheet music, post cards, playing cards, stationery, school tablets and notebooks, puzzles, games, and calendars are but a few of the paper items.

### Collecting Motion Picture Memorabilia

A myriad of paper items can be collected in myriad ways. With such a wealth of subject matter and items available, collectors tend to be selective. Favorites have a way of making themselves known in rather short order, too. Favorite movie star, favorite actress, favorite actor, favorite movie, favorite type of movie, favorite motion picture eras. To narrow it down even more, the collection can be limited as to type of paper item. Photographs only — with or without autographs — posters, books. One collector specialized in all editions of *Gone with the Wind.* Some collect old movie ads; others collect anything related to their favorite.

Collecting motion picture and theatrical autographs has become a hobby in itself apart from any other of the performing arts memorabilia. Of course, the rarest autographs are of those no longer with us. The most prominent of the departed among the movie set are Humphrey Bogart, Judy Garland, Marilyn Monroe, Rudolph Valentino, and Jean Harlow. Other noteworthy former movie luminaries are Clark Gable, Carole Lombard, Mae West, James Cagney, and John Wayne. At one time, many of these items were giveaways or available for a very nominal fee. The back pages of old movie magazines usually contained a number of ads for companies offering autographed photographs of movie stars.

Hollywood at War in World War II offers a sizable amount of paper memorabilia in itself. Many of the favorite male stars of that period went into the armed services. Those who were exempt from military service went off to war by way of USO tours, bond drives, and benefits for the Red Cross and other worthy causes. The Hollywood Canteen was a popular spot with military personnel in the Los Angeles area. They could have a few hours of relaxation, and dance or chat with their favorite stars. A similar operation in New York City was called the Stage Door Canteen.

Some blockbuster type movies have even come out with their own souvenir programs (Fig. 41).

There are a variety of sources for motion picture memorabilia depending upon what type of paper it is. Collecting autographs is dealt with in Chapter 4. Paper memorabilia dealers may be the best sources for items like posters, old tour guides and maps to stars' homes, post cards and folders featuring stars, paper dolls, playing cards, and other like items. Dealers in old magazines will probably be good sources for old movie magazines and periodicals. Sometimes special magazines were published devoted to one star. Antique shops and dealers may have some of the earlier items, though the motion picture industry is still so relatively young in comparison with other collectible areas that only the very early items may be classed as antiques.

*Figure 41.  Souvenir program for motion picture,* The Sound of Music. *(Author's collection.)*

## BROADCASTING

### Radio Broadcasting

Radio broadcasting came to the forefront during the decade from 1920 to 1930, and was then looked upon as an effective rival to newspapers, an image that it retained as it grew into a major entertainment medium.

Experiments began some years before 1920 to effectively transmit speech and music from a central sending station to owners of receiving sets. One of the leaders in this development was Lee DeForest. Station KDKA Pittsburgh, Pennsylvania, operated by the Westinghouse Electric and Manufacturing Company (at East Pittsburgh, PA), broadcast the presidential election returns in 1920. The popularity of this broadcast led to a phenomenal increase in the number of receiving sets in homes plus a corresponding increase in broadcasting stations. By 1940, one receiving set was owned by an average of 2.4 persons in the United States. Programming has expanded to suit every taste and purpose.

Four major networks were instituted as radio broadcasting grew and prospered — American Broadcasting Company, Columbia Broadcasting System, Mutual Broadcasting System, and National Broadcasting Company. With the utilization of telephone wires, it was possible to connect chains of stations that could send out identical programs. Hookups could be made nationwide and worldwide.

The United States had 675 radio broadcasting stations by 1940. Canada and Russia were next in rank. The worldwide total was fewer than 2,000. Even with the introduction of television in 1939, radio broadcasting has remained an important means of communication. FM radio broadcasting was a major development in improving radio sound quality.

### Television Broadcasting

The first television station, WRGB at Schenectady, New York, began operating on November 6, 1939. Visual images are transmitted by wire or wireless by conversion of light rays to electrical waves which are then reconverted to reproduce the original images on a receiving set.

Television did not really achieve nationwide status until the mid-1940s. There was usually one television channel in the vicinity of the larger cities, and television receiver screens resembled portholes. They were about seven or eight inches in diameter. Some dealers were inclined to put several television sets in their store windows, turned on and facing out, so potential buyers could get a good look. Since, at that time, there were more homes without television than with, it was a common sight to see a group of people gathered in front of a store window watching this new wonder.

By the 1950s, television had made such inroads into the recreational habits of the masses that radio began to feel the pinch and was forced to regroup. The networks no longer monopolize the radio airwaves completely though network news is still prominent. Local radio broadcasting has come to the fore with music, news, and talk. With the exception of some late night talk shows, most of radio's stars are local personalities. Networks and the big stars now concentrate most of their energy on television, but with the advent of cable television and the deep inroads it has made on television viewing, the networks are now feeling the pinch.

### Collecting Broadcasting Memorabilia

At approximately seventy years of age, broadcasting is the baby of the entertainment media. As such, a nice variety of paper memorabilia should still be available at reasonable prices.

Both radio and television spawned a horde of paperwork. Each had its stars, some of whom spanned both media. Besides the usual items like star photos, show manuscripts, promotional pamphlets, booklets, and brochures, there are also items like schedules, logs, commercial copy, program formats, story boards, still cards, cue cards, correspondence, memos, you name it. All this is compounded when you realize that this type of paper was and is used for each show on each network, and on a local basis for each station, in every locale, on a daily basis. Add to this all the cable telecasts.

There are also a lot of promotional items from other sources sent to stations or networks or to specific personalities on the stations or the networks. This may be true more so for radio than television since performers want to get their records played on the radio. More than likely, performers have to arrange an appearance on a television show to present new material, or they make a video. But the paperwork still goes on.

Broadcasting stations themselves may be sources for some of these paper items. Stars, local, national, and international, have their share of promotional items to give away or sell for a nominal fee. Radio used to be a big source for premiums connected with one show or star or another, but premiums aren't mentioned much anymore except possibly on the Saturday morning cartoon shows, and those are likely to be found in or on cereal boxes.

Flea markets may be a good source for old radio premiums. Stations that close down or move to other locations may be prime sources for paper items. Old stationery and other office paper, old logs, old schedules, old music charts, old *Broadcasting Magazines*, issues of *Variety*, and other periodicals may all be waiting for the takers. Stations that change their format usually have a supply of items to dispose of, too. Flea markets and thrift shops may be good sources for local items, and estate sales of local former broadcasting bigwigs may yield some choice items.

Paper memorabilia dealers may have some of the harder to find items.

## PRESERVING THE PERFORMING ARTS

Paper memorabilia connected with the performing arts ranges over such a wide spectrum that it entails almost all of the forms of paper mentioned in the other chapters of this book — prints in almost all forms including cards, newspapers, and magazines, manuscripts, documents, books, games, matchbooks, and all sorts of ephemera. Therefore, each piece of performing arts memorabilia must be considered on its own merits according to its form and handled as described in the corresponding chapter. The General Preservation Rules in Chapter 3 also apply. Follow the framing directions for prints (Chapter 6) for any items suitable for framing. Programs in booklet form should be handled like magazines.

Obviously, a variety of paper grades will also be involved in a collection of performing arts memorabilia. A small portion of it will be quite good, another small portion will be on the bad side — in the league with newsprint. The majority of it will fall somewhere in between. Whatever kind of paper it is, handle it with care to avoid further damage and impede deterioration.

Keep in mind that some performing arts items were meant to be used, and consequently handled a lot. Sheet music and scripts and any items used in the production of a show in any of the media are examples. It may not be possible to find them in mint condition. Sheet music is a prime example of wear and tear on paper. Very little of it will be found in mint condition. Scripts can be dogeared, marked with cues and other production aids, and generally showing signs of much handling on every page. Sheet music, too, may have some markings. These might also include notations on the cover regarding prices. Sometimes handwritten notations on a paper item may add to its value, depending on what they are and who wrote them if it can be determined. Do not attempt to remove any of these markings, especially on very early specimens. Besides possibly causing additional damage, something of importance may be removed.

### The Performing Arts as Collectible

Performing arts is the passionate collectible. The performing arts began as an integral part of society, yet it has taken centuries for the professional to achieve its just status in society. The image of the performer, once part of the laity, evolved into that of itinerant worker. Unstable, unkempt, homeless, second rate citizens all. To the wealthy, servants at their beck and call.

Performing looks easy and fun, yet in reality a lot of hard work goes into making it look easy and fun. It can be exhausting, exhilarating, and scary.

Memorabilia of the performing arts have long been popular with collectors. Interest in performers runs high and much memorabilia — paper and otherwise — is easily accessible. As unstable as paper can be, it is the stabilizing factor in a collection. Without the paper items to back it up, the collection has no validity. Paper gives substance to an apparently vacuous lifestyle. It secures the performer's rightful place in society.

# 11
# Newspapers and Magazines

Newspapers mirror the day-to-day happenings of their times without embellishments. The daily history of a community, a government, a world as they knew it (Figs. 42 & 43).

Magazines reflect the culture of an era, the trends, the struggles, the triumphs, the ridiculous, the sublime, the lifestyles of a country.

History books record history as events. Newspapers and magazines record history as it is happening, but on different planes. Newspapers depict the common man as he is (Fig. 44). Magazines depict him as he would like to be. History books record the events that move and change the world — charts of the Earth's and the world's progress. Newspapers and magazines record the people who move and change the world — charts of the people's progress through the Earth and the world (Fig. 45). History books hit the high spots. Newspapers and magazines fill in the gaps between the high spots.

## NEWSPAPERS

Newspapers reflect the history of the common man. The causes of the common man became the causes of the press.

The prototype of the modern newspaper can be traced back to the *Acta Diurna — Daily Events* — issued during the Roman Empire and posted in a public place. Copies were made by hand and dispatched to distant subscribers.

The first genuine regularly published newspaper was the *Avisa Relation oder Zeitung*, first printed in 1609 in Germany. In 1622, the first newspaper appeared in England, *The Weekly News* from Italy, Germany, etc., published in London. In the Western Hemisphere, the earliest news sheet was the *Relacion* issued in 1594 in Lima, Peru, but it was 1620 before a regular newspaper was published there.

Early newspapers were, by and large, a one-man operation, usually a printer with a small press and paper. He was publisher, printer, and distributor of the newspaper.

As early as 1689 in Boston, broadsides containing news were printed — under the authority of the British government, unless some individual was brave enough to publish an outlaw sheet. Throughout the history of the newspaper, the press and the government have engaged in a tug-of-war over censorship. The publisher on one side struggling for unrestricted freedom of the printed word, the government on the other side trying to exert authority to keep the press in line with government policy. Unfortunately for the first American colonists, the government exerted just as much control over press, politics, and religion as that which had caused them to flee their native country.

In 1690, Benjamin Harris of Boston published the first American newspaper, a monthly issue called *Public Occurrences Both Foreign and Domestick*. It was a small folded sheet printed on three sides. The fourth side, left blank, was reserved for notations or newsworthy events. It was a short-lived endeavor

*Figure 42. Front page of* Chicago American, *November 11, 1918, headlined "WAR OVER." (Photograph courtesy Newspaper Collectors Society of America and the R. J. Brown Archive.)*

*Figure 43. Front page of* Cleveland News, *May 7, 1945, headlined "NAZIS QUIT!" This was an "EXTRA" edition. (Photograph courtesy Newspaper Collectors Society of America and the R. J. Brown Archive.)*

*Figure 44. Front page of* Chicago American, *November 8, 1933, headlining the repeal of Prohibition: "HAPPY DAYS ARE HERE AGAIN!" (Photograph courtesy Newspaper Collectors Society of America and the R. J. Brown Archive.)*

*Figure 45. Front page of* Chicago American, *August 16, 1936, headlined "WILL ROGERS KILLED." (Photograph courtesy Newspaper Collectors Society of America and the R. J. Brown Archive.)*

since Harris did not secure a proper license and printed derogatory articles about the authorities.

Another fourteen years passed before a second attempt was made at publishing a newspaper. In 1704, Postmaster John Campbell published the *Boston News-Letter*. It lasted only eighteen years since, at that time, advertising was limited and news usually traveled faster by word of mouth.

With the issuance of the *New England Courant* in 1718, James Franklin, brother of Benjamin Franklin, was the first recognized newspaper editor. Controversial though the first issues were, the people were eager for freedom of the press and avidly absorbed any attacks on the establishment. Letters to the editor and shipping accounts were the most popular sections of the single-sheet paper.

Benjamin Franklin was apprenticed to his brother as a printer at the age of twelve and took over as publisher at the age of seventeen, but after a quarrel with his brother, left for Philadelphia where he published the *Pennsylvania Gazette* in 1729. It was quick to turn a profit, and his *Poor Richard's Almanac* published from 1753 to 1758 sold over 10,000 copies annually. Acting as a partner, he introduced the art of printing and newspaper publication to many American communities. Despite his fame and his many accomplishments, he began his will "I, Benjamin Franklin, printer...".

By 1750, with a growing need for information and licenses no longer mandatory, fourteen weeklies were operating in the six colonies. They were filling the needs of businessmen who had to be able to pass on information about the availability of any new shiploads of goods to consumers. The weekly increased to three times a week with political machination their main topic. To avoid submitting controversial comments to the press, individuals were encouraged to print pamphlets which let the newspaper "off the hook."

Disagreements between the Crown and the colonies mounted and came to a head with The Stamp Act of 1765. Rather than fight the taxa-

tion, some newspapers suspended publication. Others printed without a masthead giving the title and ownership while others said they couldn't find any stamps to buy.

Because of the Revolution, printing supplies were no longer available from England so press and type makers were encouraged to start businesses in America. Politicians now believed the press to be a very useful tool which encouraged individual independence.

Noah Webster's *American Minerva* was another early newspaper. Started in 1793 using the pseudonym "Curtius," Webster published one of the first editorial pages.

Improved presses reflected a daily increase in newspapers with some even hauling their equipment westward on wagons. The first printing press in California began operating in 1834. Soon after every city, mining settlement, and lumber town had its own paper. In contrast to the eastern papers, which often displayed high literary quality, these western journals had little or no international news but confined themselves to local expressions and happenings. Very few of these early newspapers published west of the Mississippi were preserved, so any of them are of value. Many of them came from areas that eventually became ghost towns.

First used by the *Philadelphia Public Ledger* in 1847, the cylinder press converted newspapers from a single operation to mass production, printing over 8,000 sheets an hour.

In the 1850s, there was an upsurge in popularity of magazines but, as with all wars, the Civil War generated renewed interest in daily happenings. Many newspapers were in opposition to the spread of slavery. Antiwar sheets sprang up on both sides. Newspapers were soon as divided as the nation. Also common fare in the press were pictorial scenes of the war, many by well-known artists of the time, including A. R. Wand, T. Davis, and Thomas Nast. Two popular publications of this period that, because of numerous illustrations resembled a cross between a newspaper and a magazine, were *Harper's Weekly* and Frank Leslie's *Illustrated Newspaper*. War news, as was its wont, increased circulation, and a new, more readable style evolved. It was also a transitory period for funding with less dependence on subscription money and an increase in revenue from advertisers.

Several newspapers that developed in the South during the Civil War continued to boost southern industrial progress after the war. From the 1870s to the 1890s, the newspaper established itself as a daily part of living, reflecting social and economic growth throughout the nation. Advertisements became the mainstay of survival for newspapers and collector's items themselves, in particular those concerned with new inventions, transportation, photographers, artists, silversmiths, clock makers, and illustrated cuts of patent medicine. News content included elections, executions, deaths of famous people, assassinations, and scientific advances. Even early comic strips are collectible.

A word of caution. Many newspapers reporting famous events have been reprinted, sometimes just a few years after the actual event, which makes distinguishing between the two nearly impossible. Patent medicine companies, for example, printed newspaper copies of Lincoln's assassination which can be dated correctly only by testimonial dates on the back pages. Suspect newspapers should be studied carefully to determine authenticity.

### Collecting Newspapers

Ever since newspapers have been available to the masses, people seem to have had a natural propensity for saving newspaper accounts of events likely to have long-term effects of national or worldwide intensity. Front page items and headline stories would be retained. Clipping newspapers has long been a popular avocation, too. Recipes, information, advertisements, coupons, news items of local import are the norm for clippers.

For the collector, the entire newspaper is the prize. The value can be drastically diminished if any part of a newspaper is missing, however, in the case of 20th century newspapers, which have several sections, the front section

only retains about ninety percent of the collector value.

Newspapers don't necessarily have to contain a significant historical news event to be collectible. Newspaper of a "no-news" day are called "atmosphere" newspapers. The majority of historical dates fall into this category. Of course, the value of an "atmosphere" paper is not as great as one with significantly historical content, but its contents offer the reader the opportunity to get a feel of what that era in time was like. A 200 year old newspaper, for example, may contain ads for runaway slaves, ships' schedules, jobs wanted, and articles on such topics as mermaids, ghosts, hangings, and sea voyages. Newspapers document day-to-day lifestyles and living, and with or without headline news, contain information one is not likely to find anywhere else.

There are many ways to collect newspapers, other than for their historical content. Unique or unusual titles of newspapers — *Cupid's Sitting Room*, *What's Next?*, the *Ubiquitons*, *Tack-Room*, and *The Bitter-Sweet* are examples. First and last issues. Centennial or anniversary issues. Those with intricate or decorative nameplates/mastheads. Newspapers with engravings. Recent newspapers from around the world.

Newspapers are graded as either "collectible" or "not collectible." Collectible condition means the newspaper can be easily read with no danger of pieces chipping away and the paper is otherwise sound. Collectors do not want to buy papers that are brittle, fragile, falling apart, or with pieces missing. If only the front page is present, the value is usually 25% of a complete edition. Up to approximately 1870, newspapers were printed on rag paper, and for this reason, newspapers prior to 1870 remain in better condition than 20th century ones. Newspapers of the World War I era (1914-18) are hard to find in collectible condition because of the excessive acid content of the paper.

The best source for old newspapers is from historic newspaper dealers, and there are many. Most of them issue mail-order catalogs on a regular basis, and offerings include newspapers from the 1600s on up to the present. The prices are the most realistic, and there are thousands of newspapers from which to choose.

*A Primer on Collecting Old & Historic Newspapers* is published annually by Rick Brown of the Newspaper Collectors Society of America. It contains more detailed information about collecting newspapers, and includes a price guide and an application for membership in the NCSA. The address is: NCSA, P.O. Box 19134, Lansing, Michigan 48901.

### Preserving Newspapers

Newspapers were and are one of the original throwaway items. Certainly there was no reason to keep them for any length of time to clutter up the premises. But some did survive. Many later newspaper issues are harder to find than some of the earlier ones since the early paper stock was of a much better grade.

Preserving newspapers is a matter of maintaining those in good condition against damage and deterioration, and preventing further damage and deterioration to those with minor imperfections or in danger of deterioration from acid build-up in the paper.

It would be impractical to attempt to deacidify all collectible newspapers, though it could probably be done to very rare and valuable ones. The solution lies in attempting to save the paper as it is and delay any deterioration as long as possible.

Newspapers should be stored flat, unfolded to the size of the front page. Special Mylar newspaper-size envelopes are available that offer archival storage while giving complete visibility to the contents. They are available in several sizes ranging from 11″ by 17″ to 24″ by 36″.

Acid-free newspaper storage boxes are also available. They are manufactured of archival quality board and lined with heavy white bond for extra protection of contents. The top telescopes to give double stacking strength. These boxes are available in three standard sizes, but can be made in special sizes for particular requirements.

These simple preservation methods will do much to protect the newspapers from atmospheric conditions — chemicals in the air, dust, insects, and light. It is not always possible to keep room temperatures at a constant level in one's home, but care can be taken to store newspapers, in their acid-free containers, away from excessive heat, light, and moisture.

Care should also be taken not to seal the Mylar envelopes so that air cannot get to the newspapers at all. This could be a built-in trap for condensation. Newspapers should not be packed tightly in the storage boxes nor should the boxes be sealed tightly for the same reasons.

Because of the acid content of some newsprint, it is best to keep newspapers from rubbing against each other. If one should begin to deteriorate, it could damage all the rest in the box.

## MAGAZINES

Magazines may be a bit underrated, but deserve to be recognized as purveyors of high-quality journalism and artwork. Frequently, they are aware of the newest trends or styles before the daily newspapers. Undoubtedly, their audience is vast. Noted writers Tennyson and Longfellow for instance, always realized the potential of magazines in reaching people. Most often a magazine is issued periodically — monthly, bimonthly, etc. — but even those issued on an occasional basis may be considered periodicals.

Benjamin Franklin was the first to conceive an American magazine, but he was beaten to the presses in 1741, just barely, by Andrew Bradford and his *American Magazine, or A Monthly View of the Political State of the British Colonies.* Early attempts at publishing magazines were almost destined to fail because of lack of interest and the illiteracy rate among the masses. This was during a time when a few thousand subscriptions were considered a generous circulation.

Much of the content of these early magazines was not original but copied from recent books and newspaper accounts. It soon became apparent that originality was the key to success, and publishers begged noted authors for contributions of original works. Women had a hand in publishing some of these early magazines probably because the periodicals were female-oriented and dealt with subjects more interesting and familiar to women.

In 1794, magazines were given special postage rates which resulted in an increase in publications. Regrettably, most of the magazines did not require advance payment so collecting subscription fees was something else. Advertising had yet to reach its potential, with mostly book and pamphlet ads limited to the back pages of the periodicals. Many publications failed during the Revolutionary War when materials from England were cut off. With independence came reason enough to try again, and the new periodicals that followed were not only rife with illustrations, but also branched out to include humor, poetry, and music. Magazines also began to target specific audiences such as women and children. Women's magazines often reflected thought-provoking ideas, daring clothing styles, social injustice, women's liberation, and later, the suffragettes' struggle for recognition. In contrast to today's children's magazines, children were treated as persons of intellect, and early children's magazines were modeled after similar adult counterparts.

Fiction and short stories were added by popular demand during the first quarter of the 19th century.

The fifty year period from 1830 to 1880 saw the extension of specialization in publications: mechanical reviews, scientific journals, farmers' guides, and religious monthlies.

Magazines published during the latter part of the 19th century through the early 1900s, though just as diversified, also reflected an increasing awareness of reader intelligence. The reader had a choice of several publications devoted to a single subject, and competition was keen to attract new readers.

Magazines published from 1880 through the 1920s are collected mainly for signed artist illustrations and advertisements. Covers drawn by Frederick Remington, Norman Rockwell, and Maxfield Parrish are examples to note. Article illustrations by Howard Pyle, Kate Greenaway, and Rose O'Neill, creator of the Kewpie doll, can also be found.

### Collecting Magazines

A conservative estimate of the number of periodicals published over the years since those first magazines appeared in the 1700s, is tens of thousands. Most of these old or back date magazines share one common denominator, while not always collectors' items in themselves. They are bought for reference material or for the need of a special article contained therein.

Rigid condition standards are all but impossible to set for old magazines as a whole. One cannot expect issues dating from 1900 to be in entirely fresh condition, and those of 1850 or earlier will certainly reflect some soil and deterioration. Regardless of age, collectible magazines should have covers intact and the covers should not be loose, pages should not be missing or reflect clipped out areas, and there should be no serious staining or other outward damage.

Collectors prefer magazines in unbound volumes, especially the rarities. However, assembling sets of pre-1900 titles may be very difficult without acquiring some volumes in bindings. Original owners, and often subsequent owners, sometimes had them bound. Considering this, collectors may in time become more receptive to bound volumes.

Some collectors specialize in "first editions" of magazines. those dating from about World War I up to the 1960s and 1970s are the most sought after. Special editions of some magazines are also collectible (Figs. 46 & 47). Magazines with brief publishing histories may prove to be the sleepers of magazine collecting, especially if they were nicely crafted publications with good illustrations.

Some dealers tend to price magazines by age alone, but this does not give a fair picture of the actual values. Certain magazine issues may be worth more than others of similar dates because of content. Others may be worth less because

*Figure 46. This* Life *magazine, dated February 9, 1962, previewed the 1962 Seattle World's Fair which opened April 21 of that year. (Author's collection.)*

*Figure 47. The December 1953 cover of* PLAYBOY *magazine featuring Marilyn Monroe. (Copyright © 1953 by* PLAYBOY. *Reprinted with permission.)*

there is less demand for them. Auction sales are apt to be more accurate in determining a price.

No doubt the best place to obtain magazines in collectible condition is from a dealer. Dealers also will have the harder to find issues or be able to get them for you, given a little time. Back issues of more recent magazines and issues of defunct magazines also are usually available from dealers. Most of these dealers accept mail-order sales.

Another good prospect for magazines is estate sales. Like other paper items, they are usually an afterthought at these sales and resigned to attics or storage areas. Condition will not always be the best, but who knows when and where a real find will surface? Flea markets, thrift shops, and garage sales are other options.

### Preserving Magazines

Most magazines are made of a much better grade of paper than newspaper. Often magazine paper is coated for ease in absorbing inks and because it looks and wears better. That does not mean that some deterioration won't occur in time. The paper used for some early magazines was but a shade or two better than newsprint and could turn yellow and crumble like newsprint in time; perhaps not quite as quickly as newsprint. It's a bit ironic that some of the finest writing and artwork appeared in magazines that could not stand the test of time.

Magazine-sized archival quality Mylar envelopes are available to provide safe individual storage. Vertical shelf files made of either extra-strong, acid-free 200 lb. test corrugated board, or acid-free board, or acid-free polypropylene can be used in conjunction with the Mylar envelopes. All the files come in a variety of sizes to fit most magazines.

The acid-free corrugated board files are the most economical and come with pressure sensitive labels. Some assembly is required. The acid-free board files come set up and ready to use. The acid-free polypropylene files will not scratch, dent, peel, or fray under normal conditions, nor will they cause damage to paper stored in them. They are available in a selection of colors from bright to sedate, and with either closed or open backs.

For those who prefer to box their collections, acid-free hinged top file boxes are available. Unless a magazine is in fragile condition, Mylar sleeves are not necessary with these boxes, but acid-free backer boards between each magazine are recommended so the magazines will retain their shape and not buckle. These files are stackable and have a pull tab on the front for easy retrieval when stored on shelves. Magazines should be packed with breathing space and for easy removal of a desired one without damage to the others.

## NEWSPAPERS AND MAGAZINES AS COLLECTIBLE

Newspapers are the literature of the common man — the diaries of the day-to-day happenings as they happen. Magazines are an embellishment of newspapers. They add flesh to the stark detail of the newspaper report.

Both are the documentation used by historians in recording the history of an era. Sometimes they are the only documented evidence of an event. The thread of the history of mankind is spun through man's efforts at recordkeeping. Newspapers and magazines are the ultimate in man's recordkeeping — first-hand reports from the scene of the action, sometimes with illustrations. Collecting newspapers and magazines is collecting history in the making.

# 12
# Literary Items

For a piece of writing to be properly designated as literature, it should meet two criteria:

1. It must be so arranged and ordered that it will appeal to the heart and mind of man, or to put it more simply, it should appeal to the imagination. The author should be able to express or communicate effectively the emotion or idea that possesses him — he must have "style."

2. It must have significant content. Without style, a work is not literature at all. Without significance, it cannot be great literature.

Literature which meets this criteria constitutes our most valuable record of the inner life of man. Nowhere is the history of man's spiritual existence — the life of humanity — so thoroughly and fundamentally presented as in the world's greatest masterpieces of literature. It is what elevates man above his mere animal existence. It provides a standard of values for our human activities. It gives us the meaning of human history — the logic of life.

The "world's greatest literature" generally includes only the literature and literary tradition which was first developed in Europe by the Greeks from where it was passed down through the Romans to the modern European nations which in turn spread it to the colonies they founded. This literature included the Bible which came from farther East. There has also been a smattering of influence from Persia and India, however, the literary traditions of the Hindus, the Persians, and the Chinese, for the most part, have remained largely alien to the western nations and are not considered to be a part of that literary heritage.

## AMERICAN LITERATURE

### Beginnings

American literature, like that of other people who have emigrated from lands already in an advanced stage of culture, has no native roots. American writers brought their traditions and a rich literary heritage with them, but faced with a new and stubborn land to conquer, they had little time to devote to writing. It was some time before their writings reflected the consciousness of a people of an independent land with an individuality and a life of its own.

Literary history in America had its beginnings during colonial times — 1608-1775 — with such accounts of life, travels, and adventures as in the simple, direct narrative of John Smith's *True Relation of Virginia* (1608) and a more pretentious work, *A Map of Virginia with a Description of the Country* (1612). The latter is similar to many English pamphlets published in London during the 17th century and written to draw attention to America and other distant parts of the world. Some New England writers also wrote narratives similar to John Smith's *True Relation*.

Poetry also came to the fore. A forty-four line epitaph on Nathaniel Bacon, the insurrectionist leader in Virginia, is looked upon as the "one really American poem" of the 17th century. It is designated as one of a large number of elegies produced in the colonies at that time, especially by the New England clergy.

## The Revolutionary Period

The next notable stage in American poetry, the Revolutionary Period, (1775-1800), was marked by ballads and satirical verses. The best known of the purely humorous ballads of the time was Francis Hopkinson's "Battle of the Kegs." One of the best longer pieces of humorous verse in early American literature was Joel Barlow's mock heroic "Hasty Pudding." The most effective of the many political satires of the period was John Trumbill's "McFingal."

The first of the American poets was Philip Freneau, who had no equal in the Revolutionary Period in quality and range of subject and style. Though he is famous for his romantic lyrics primarily of the sea and nature, he first became known for his satirical verse. His poems such as "Eutaw Springs" and "The Wild Honeysuckle" reflect the spirit of the English romantic poets.

The most important of all the writings of this period were the eighty-five essays included in the collection known as *The Federalist*. They were written by Alexander Hamilton, James Madison, and John Jay and first published in the *Independent Journal of New York* in 1797 and 1798. More than anything else, they were influential in bringing about the adoption of the Constitution. They are still priceless contributions to American political history and literature.

*The Prince of Parthia*, a romantic tragedy by Thomas Godfrey, was the first American drama. It was first presented at the Southwark Theater in Philadelphia in 1767. *The Contrast* by Royall Tyler was the first American comedy to be presented by a professional company. It was produced in 1787 in New York. Tyler wrote more than fifty plays, most of which were successful. James N. Barker and John Howard Payne were other playwrights of this era.

## 19th Century Literature

The first two centuries of American writing paved the way for rapid development during the first two decades of the 19th century.

William Cullen Bryant, lawyer, successful journalist, and publicist, was the next American poet after Philip Freneau. His literary career spanned almost seventy years — from "Thanatopsis," written when he was eighteen years old, to his translation of Homer, the work of his declining years.

The work of Charles Brockden Brown marked the beginning of American fiction in the longer novel form. He predates Cooper in adventure and Poe in his use of mystery and horror. His first work was *Wieland* in 1798. His best was *Edgar Huntley*.

James Fenimore Cooper's reputation was made with *The Spy*, a romance of the Revolution written in 1821. His greatest work is *The Leatherstocking Tales*, a series of five novels about frontier life, published between 1823 and 1841, and centered around a great trapper and his Indian friends. The most gripping of the five is *The Last of the Mohicans*.

Ralph Waldo Emerson was the prophet of the idealism that ruled the literature of the three decades prior to the Civil War, a period that might be referred to as the Golden Era of American Literature. His essays, poems, and addresses emphasized the importance of the individual as a spirit. *The American Scholar*, his Phi Beta Kappa address, has been called the American "Literary" declaration of independence. Henry David Thoreau in *Walden*, which is rich in reflection, wrote of his efforts to withdraw to a simple life. Nathaniel Hawthorne and Herman Melville were the premier novelists of the era. Hawthorne's chief volumes were *The Scarlet Letter* in 1850 and *The House of Seven Gables* in 1851. Melville published *Typee* in 1846, after spending his youthful years as a seaman. It chronicles four months in the Marquesas. His *Moby Dick* was published in 1851. It is only in recent years that Melville has been truly appreciated.

Of all the poets to emerge in the mid-19th century, Edgar Allen Poe and Walt Whitman were by far the greatest. "The Raven," "Israfel," "Ulalume," and other of Poe's poems achieve their effects by a haunting musical quality and an eerie power of suggestion evoking an atmosphere in counterpoint to the intellectual content. Whitman, with "Leaves of Grass" in 1855, was the first of the free verse poets and, though he created a sensation, his long crashing lines disturbed many. His frankness of expression was even more disturbing. He aspired to be the poet of democratic America, and his genius is now fully recognized.

In contrast, Henry Wadsworth Longfellow and John Greenleaf Whittier were of the New England School of poetry. Longfellow's narratives and simple didactic poems made him a household poet. Because he was a teacher, a translator, and a diligent gatherer of material from the literature of the world, he exerted a profound influence on the culture of his time. Whittier, with scanty formal education, was more limited. His poetry like "Snowbound," which focuses on New England life, secured for him a permanent place in American literature. Oliver Wendell Holmes, with his polished verse of humor and sentiment and his written essays published as *The Autocrat of the Breakfast Table*, maintained his hold upon a wide following for many years.

Among the orators and statesmen of this period were Daniel Webster, Rufus Choat, Edward Everett, Charles Sumner, and Wendell Phillips. Their contemporaries from the south were Henry Clay, Robert Y. Hayne, and John C. Calhoun. To these must be added the name of Abraham Lincoln, for his Gettysburg Address, if nothing else.

The unqualified master of American humor of this time was Samuel L. Clemens, Mark Twain. He wrote numerous sketches and books. *Innocents Abroad* and *Life on the Mississippi* are examples. Novels like *Tom Sawyer* and *Huckleberry Finn* put him in the top rank of American novelists. He was probably one of the three or four greatest of the century.

## At the Turn of the Century

Novels rose to the fore at the turn of the century and continue to be popular favorites. The novel of free action in far times and places seems to have carved out a special place in American literature. Lew Wallace's *Ben Hur*, published in 1880, is still widely read. Jack London's stories were of this same genre but vastly superior in literary quality. Nordhoff and Hall's more recent *Mutiny on the Bounty*, has the same basic appeal. There were also many romantic novels, usually dealing with the Revolutionary or Civil War. Winston Churchill, Paul Leicester Ford, and Marey Johnston wrote in this vein as did Thomas Nelson Page, who is notable for his Southern perspective. The third great American novelist, Henry James (1843-1916), followed an opposite trend, exploring a subtle realism of the mind. His most important works include *The American, Portrait of a Lady*, and *The Golden Bowl*. Edith Wharton with *The Age of Innocence* followed his mode.

## The 20th Century

Theodore Dreiser with *Sister Carrie* in 1900 and *An American Tragedy* in 1925, opened the doors to the extreme realism of the later years. With *Main Street* in 1920 and *Babbitt* in 1922, Sinclair Lewis established his reputation for satires on the small town and business. His best novel is *Arrowsmith*. F. Scott Fitzgerald was the spokesman for the younger generation of the 1920s. Ernest Hemingway was a novelist of range and seriousness. Witness *A Farewell to Arms* and *For Whom the Bell Tolls* in 1940. Representing the historical novel form are such later works as Hervey Allen's *Anthony Adverse* and Margaret Mitchell's *Gone with the Wind*. Thomas Wolfe, *Look Homeward Angel*, and Nobel Prize winner, William Faulkner, *Sanctuary* and *The Sound and the Fury*, should not go unmentioned.

Among the dramatists of the 1920s and 1930s were the great Eugene O'Neill with among others *The Emperor Jones* and *The Hairy Ape*, Maxwell Anderson with notably *Winterset* and

*High Tor*, Elmer Rice with *Street Scene*, Robert Sherwood with *The Petrified Forest*, Marc Connelly with *Green Pastures*, Tennessee Williams with *A Streetcar Named Desire*, and Thornton Wilder with *Our Town* and *The Skin of Our Teeth*.

The short story gained popularity with the publishing of Washington Irving's narratives in *The Sketch Book*, and continued to gain popularity through the tales of Edgar Allen Poe and Nathaniel Hawthorne's character study problems. Poe established a pattern for the detective story, introducing the character of Monsieur Dupin, the first of a long line of literary sleuths. Notable among them are Arthur Conan Doyle's Sherlock Holmes, J. P. Marquand's Mr. Moto, and Earl Derr Biggers' Charlie Chan. Many novelists also wrote short stories, including Henry James and Ernest Hemingway. A few writers, notably Bret Harte and Joel Chandler Harris, built their reputations on short stories alone. Also popular early in this century were the stories of O. Henry (William Sydney Porter) with their clever surprise endings.

A revival of interest in poetry took place in 1912 with the publication of *Poetry: A Magazine of Verse* and many other small magazines. Carl Sandburg, Edgar Lee Masters, Vachel Lindsay, Amy Lowell, and Robert Frost all achieved prominence with their diverse styles. In the 1920s, Edna St. Vincent Millay excelled in the sonnet, and Stephen Vincent Benet's best work dealt with American themes. Prominent among contemporary poets are a large number of writers whose sincerity and technical skill destine them for a permanent niche in literature. These include Robert Hillyer, Archibald MacLeish, Wallace Stevens, e.e. cummings, Marianne Moore, and Theodore Roethke.

## COLLECTING LITERARY ITEMS

Collecting literary items has been a popular avocation for centuries. For the book lover, all the books in the public library cannot take the place of a shelf or two of one's own books, whether home is a one-room apartment or a stately mansion with dozens of rooms. Most book lovers — bibliophiles — select their books according to their own tastes. The astute bibliophile learns to cultivate that taste.

The oldest discoverable collections of writing contain well-developed narratives in the form of myths and legends. A myth, a tale of ancient origin, usually tells some imaginative account of the origin of gods, various human arts, or natural phenomena. The legend is similar to the myth, but is more directly concerned with the deeds of men. Over the centuries, many of these tales were combined by master storytellers into epics — stories of the lives and deeds of heroes. *The Iliad* and the *Odyssey* are examples. The word "epic" is from the Greek "epos," which means speech or song, because these stories were told or chanted for generations before they were actually written.

From the fragmented information which has been passed down to us about the bibliophiles of the Roman Empire, it appears evident that there were some modern features about book collecting of those days. Because of the abundance of educated slave labor, books were inexpensive, and book collectors could center their attention on refinements similar to those of present-day book collectors. By contrast, books were expensive in the Middle Ages, and until almost the beginning of the 14th century, there were few libraries for reading purposes. Royalty and the wealthy found pleasure in owning the best books, of literary and scholastic merit, in as many subjects as possible. These were usually finely written and illuminated manuscripts. The same ideals were carried out after the invention of printing, but they could now be done on a larger scale. Libraries were formed in the 16th century by Archbishop Cranmer, Lords Arundel and Lumley, and historian De Thou, which were essentially students' libraries. Classification of the books themselves and the catalogs was often done to reveal which books had been acquired in all the different fields of human knowledge.

The purpose of literature is two-fold — for learning and for inspiration — the "literature of knowledge" and the "literature of power." Literature of knowledge refers to reliable volumes containing the things one needs to know or wants to refer to on occasion — dictionaries, encyclopedias, histories, sciences, etc. Literature of power refers to the books that inspire ideals and feed the imagination — great biographies, classic stories, essays, and poetry.

This private, personal library not only reflects the interests and tastes of its owner but, as it grows and expands, it also will be an accurate index of its owners changing intellectual requirements and emotional needs.

## COLLECTING FIRST EDITIONS

Collectors of first editions should understand the terminology of this phase of book collecting.

An "edition" refers to the total number of books printed from one set of plates or from one setting of type.

An "impression" or "printing" is the number of copies printed at one time. If the demand for a book is not met by the number of copies produced by the first impression or printing, the publisher orders the printing of additional copies from the same plate or type. These additional copies are called a "second impression" or "second printing" even though they are actually part of the first edition.

Book collectors consider the term "first edition" applicable only to the "first impression" or "first printing." This usually can be determined from the title page and copyright page. The book is likely to be a first edition if the copyright date and the date on the title page are the same. Sometimes a book is copyrighted a year or more before publication so a difference in dates does not always preclude the possibility of a book being a first edition. The words "first edition" appear on the title page of some first editions.

Some publishers use special marking for first editions. In some books, the month and year of publication appear below the copyright notice with the date of subsequent prints added. If only one date is listed, the book can be immediately recognized as a first edition. Other publishers

use the date on the title page of the first edition but omit the date on subsequent printings. Still other publishers use an identifying letter beneath the copyright notice.

Later, if the plates or type become worn, new plates may be made or new type may be set, and the book reprinted. All books printed from the second set of plates or type are called the "second edition."

In these later editions, a phrase such as "Second printing," "New edition," "Second thousand," "Revised edition," "New edition with illustrations," "First printing, (date)," "Second printing, (date)," "Published," or "Reprinted (dates)" often appears on the title page or copyright page.

## PRESERVING LITERARY ITEMS

Deterioration problems of books are multiplied with each page. Single layer paper items can be separated from each other so that damage which may have occurred to one item will not be transferred to other like items. The multiple pages of books prohibit this. Books must be dealt with intact. Consequently, multiple-page deterioration occurs since, at the onset of damage, the offending pages cannot be removed and separated from those that still may be untouched by deterioration. Museums and libraries sometimes take a book apart and deacidify the pages separately, but that is not a practical alternative for the individual collector.

### General Guidelines on Environmental Standards for Books and Manuscripts

1. Insofar as it is practical without violating the basic reason for a library, books should be separated from people. With a home library, that may not be possible at all.

   Environmental conditions which are the most favorable for people are not the same as those which are conducive to the preservation of books and manuscripts.

2. Temperature: Temperatures that range from

68 to 74 degrees Fahrenheit are the most favorable for the preservation of paper items including books and manuscripts. A temperature of 72 degrees Fahrenheit is often cited because that is a comfortable temperature for people. When books can be stored in separate areas away from people, lower limits of temperature can be considered, but the temperature and humidity of any reading room must also be regulated. Condensation will occur if books stored below a certain temperature are brought into an unregulated people area for use. With a maximum temperature of 76 degrees Fahrenheit, and maximum relative humidity of 50% in a reading room, books could be stored at a temperature of as low as 57 degrees Fahrenheit without moisture damage from condensation.

It is known that temperature and humidity variations are damaging to paper. Such damaging effects are magnified many time when considering a whole book, which is composed of materials with differing responses to temperature and humidity.

3. Humidity: With temperature, an ideal can be stated based solely on practical considerations, but that is not the case with relative humidity. There is also a scientific disagreement as to what the optimum is. The reasons are two-fold:

   a. Two conflicting but valid factors enter into humidity control: On the one hand, increased moisture content increases the rate of deteriorative chemical reactions while reduced moisture content reduces the flexibility of paper thus increasing the likelihood of brittle paper breaking down from use. Because of the nature of a whole book as opposed to a single sheet of paper, there is no way to accurately balance these two factors. Natural adhesives are particularly subject to deterioration which in turn breaks down the book's structure.

   b. Add to this the fact that different book materials react differently to changes in moisture content. Cover boards which may be flat at one setting will not be so at another, because the tensions were balanced at the first setting.

   Fluctuations in humidity seem to be considerably more serious than fluctuations in temperature. Some of the effects of extreme humidity changes are visible to the naked eye while the effects of temperature variations may be seen only under a microscope.

4. Air Cleanliness: All impurities in the air are harmful to books and manuscripts. Sulfur dioxide is the most serious gaseous pollutant, but oxidants such as nitrogen oxides and ozone are also important.

   Though its effects tend to be more superficial than those of the gases mentioned above, dust settling on books is disfiguring. When this dust on books combines with the perspiration and skin oils of people handling them, the result is fingerprints, which are virtually impossible to remove. The necessary handling to dust books is also damaging. Some libraries and museums use filtering systems, but these are impractical for the home library.

5. Ventilation: Enough air, as clean and temperate as possible, should circulate to maintain a balanced climate with no stagnant areas. Books should be removed from the shelves from time to time so that air can circulate through the pages. Ripple the pages carefully a couple of times to separate them.

6. Light: Three factors determine the degree to which light causes damage to books and manuscripts.

   a. The spectral distribution of the light.
   b. The intensity of the light.
   c. The length of time that the books and manuscripts are exposed to the light.

The spectral distribution of light ranges from cosmic rays on the short end to radio waves on the long end. Somewhere in between range the ultraviolet, visible light (violet, blue, green, yellow, orange, red), and infrared, listed in order of increasing wave length. The shorter end of the spectrum is the concern of paper preservationists. Calculations are that radiation in the approximate middle of the ultraviolet range has a damage factor of 145 times that of green light which is in approximately the middle of the visible spectrum. The damage factor is very slight as the wavelength increases but still exists as long as oxygen can get to the book or manuscript.

Ultraviolet radiation is abundant in daylight and fluorescent tubes while incandescent lighting units contain negligible amounts. Lighting levels should be kept as low as is consistent with efficiency of whatever activities occur in the areas of book and manuscript storage.

Obviously, creating rigid library conditions in the home would be impractical, if not impossible, but the general guidelines can be instituted to some extent. For practical purposes in storing literary items in the home, moderations in temperature, humidity, atmospheric conditions, ventilation, and light should be observed. Some will be more difficult to maintain than others. The amount and location of space allotted to a library will greatly determine how well the guidelines can be carried out, but whatever effort is made is a step in the right direction.

## Rare Books

Obviously, if rare books are involved, these guidelines are imperative to the proper preservation of these items. Besides their aesthetic value, deterioration could be a deciding factor in their monetary worth.

Adjustable rare book storage boxes are available. They are made of acid-free, soil-resist-

ant boards, scored every ¼" for ease in folding. Each box comes in two sections which are criss-crossed, allowing flexibility in fitting the box to the book size. Special self-adhesive Velcro closures are included to attach to complete enclosure of the book. These boards are available in sizes ranging from 6" by 14" to 14" by 36".

## Storing Manuscripts and Loose Papers

Acid-free envelope storage binders are available for storing manuscripts and loose papers. The covers are made of sturdy sixty point board which protects the contents during handling, circulation, or storage. The spine of the binders is made of a high thread count cloth for long life and handling strength. They are available in several different sizes.

A variety of archival quality storage boxes is also available. Some are for upright storage while others are flat and stackable. For upright storage, it is suggested that manuscripts be inserted in acid-free storage binders or folders first to support the manuscripts or loose papers properly.

## Shelving

Proper shelving and book supports are prime considerations to avoid further damage to books and manuscripts. Shelving should be smooth and free of sharp edges and corners which could cause damage to books. Steel shelving with a smooth baked enamel finish is preferred. The shelving should be adjustable vertically to accommodate different size books. The bottom shelf should be at least four inches from the floor to allow for air circulation and prevent possible water damage. Standard metal filing cabinets with baked enamel finish for flat files are also acceptable.

Wooden shelving should be coated with three coats of a polyurethane varnish that does *not* contain formaldehyde, and allowed to dry for several weeks. As an alternative, wooden shelving can be lined with 5 mm polyester film held in place by double-coated 3M #415 tape.

The film and tape are available from suppliers of archival quality storage materials.

It is extremely important that books be held firmly upright on the shelves to ensure their health, but not so tightly that it is difficult to remove them. Book supports should be thick enough so they are visible and the contents of the books are not damaged by inadvertently forcing them over the bookend. The most common type of bookend with a tongue that slides under the bottom of adjacent books, is not really ideal.

## LITERARY ITEMS AS COLLECTIBLE

Literature is the collectible of substance. Literature is the center of knowledge. Man can exist without literature, but with literature, man lives.

Collecting literature should mean more than just having a shelf of fine books and manuscripts on display. Literature admits the world to anyone who takes the trouble to open the door.

Literature also should be collected — and preserved — for future generations who may not ever see books except in museums. It is the literature of man that preserves the history of past generations. Without literature, there would be no link to the past. For man to know where he is going, he must first know where he has been.

# 13
# Puzzles, Games, and Children's Items

The natural exuberance and energy of children puts wear and tear on anything that comes in contact with them. Whatever they have in the way of playthings gets picked up, put down, tossed in the air, kicked, patted, squeezed, batted, slapped, caressed, chewed, kissed, stepped on, and whatever else pops into young minds — not once, but innumerable times.

Paper items are among the heavy casualties of this "child's play." Unlike a doll or a wagon, paper items usually can't be put back together again. The one saving grace for some early children's items was that often children didn't have many toys, and learned early on that if a toy was damaged beyond repair, there just might not be another one to replace it. Consequently, some early children's toys did survive, including some early paper ones, though few are found in mint condition.

Many early toys were handmade or fashioned out of available materials since, in most households, the budget couldn't be stretched to spend on unnecessary items. Children would search through trade and dress catalogs for figures to use as paper dolls or furniture for a cardboard playhouse. Sometimes the catalog was utilized as a scrapbook for pressed flowers, clippings, trade cards, visiting cards, lace and ribbons, and locks of hair. Girls learned to sew at an early age, and made clothes from fabric scraps to dress their paper dolls. Children were also

encouraged to make other things of paper — Christmas ornaments, rewards, certificates, autograph albums, storybooks, and games. Evidently, these children treasured their paper toys because many fine examples can be seen in museums and an occasional antique show.

All children's items are and were meant to be handled, and paper items of any kind reflect the ravages of handling more than items of other materials. Books, jigsaw puzzles, games, and paper dolls are the major types of children's paper items, with countless variations of each. Space limitations preclude mentioning all the types of children's paper items, but we will touch on the major ones. It is duly noted that adult versions of games and puzzles also exist.

## CHILDREN'S BOOKS

Children's picture books with woodcut illustrations date from the 1600s. The illustrations while being imaginative also could be terrifying — to a child. Morality played a big part in many of the stories. Early prints depicted children being punished for disobedience with the rod prominently displayed. At the turn of the 1800s, chapbooks — paper pamphlets — featuring morality tales of occupations like "dairyman," adventures, the sea, stories of young people, picture alphabets, and sermons often contained crude pictures called "elegant cuts." A typical mid-19th century children's publication might contain histories, arithmetic and grammar exercises, nature studies, rhymes, prose, limericks, or puzzles.

### McLoughlin Brothers

McLoughlin Brothers of New York was one of the most prolific producers of children's paper items — story and alphabet books and other paper toys (Fig. 48). John McLoughlin immigrated to this country from Scotland in 1819 and went to work for a manufacturer of printing presses. He developed an interest in that work and studied printing in his spare time. In 1827, he purchased a hand press and the necessary accessories and became a printer. He had also developed an interest in children's books, and in 1828 brought out a children's book of semi-religious stories. After this single venture into publishing, he merged with a competitor named Elton, and together they developed a business which in time achieved a moderate success. Around 1850, both men retired and John McLoughlin, Jr. took the reins. Joining the company as a teenager, he learned the trade and by the age of twenty-one he became a partner. The company name was amended to John McLoughlin successor to Elton & Company. McLoughlin, Jr. was very progressive and had a sharp eye for new improvements in lithographic printing methods.

In 1850, the John McLoughlin New York City business, which had been located on Division Street off Chatham Square, burned to the ground. He moved to a larger location at 24 Beekman Street. That same year his brother Edmund joined the firm, and in 1850 the company became *McLoughlin Brothers*. In 1864, business had increased so much that a move to larger quarters at 30 Beekman Street was necessary. Business was slowed down by the Civil War, but expansion plans and the development of a newly designed line went on. In 1870, they moved to what was said to be the largest color printing plant in the country, in Brooklyn, New York.

*Figure 48. Book,* Children from the Bible, *published by McLoughlin Bros., Inc., 1930. (Author's collection.)*

A McLoughlin series published during the 1870s was the Uncle Frank series of story books. Other series were the Little Folks and Familiar Stories. Among the Familiar Stories were *Tom Thumb* and *Cock Robin*. Die-cut books, in the shape of animals, dolls, or children, first appeared at the end of the century. The enclosed pages were cut to conform to the cover.

Color picture books and paper dolls from England and Germany were McLoughlin's major competition at that time. Tuck, Routledge, Warne, and Nister were all exporting beautiful paper products. These issues were not protected by the United States copyright laws so McLoughlin Brothers copied them and published them at lower prices. Reliance on English and German illustrators had all but disappeared by the 1890s while American artists like Thomas Nast, Justin Howard, and Henry Herrick came to the fore, and McLoughlin Brothers wasted no time acquiring their services when possible. Nast, a political cartoonist, created the American image of Santa Claus (Fig. 49) which can be found in the

*Figure 49. Reproduction of illustration by Thomas Nast, "Merry Old Santa."*

duced by Dean & Son of London and Ernest Nister of England and Nuremberg, Germany. Introduced in Dean's books were hand-colored woodcuts of hinged figures and movable objects. Old Mother Hubbard sweeping her floor is an example. Fold-out books incorporated figures and scenes that popped up when opened. In 1883, Palmer Cox created the Brownies which first appeared in *St. Nicholas* magazine in a story titled "The Brownies Ride." Eventually, their escapades appeared in the pages of *Harper's, Young People, The Youth's Companion, Wide Awake, Ladies' Home Journal,* and sixteen books. They lent their images to other paper toys — games like Blindman's Bluff, and paper dolls with interchangeable heads. A similar 20th century version (circa 1940) were William Donahey's "Teenie Weenies," miniature, childlike creatures who lived in a shoe.

Many famous women illustrators created children's storybook or magazine characters. Prominent in the field were Kate Greenaway, Rose O'Neill, and Grace Drayton. Kate Greenaway's quaint drawings of stylishly dressed country children (Fig. 50) have remained popular for nearly a hundred years. The cherubic Kewpie Dolls were Rose O'Neill's creation. Grace Drayton created the original Campbell Kids and the Dolly Dingle paper dolls (color section).

McLoughlin edition of Clement Moore's *Visit From St. Nicholas*. Justin Howard is believed to be the originator of the Uncle Sam figures.

### Other Popular Children's Books

Other popular children's books were mechanical books — "flip" books with divided pages which, when flipped, changed the head or body of an animal; and hole books that might picture the path of a bullet or other object through a series of holes in each page. These date from the 1890s to the early 1900s.

The first notebook of any kind in the United States was Dunigan's multiplication tables for children that had cutouts over answers on each page. After the 1840s, movable books were pro-

### Milton Bradley

Edmund McLoughlin retired in 1885, and twenty years later John McLouglin died. At that time, John McLoughlin's two sons, James and Charles, had control of the company, and it remained a family enterprise until 1920 when Charles died. It was then that the company was sold to a Springfield, Massachusetts competitor, Milton Bradley.

Born in Vienna, Maine in 1836, Milton Bradley entered the Lawrence Scientific School (later to become a part of Harvard University) and attended for three years before the family moved to Hartford, Connecticut. He later moved to Springfield, Massachusetts where he worked as a draughtsman for several firms. Subsequently,

*Figure 50. Reproduction of illustration by Kate Greenaway, "The Tennis Player."*

credited with the creation of the jigsaw puzzle though forerunners made of baked clay can be traced to ancient Egypt. In 1762, Spilsbury was looking for a way to market his elegantly engraved maps. He conceived the idea of gluing the maps to thin cedar and mahogany panels which were then cut in sections. They were to be reassembled by children as a learning tool.

Spilsbury's creation proved successful, spawning many imitations and inspiring a host of puzzle fans. For years, maps were the only puzzle subjects, but eventually other subjects were introduced — colored lithographs of people, nature, and machines.

The technology of the jigsaw puzzle has advanced considerably since Spilsbury's first effort, but the basic process has remained the same for many years. Making a puzzle is still a lot more time consuming than working one. A whole year is required to complete the design, printing, cutting, and packaging stages.

Jigsaw puzzle aficionados now span all age groups, and the puzzles range from the simplest one of just a few pieces for the youngest to 3,000-piece intricacies that can intimidate all but the most dedicated jigsaw puzzle fans.

Though there seem to be endless varieties of

he took a lithography course in Providence, Rhode Island. He began doing lithographic work in 1860, and that same year published his first game, *The Checkered Game of Life* (Fig. 51), which remained a popular seller until after the turn of the century. At about the same time Bradley opened a factory in Springfield in 1870, his father, Louis Bradley, joined the firm. In 1882, the factory was moved to another Springfield location as it continued to expand. The company employed over 500 people at the turn of the century and were producing over 400 games and puzzles as well as other playthings.

## JIGSAW PUZZLES

A London printer named John Spilsbury is

*Figure 51. The first Milton Bradley game, The Checkered Game of Life. (Photograph courtesy Milton Bradley Company.)*

jigsaw puzzles — square, rectangle, round, vertical, three-dimensional, solid-color, multiples all mixed up in the same box, etc. — the varieties that have remained popular for generations are scenic, animal subjects, and nostalgic themes.

The hardest puzzle currently on the market is reputed to be one with the same picture on both sides, with one rotated 90 degrees from the other, and with the pieces cut so that it is not possible to determine which ones are for the top.

Milton Bradley got into the puzzle market a bit later than McLoughlin, but they weren't long in becoming serious competition. Their 1896-97 catalog boasted of "the cheapest and best dissected map of the United States ever published." Also part of their offerings were pictures dissected in squares so they could be constantly shifted into innumerable exciting combinations. The animated forest, the farmyard, and the wild west show were examples. Another outstanding puzzle was the smashed-up locomotive (Fig. 52). It pictured a colorful early locomotive and tender in 58 sections, none of which were constructed with the interlocking feature of McLoughlin puzzles. The parts of the locomotive were marked on the pieces: headlight, smoke box, boiler, etc. The tender was also marked similarly. The puzzle came packed in a wooden box with a hinged lid on which there was a paper label picturing the smashed-up locomotive. Most puzzles came with a pattern sheet, but it was thought that since it was already known that the finished product would be a locomotive, a pattern sheet might diminish interest in the puzzle. Another Milton Bradley puzzle of that same period featured six horse-drawn fire wagons all in a row. The complete puzzle measured 84″ by 84″! A similar puzzle pictured a complete train of locomotive, tender, and five cars and measured 96″ long! From 1909 to 1914, Milton Bradley catalogs offered a wide selection of boxed puzzles including nursery tales, historic places or personalities, United States maps, farm scenes, circus, Santa Claus, and on and on.

An innovative variation of these puzzles were sliced objects and animals, with four to six

*Figure 52. One of Milton Bradley's early and popular puzzles, The Smashed-Up Locomotive. (Photograph courtesy Milton Bradley Company.)*

slices to a complete picture. They included word labels that taught spelling.

Competitive with Milton Bradley were Parker Brothers catalogs from 1916 to 1919. Items were similar in size, subject matter, and price. In addition, a 1917 and 1918 catalog insert listed a selection of adult puzzles — about 200 — beautifully colored and reproduced from well-known paintings of the past. Called "Famous Pastime Puzzles," they ranged from 100-piece puzzles for a dollar to 1200-piece puzzles for twelve dollars. This line was still listed in Parker's 1940-41 catalog, but backed with wood and priced at eighteen dollars for the largest puzzles.

## GAMES

Games have been around since the beginnings of humankind. Besides finding ways to communicate, ways to other lands, ways to ply a trade, and ways to decorate his surroundings, man also found ways to entertain himself and others. Man seems always to have sought competition, either with himself, other humans or animals, or with nature: running races, stalking game, fighting other men or animals, pitting animals against each other, climbing mountains and swimming rivers. Once paper became a viable commodity, the creation of games made of paper or cardboard or in part paper or cardboard was a natural progression.

Parlor games were a popular pastime of the 1880s, and attracted adults as well as children. Most were educational in nature — instructing in letters, matching pictures, and of historical, geographical, or patriotic subjects. These games are, of course, more valuable in original condition with all pieces intact, but mint sets aren't so easy to come by. Game boxes, with their colorful lithographed labels, have become collectors' items in themselves.

Panoramas and dioramas were popular in the 1870s. A panorama was a mechanical toy that consisted of a long strip of lithographed pictures wound around a wooden dowel with a roller at each end. It was turned by a crank which was set into a box with an opening. A moving picture was produced when the crank was turned. Panoramas had been enjoyed by European children for several years before Mc-Loughlin Brothers and Milton Bradley introduced them in America. The diorama resembled the panorama with the exception that the box was more like a three-dimensional theater displaying cutout figures or objects that were moved by means of pulling a string or wire fastened to the side.

## PAPER DOLLS

The ancestry of the paper doll reaches back centuries before they were introduced as children's playthings. In China at the time of Confucius, 475 B.C., the custom was to burn a paper image or representation of the deceased person at the funeral service as a means of purifying the body before the spirit left it. In Japan, since the year 900 A.D., small cutout figures called "Katashiro" have been used in cleansing ceremonies. The "Katashiro," symbolizing the human form, is purchased from a priest at a believer's shrine.

The believer takes it home, paints on it the characters of the believer's name, the believer's birth date and sex. The believer then breathes on the figure and rubs it all over his body to transfer any diseases or impurities to the "Katashiro." The "Katashiro" is then returned to the shrine and the priest disposes of it in a a mass religious ceremony.

### The Pantin

Another form of paper dolls was the 18th century "pantin," named for a city near Paris. Pantins were usually printed on sheets in six parts — the head, torso, arms, and legs. The sheets were mounted on cardboard, and the various parts were appropriately painted and cut out. It was really an adult diversion with the limbs of the doll attached loosely to the body so that when pulled by a thread, the doll appeared to be dancing. Later on metal fasteners were used. Favorite subjects were clowns, jesters, and harlequins.

Pantins became such a craze in France, the fad eventually wore itself out. The pantin is related to the jumping jack, which was a toy in ancient Egypt, rediscovered in 18th century France. It found its way to Germany where it was called the "hamplemann." Eventually, it appeared in England where it was given its present name jumping jack. In its various incarnations, it was made of materials other than painted cardboard.

### The First Paper Dolls

England is credited with the invention of the paper doll as we know it today. In 1790, an eight inch, one-sided paper doll with a wardrobe of six changeable pieces of paper clothing appeared on the market. It proved to be a popular idea which quickly spread to France and Germany. The French publishing Pellerin family, which had produced many of the earlier pantins, issued several sheets of paper dolls. Included on the sheets were changes of clothing in the latest styles, stylish wigs, beautiful headdresses, and other accessories suitable to a lady of that time. An extremely rare and very fine early set depicts Napoleon and outfits worn during the highlights of his career, between 1769 and 1821. Other English paper dolls soon followed that first set. Early publishers were S & J Fuller and Raphael Tuck & Sons Ltd.

In the early 1800s, England and France produced storybook dolls, but it was the mid-19th century before they were printed in America.

### American Paper Dolls

The first known commercially published American paper doll was issued by J. Belcher of Boston in 1812. It resembled and bore the same title of an S & J Fuller issue called *The History and Adventures of Little Henry*, which was issued in a small book containing a moral story with hand-colored illustrations. Each illustration depicted a young boy in appropriate costume but with no head. There was a horizontal slit at the neckline to accept the neck tab of a single boy doll's head which was supposed to be moved from illustration to illustration to follow the story.

Dolls were boxed and sold to adults as well as children beginning in the 1850s, and *Godey's Ladies' Book* published a sheet of cutout paper dolls in 1859, the first to appear in an American magazine. Most of these original boxes, with lithographed designs, were either discarded or ruined and are difficult to find. Paper doll collectors consider the *Godey's* issue a real find.

Late in the 1850s, a line of full-body paper dolls and dresses in paper envelopes was issued by Brown, Taggart & Chase of Boston, Massachusetts. Other notable but limited producers of paper dolls of that time were Clarke, Austin & Smith of New York City, Degen, Estes & Company of Philadelphia and Frederick A. Stokes Company of New York City. McLoughlin Brothers were by far the leader in this field, probably with a greater paper doll production than all its American competitors combined. Most of their sets were printed on uncut sheets which were folded and inserted into an envelope decorated on the face and listing other offerings on the back. Also printed were paper furniture sheets or cards depicting parlor sets, drawing rooms, and bedroom sets.

Early in the 1900s, Dennison Manufacturing Company issued boxed sets with paper figures, tissue, crepe paper, lace and other trims, and instructions for making clothing. The jointed dolls, made by Littauer & Bauer of Germany, were embossed in the form of babies, young children, girls, and women. Parker Brothers issued a similar set in 1917.

Some paper dolls in the early 1900s were published on the front of postcards. But few have survived since they were sent to children and meant to be cut out. After the turn of the 20th century, sheet paper dolls were printed in nearly all women's magazines among them *Good Housekeeping*, *McCall's*, and *Woman's Home Companion*.

Toy paper soldiers were made to appeal to boys, but few have survived since boys will be boys. They date from the 1870s through the 1890s. Some could be mounted on wooden forms. Others could be cut out and fastened to wooden stands.

### Celebrity Paper Dolls

A series of movie actress and actor paper dolls, which pictured famous movie personalities of the time with the costumes worn in their starring roles, was issued by Hollywood Dollies, Inc. of New York City in the 1920s. Included were Colleen Moore, Rudolph Valentino, and Tom Mix.

A great variety of movie star paper doll books were offered in the late 1930s and early 1940s. These glamorous stars came with an assortment of the beautiful gowns and other clothing worn in their motion picture roles. Among the popular ones were Sonja Henie, Clark Gable, Rita Hayworth, Alice Faye, and Shirley Temple. The color section of this book pictures a recent reproduction of a Shirley Temple paper doll book which featured three different sized dolls of the little star. One doll comes with a back as well as a front view which can be glued together to form a double-sided doll. The clothing can be folded over to cover both sides of the doll.

From 1940-43, paper dolls took on the military look of World War II — Harry the Soldier, Dick the Sailor, Wacs and Waves, Bride and Groom Military Wedding Party. By 1944, fewer paper doll books were published as the shortage of paper and manpower became more apparent.

Television stars came to the fore in the 1950s with, among others, Fess Parker, Pat Boone, and Elizabeth Montgomery. Also in 1950, Milton Bradley introduced "Magic Mary," a novelty paper doll utilizing concealed magic to hold the dresses in place and eliminating tabs. Late the same year, three other sets in this series were offered.

Hundreds of paper dolls have appeared over the years in magazines and newspapers and in inexpensive books. No one could begin to list the thousands that have appeared since that first English paper doll in 1790.

## COLLECTING CHILDREN'S PAPER ITEMS

Often children's items, in any form, are collected as an adjunct to other collectibles. Some glass and china collectors also collect children's toy dishes. Some antique furniture collectors also collect children's antique furniture. Our ancestors patterned many children's items after the adult counterpart. Most of the items in this chapter also have adult versions. Some collectors want whatever fits into their collecting category, and that includes paper items. Doll collecting can also include paper dolls. Railroad buffs might want that "Smashed Up Locomotive" puzzle. Whatever the reason for collecting, paper children's items add a decided extra dimension to a collection.

Collecting children's items for their own intrinsic value is a pleasant pursuit, too. Some collectors want only little girls' items while others want only little boys' items. A nice aspect of collecting paper items is that most of them are not bound by gender. Anyone can play. A puzzle is a puzzle. A game is a game. A book is a book.

Since children's items were meant to be used, meaning "handled," finding anything, especially paper items, intact and in mint condition borders on the exceptional. Items, intact and in their original box or other container, are coveted. Some children's paper items were meant to be used and discarded when they ran their course, if they hadn't fallen apart first.

The usual sources for other paper items may be the best bets for children's items, too. Paper memorabilia dealers, antique dealers for very early items. Flea markets, garage sales, and estate sales may yield some finds.

## PRESERVING CHILDREN'S PAPER ITEMS

The preservation of those children's paper items still to be found may be more a case of attempting to prevent further deterioration than preserving something that is complete and undamaged, so that deterioration will be held to a minimum.

Storing these paper items properly may go a long way toward retarding further deterioration though it probably won't stop it altogether, particularly if some damage is already evident. Many children's paper items were not made from the best paper, and those that were may not appear so after being subjected to "child's play." Proper storage will keep paper items from creasing, wrinkling, buckling, and warping, which contribute to the deterioration by breaking down the paper fibers. Storing in an acid-free and dust-free environment will help shield the items from atmospheric conditions that can cause deterioration. In short, it can't eliminate the damage that has already been done, but it can eliminate some of the elements that would cause further damage.

Like some other paper collectibles, children's items span the spectrum of paper forms. Each item should be judged on its own merits in devising the proper preservation methods. Mylar sleeves and bags are available in a variety of sizes as are acid-free containers and boxes.

Whatever seems fitting for an item is the method of choice.

Items constructed of or incorporating acid containing papers can be treated to remove the acid residues and ensure against further deterioration that way. It is an expensive procedure, but may be the only answer for extremely valuable and/or rare items. It is best to consult experts and not attempt this yourself.

Since many children's books are about the size of regular and digest-size magazines, archival Mylar envelopes and acid-free boxes for magazines should work well. These should also be stored upright and packed with breathing room but not leaning. Archival acid-free boards can be interspersed between the books, if necessary, to keep them from bending and warping.

## CHILDREN'S ITEMS AS COLLECTIBLE

Though many types of paper collectibles have an air of nostalgia about them, children's paper items possess an aura all their own. Childhood is the time of innocence that once lost, can never be regained. Children's paper items are the documentation of this innocence.

Childhood years are the formative years of one's life. The adult within a child is molded and shaped by the actions and events of those formative years. The actions and events evolve from the child's environment. Part of that environment is the child's possessions which hold a special place in his world. Paper items are a part of those possessions. These paper items are not necessarily written documentation, but more than likely illustrated documentation. They offer pictures, in the form of toys, of long past childhoods. We may not be able to go home again, but we can bring a bit of home to us — a part of the innocence of childhood.

## PLAYING CARDS

Though no clear dates have been established for the invention of playing cards, earliest records indicate they were first used by the Chinese, who also were first with paper, in the early half of the 12th century. Hindus stake their claim to being playing card originators, and it is know that they, as well as the Persians and Chinese, had playing tablets or counters arranged in "suits" with painted devices depicting royalty and rulers and various emblems.

Cards seemed to have followed a similar route as that of paper in finding their way from the East to the West. The thought is that a fleeing Hindu tribe carried the cards into Egypt from where they found their way to Italy and Spain in cargos of spices and silks. From there playing cards were brought to France by raiding soldiers and thereafter to England and America.

These very early decks of cards were painted by hand and incorporated a variety of materials — thin sheets of wood, ivory, metal, and dried leaves. Also known to exist are cards of canvas, leather, embroidered silks, small tiles, and tortoise shells. The first American settlers introduced cards of leaves, bark, sheepskin, and deerskin which were hand cut and painted. One of the leading card-paper manufacturers of the 18th century was Benjamin Franklin. Franklin used some of his own cards as insulation in the electrical friction machine he built in 1731.

One of the earliest mentions of playing cards is in the treasury records of Charles VI of France. He authorized payment of fifty-six sols to the painter Gringonneur, for the illumination of three decks for the amusement of the king. The date was 1392, which predates the invention of printing.

### Card Designs

Each country adapted the suit signs on cards to their own designs. Spaniards and Italians preferred Swords, Cups or Chalices, Coins, and Batons. Italian cards appear to have been in the form we know as a tarot deck which contained seventy-eight cards: twenty-two trump cards with symbolic designs and fifty-six number cards including four court cards — king, queen, mounted knight, and page. France opted

*Figure 53.  French playing card circa 1540. (Photograph courtesy The United States Playing Card Company.)*

*Figures 54 and 55.  German playing cards circa 1460. Hand-colored block prints, they are the four, five, and nine of "leaves." German suit signs were leaves, acorns, hearts, and falcon bells. (Photographs courtesy The United States Playing Card Company.)*

for the familiar spades, hearts, clubs, and diamonds (Fig. 53). Germany and Austria used a variety of bells, hearts, leaves, and acorns (Figs. 54 & 55). England borrowed the French suit signs and America's were patterned after the English. American card manufacturers did try to introduce Americanized versions of the suit signs, but they met with scant acceptance by the general public.

The handmade nature of these cards meant that only the most affluent could afford this luxury. The Germans began to produce cards for the masses in the 1400s after the invention of printing. They were the first to alter the designs of the cards from their Italian counterparts.

About that same time, the French designed their own deck. They discarded the twenty-two trump cards of the tarot deck and combined the knight and page into a single card — the jack — making fifty-two cards. They also designed the suits as used today — spades, hearts, diamonds, and clubs — and simplified the suit symbols using flat, simple designs in two colors, red and black.

## Court Card Designs

One must keep in mind that these card designs reflect their times — the Middle Ages — replete with knights in shining armor. The court (face) cards were representative of the heroes of the time. The use of court cards — kings, queens, and knights — reflected recognized society as it was then. The structure of medieval society is reflected in the four suits: spades (swords), the military; hearts (cups or chalices) represent the church; diamonds (coins) the merchant class; and clubs (batons), agriculture, which was the basis of medieval life.

The French also printed names on their court cords to identify them. The king of spades is David. On French cards he holds a harp referring to the Psalms he wrote. On English cards he carries a large sword belonging to Goliath whom he slew. The king of hearts is Charlemagne and he swings a sword over his head. The king of diamonds is Julius Caesar who carries a battle axe. He is shown in profile because his appear-

ance was known only from coins struck in his lifetime. The king of clubs is Alexander the Great. He holds an orb, the symbol of the world that he conquered. The four kings represent the four civilizations which made up the Western culture: the Hebrews, the Holy Roman Empire, the Romans, and the Greeks.

The queen of spades is Pallas Athena, Greek goddess of wisdom and war. She is the only armed queen. The queen of hearts is Judith of Bavaria, daughter-in-law of Charlemagne, married to his eldest son, Pippen. The queen of diamonds is Rachel, wife of Jacob and mother of the twelve sons who founded the Twelve Tribes of Israel. The queen of clubs is Argine, considered to be an anagram for the word "regina" or "queen."

The jack of spades is Hogier, a Dane and knight of Charlemagne. In early single-ended cards, he had a dog at his heels for he was the patron of the chase (Fig. 56). He carried a halberd or large sword on French cards, a marriott or beribboned pike on English cards. He is shown in profile. The jack of hearts is "La Hire" whose name was Stephan de Vignoles, a knight in the court of Charles VII. He carries a battle axe surrounded by "faces," a symbol of authority. The identity of the jack of diamonds is less definite. Some early decks identified him as Roland, while later ones identified him as Hector. He carries a "Welsh hook" or weapon. The jack of clubs is Lancelot, chief knight of King Arthur's Round Table.

Each area of France had its own design variations to help the government levy taxes on the cards, although the general design and identity of the court cards were the same.

The designs of cards were limited by early printing techniques. They have changed very little through the ages, refined only by technical improvements. Card players, being a superstitious lot, are reluctant to change anything that could change their luck!

## Double-Ended Cards

Double-ended cards did not become acceptable until the middle of the 19th century,

*Figure 56. French playing card circa 1540 depicting Hogier, patron of the chase. (Photograph courtesy The United States Playing Card Company.)*

although there were earlier isolated examples. During that same time, various ways of indexing the cards were tried: miniature cards in the corners, numbers and suit signs running around the borders for example. Eventually, the index system found on today's cards was accepted.

## Decorative Card Backs

Decorations on the backs of cards are a rather recent innovation. The backs of most of the early cards were quite plain and without designs or coloring. Colored backs and some simple one-colored designs began to appear on French and German cards in the early 1800s. From the beginning, the backs of Italian cards were decorated with wood-block designs of figures and

flowers and occasionally a coat of arms. Russian card backs exhibited work of great precision in rich colors. English card backs of the early 1800s were stained yellow instead of the conventional white.

A patterned back in red and white was introduced by Reynolds and Sons in 1845, and several years later a design in white and gold centered by a harp was issued. De la Rue and Company, in London, was responsible for the first really artistic development of playing card backs. Depictions of historical events and places of interest began to appear on the backs of playing cards.

## Presentation Packs of Cards

In 1882, the Worshipful Company of Makers of Playing Cards in London began to issue presentation packs of specially designed and printed cards for a limited edition of 150 for private distribution, made up in leather cases of two packs each. The designs for the card backs were selected from a public competition. The Arms of the Motto of the Company were worked into the design which depicted the outstanding event of each specific year in England. Kendall issued cards commemorating Queen Victoria's Diamond Jubilee in 1897, which depicted on the back an excellent portrait of the Queen. Each succeeding crowned head has been pictured on the backs of cards which included their Crowns, Crest, Royal Regiments, and other royal symbols. Royalty from other countries — France, Denmark, Sweden, and Spain for example — have been pictured on the backs of cards as well.

## American Playing Card Backs

The first American card backs were also plain, but early in the 19th century, 1810-19, cards appeared in Philadelphia depicting likenesses of George Washington and John Adams in medallion style on a printed background. Cards with patriotic and partisan backs were issued during the Civil War. These displayed Confederate flags, the Stars and Stripes, Union generals, and the "Monitor and Merrimac."

### Squeezers

The year 1854 marked the introduction of "Squeezers," cards showing an index — number or value of card — in the corners. This bright innovation made it possible to squeeze the cards together in the hand and still read them. Earlier cards without these corner indices had to be spread out to be identified correctly.

Advertising cards, also in the form of squeezers, were first issued in 1871. In the 1880s, many special interest designs began to make their appearance — colorful portraits and pictorials depicting people and places of the time. From 1885 to 1895, many of these cards, in series, were enclosed in packages of cigarettes and are highly coveted by collectors.

### American Souvenir Packs

Souvenir packs were first seen in 1893. These depicted a different photographic scene or subject — topical or historical — on each. One of the first decks of this type commemorated the World's Columbian Exposition of 1893 in Chicago. These advertising cards gained momentum and today cover many and varied fields of interest.

Transportation cards are some of the most prized. These advertise modes of travel — steamships, railroads, and airlines. Educational institutions, state cards which show maps, seals, historical places and buildings, and state flowers, hotels, inns, nightclubs, and restaurants are all represented on the backs of cards. All forms of consumer goods and merchandise, business and politics are also represented.

Modern playing cards date from about 1925 and include paintings of the Old Masters and contemporary artists, and museum treasures picturing beautiful and rare objects of art.

### Children's Playing Cards

An interesting sideline to playing card collecting is children's playing cards. The only real resemblance to regular playing cards is the shape and that they come in packs. Most of them are based on the simple premise of matching

*Figure 57. Cards from game of Authors. (Author's collection.)*

identical pictures or subjects. Authors is a good example (Fig. 57). Authors and Old Maid are two long-time children's favorites. Old Maid has the added dimension of not getting caught with the Old Maid card at the end of the game. The fun was in passing it on to the unsuspecting. Other card games are Capital Cities, Peter Coddle, Husking, and Fortune Telling.

## COLLECTING PLAYING CARDS

Collecting playing cards may seem like a frivolous avocation to some, perhaps looked upon as the pursuit of an inveterate card player. But consideration should be given to the fact that playing cards are also a a form of the print. Historical societies in this country and print collections throughout Europe include old playing cards as examples of early printing and engraving as opposed to their functional role as tools of games.

Acknowledging and emphasizing the importance of collecting playing cards is the fact that large and valuable collections can be found in many museums worldwide — the British Museum, The Librarie Nationale, museums in Munich, Dresden, Vienna, and Nuremberg, and the Smithsonian in Washington, DC. The Royal

Asiatic Society has in its collection a deck of cards purported to be a thousand years old! The most comprehensive playing card collection is the Playing Card Museum maintained by the United States Playing Card Company in Cincinnati.

Originally, collectors wanted only complete and full decks of cards. Today, collecting single card backs has grown into a widespread hobby. Decorated card backs are a rather recent innovation, and represent another facet of print collecting. The subject matter of pictorial backs is almost endless with hundreds of divisions and many thousands of designs. It's a matter of preference whether a collector saves all designs or restricts the collection to certain subjects. Subjects include scenery, ships, birds, florals, people of all countries, horses, and dogs. One deck can supply fifty back collectors. A variation of back collecting is to save only jokers, and an extensive collection can contain a thousand different jokers. Valuable decks should not be broken up this way. A deck can be considered complete without a joker, but if a joker was included, the value of the deck and its desirability as a collectible is diminished.

Playing card dealers are probably the best bets for full decks. The usual method for building a collection of card backs is by swapping and trading with other collectors. There also are playing card collectors' organizations that can aid collectors in learning more about their hobby and in finding suitable specimens.

## PRESERVING PLAYING CARDS

Obviously, playing cards were meant to be handled. Modern ones have been made with a variety of finishes to ensure ease in shuffling, dealing, and the handling involved in playing a game of cards, as well as to deter wear and tear. Eventually, cards did and do show wear and tear — creases, dogeared or turned corners, faded spots, water marks, lack of resiliency — that makes manipulating them all but impossible. Serious card players know when it is time for a new deck. Consequently, finding an old deck in mint condition may never happen. Finding a complete deck intact in its original container may be just as difficult. The French cards pictured in Figures 53 and 56 were discovered, in near pristine condition, inside the binding of a book when it was re-bound several hundred years after being written. The book was purchased in 1841 by William Chatto who had it re-bound shortly after that, and discovered the cards at that time. Paper was too precious to be casually discarded and waste was recycled so the cards became padding for a book cover.

Children's playing cards will probably show even more wear and tear. Children are inclined to use their playthings in other ways than originally intended, and playing cards are one of the easiest playthings to manipulate. Toss them into a hat. See how far they can be flipped across the room. Sail them through the air like a Frisbee. Complete decks of old children's playing cards in mint condition may be all but nonexistent.

Preserving playing cards can be done much like other cards. (See Chapter 7.) Acid-free albums with sheets of Mylar pockets can be adapted to display individual card backs. The Mylar pockets come in a variety of sizes. Acid-free photograph albums with Mylar pockets will work as well. Acid-free boxes and containers in a variety of sizes are adaptable for storage of complete decks.

## PLAYING CARDS AS COLLECTIBLE

Playing cards are the versatile collectible. In addition to being a very distinctive form of print collecting, playing cards also have a history of their own which parallels that of the history of printing. Each new innovation in printing found its way to playing cards. The designs of playing cards are steeped in religion and history. Early specimens are well defined representations of life at that time.

In addition to being collectible in their own right, playing cards are also collected as part of other collections. So many varieties of playing cards have been issued that whatever the subject matter of a collectible, there is probably a deck of cards that fits it. Deal yourself in.

## COMIC BOOKS

The history of the American comic book industry spans three-quarters of a century. During that time, it has seesawed up and down the success charts of the publishing world — on top one day and down the next and over again. Comic books reached their peak during the 1940s when they were the largest selling magazines in the world. Each year 70 million readers bought over 600 million copies. Today, only half that amount are sold. With all its ups and downs, the comic book industry has managed to survive.

The first comic books were made up of reprints of old newspaper strips. In an effort to sell more papers, the *Chicago American* printed the first comic book in 1911. It was a collection of "Mutt and Jeff" strips 18" by 6". It sold 45,000 copies, but despite its success, other publishers did not take to this new idea until 1929. That was the year George Delacorte published the first four-color comics sold on newsstands. It was called "The Funnies," but despite the fact that the stories and art were all new, it lasted only one year.

Harry Wildenburg of the Eastern Color Printing Company in New York originated the modern comic book in 1933 when he devised a new format. He folded four 36" by 23" newspaper pages to make a sixty-four page book of newspaper reprints which measured approximately 8¾" by 11" to 14". A salesman for Eastern Color, Max Gaines, sold companies like Procter and Gamble and Canada Dry on using comics as giveaway advertising bonuses. They were so popular that Gaines was convinced the public would buy them as they did Big Little Books. To test the market, 35,000 copies were distributed to chain bookstores. Their success led to a quarter of a million copies of Famous Funnies No. 1 being printed for newsstands; it was the first comic book to be published on a regular monthly basis.

Other publishers weren't long in getting into this new field, and about a dozen other titles appeared on the newsstands. These were mostly reprint rights and, after the rights had been exhausted, the publishers had no choice but to find some original material. The first regular comic book to use material specifically written for comics was "New Fun Comics" published by Malcolm Wheeler-Nicholson in 1935. The name was later changed to "More Fun Comics."

Many publishers had been hit hard by the Depression, and the country was still feeling the panic of 1937. In an attempt to keep his presses going, Harry Donenfeld bought National Periodical Publications from Major Nicholson. He published the first comic book using original material and devoted to a single subject, the format for comics today. It was called "Detective Comics" and was concerned with the struggle between law and order and good and evil. National Periodical Publications is commonly known as DC Comics.

Comics did not attain the popularity of other magazines until Action Comics No. 1, featuring Superman, was issued in June 1938, marking the beginning of the Golden Age of Comics. Superman (Fig. 58) captivated the American public and paved the way for many other now historic comic characters — Batman, The Human Torch (Fig. 58), Captain Marvel, and Wonder Woman are but a few of these costumed fantasy heros. Though these super heroes predominated, comics that were comical were still around — Archie, Donald Duck (Fig. 59), Porky Pig, Little Lulu, Bugs Bunny, and Blondie. Many of these funny ones are still making us laugh. Some newspaper comic strip heroes and heroines also appeared in comic book adventures — Little Orphan Annie, Dick Tracy (Fig. 59), Lil' Abner, etc.

The Golden Age lasted until after World War II, when the comic book novelty faded. Sales were down. Publishers tried new subjects to regain the public attraction — funny animals, love, adventure, crime, but nothing seemed to bolster the flagging industry until a few publishers issued stories of violence, horror, and science fiction. Max Gaines' son, William, inherited Educational Comics, later to be called Entertaining Comics, and in 1950 began "The EC Era" with "Crypt of Terror," "The Vault of Horror," "Weird Science," and several other equally gruesome titles, moving in a new direction which appealed

*Figure 58.    Three of the thousands of collectible comic books. These feature Bat Man, The Human Torch, and Superman.*

*Figure 59.    Collectible comic books of other genre: Donald Duck and Dick Tracy.*

to more mature audiences. The industry was not without its critics who blasted the new trend as inappropriate for a mass medium which was rooted in appealing to children. Critics equated comics depicting crime, sex, and violence with antisocial behavior in children that could be harmful to the normal development of young minds.

A noted child psychologist, Dr. Frederic Wertham, published a harsh attack on comic books in 1954 which led to an investigation of comic books by the United States Senate Subcommittee on Juvenile Delinquency. The Subcommittee's findings failed to resolve anything, but the comic book industry felt compelled to clean up its act. That same year, the major publishers formed the Comics Code Authority (CCA) and devised a strict self-censoring of comic book covers in 1955. Besides proscribing the use of brutal torture, physical agony, nudity, rape, excessive bloodshed, gory and gruesome crime, lust, sadism, and masochism, certain types of behavior and language were also banned. Some publishers, artists, and writers felt their creativity was too restricted and left the industry for other fields. But many parents still had objections to comics, and young readers found more allure in television. Another era of comic book history had run its course.

With the publication of "Showcase No. 4" in 1956, featuring the Flash, DC began a revival of superheroes. To some, that was considered the beginning of the Silver Age of Comics. Publisher and mastermind behind Marvel Comics, Stan Lee, published the first issue of "The Fantastic Four" in 1961, which was the rage of the sixties and revitalized the industry. Many refer to it as the Marvel Age of Comics. Lee made the costumed hero popular again when he introduced Spiderman, the Incredible Hulk, and Thor. He also revived many heroes of the 1940s — the Spectre, the Human Torch, Sub-Mariner among them. But what really triggered a monumental rebirth of the comic book industry was the emergence of a new type of superhero — more up-to-date, more human, more relevant. Heroes, but

like real people in real life situations who appealed to adults as well as children. Considered the best-selling comic book hero, Spiderman, for example, is a science teacher with financial and romantic problems. Marvel proved to be a trendsetter, and by the mid-1970s, these new superheroes were so popular that Marvel had become the largest comic book company in the world.

Better written and better drawn than ever before, comics gained recognition as a highly developed and uniquely American art form. Courses in the study of comics were offered in high schools and colleges nationwide — pointing up the sociological and artistic merits. Many learning specialists approved of the reading of comic books as a supplement to regular reading material which could enrich the vocabulary and stimulate the imagination.

By the end of the 1970s, comic book readership was on the decline again. Inflation forced increases in the prices of new comics, while production quality — ink, paper, reproduction — deteriorated. Many companies folded while Marvel and DC, the leaders of the pack, were forced to make big cuts in their list of titles. Even with slipping sales, Marvel managed to report profits from its comic books, but most of it resulted from licensing fees for the use of the comic heroes in product promotion and from the use of their images as cartoon characters in mass media productions.

The 1980s appear to be a period of flux in the comic book industry. Artist and writer are discontent because, from their point of view, the comic book is no longer the main attraction but a tool for promoting other industries. The comic book industry has yet to settle on a direction but the comic book, like the phoenix, keeps rising from its ashes to soar anew.

### Comic and Fantasy Magazines

Over the past thirty or so years, a new breed of comic magazines was spawned. They are published as magazines, not comic books and, as such, are not bound by the Comic Code Authority (CCA). The most successful of this genre is

"MAD." It was created in 1952 by Harry Kurtzman for Entertaining Comics as an unconventional, absurd comic book satirical in context. After the CCA imposed its code, "MAD" was transformed into a larger format, forty-eight page, black-and-white magazine selling for twenty-five cents, and outside the jurisdiction of the CCA. It became even more successful, and today sells more than two million copies per issue.

Warren Publishing Company published several black-and-white magazines resembling the EC "new trend" horror comics — "Creepy," "Eerie," and "Vampirella." Other popular magazines of this genre include "Cracked," "Crazy," "Heavy Metal," "The Rampaging Hulk," "Marvel Preview," and "Howard the Duck."

## BIG LITTLE BOOKS

These small, stiff-covered books, first seen in the mid-1930s, were the forerunners of the modern comic book. There were a number of different types of these books. Besides "Big Little Books," there were "Big Big Books," "Better Little Books," "New Better Little Books," "Penny Books," "Nickel Books," and "Top Line Comic Books."

Big Little Books were usually 3¾″ by 4½″, and 1½″ thick with from 248 to about 460 pages. Generally the story appeared on the left-hand page and a single picture on the right-hand page illustrating the text on the opposite page. The picture was usually in color, sometimes in black and white. Each picture had a descriptive caption beneath it rather than dialogue or thought balloons like comic strips or books. Most of the artwork was of more or less average quality, but some outstanding artists did work on some of the early Big Little Books. Among these artists were Hal Foster, Al Capp, and Chester Gould. Many popular comic characters appeared in these books including Blondie, Bugs Bunny, Flash Gordon, The Lone Ranger, and Mickey Mouse.

These may be the sleepers among children's books. They have not been publicized like comics, and collectors haven't shown much interest,

and the highest priced ones are worth but a fraction of the value of the top-rated comic books.

## COLLECTING COMIC BOOKS AND BIG LITTLE BOOKS

Generally speaking, the most valuable issue of any comic is the first issue. Those in which popular comic characters made their first appearance in comic book forms are the most valuable. With very rare issues — a dozen or fewer recorded specimens — prices can reach four figure levels.

Depression era and World War II era comic books are among the most scarce. During those difficult years, comic books were read and swapped and hoarded until someone's mother decided it was time for a little cleaning out. The comics were relegated to paper drives or sent overseas to a member of the armed forces.

Prices can vary from dealer to dealer for the same specimen. Regional demand, condition, or a greater demand from collectors for a particular comic at one dealer than another are some of the considerations.

Condition counts in evaluating comic books. Covers should be intact with no noticeable soil, stain, or creases to realize full value. Comic books dating prior to 1940 are acceptable with minor defects. Rare comic books are sometimes cleaned and repaired before selling, which can increase the value.

Some Big Little Books are also scarce because not all of them were printed in large quantities. Paper used for these books was just a few degrees better than newsprint. Many comic book dealers have Big Little Books, too.

Even with their checkered history, comic books were issued in great abundance, and it would seem impossible to collect on a general basis. Even specialists in one or two types can amass a sizable collection.

Comic book dealers are the best sources for collectors. Flea markets, garage sales, and estate sales are possibilities, too, though condition may be questionable. Paper memorabilia dealers also may have some.

## PRESERVING COMIC BOOKS AND BIG LITTLE BOOKS

### Comic Books

Comic books were originally designed as inexpensive, throwaway after use items, to be produced as cheaply as possible, using low-quality paper. Though collectors today would prefer to have their treasures on a better quality, longer lasting product, paper used for comic book production is still low-grade acid paper. Protecting them from the start is the only way to avoid deterioration a few years hence. The books can be deacidified, but it's a rather long process, and apt to be expensive. It may be advisable for some very rare issues, but is best left to experts.

Comic books should be stored upright, if possible, in acid-free boxes. Care should be taken not to pack them too tightly. Leave a little breathing room, inserting acid-free backer boards to fill any empty space. These boxes, with covers, will store as many as 180 regular sized comics. They are available in Golden Age and Magazine size too. Acid-free comic book slipcases and flip-top comic book boxes are also available. Both are meant for upright bookshelf storage which gives a collection a library look. The slipcase is open at the top and on one side, exposing the comics somewhat, and the flip-top box comes with a tuck-in lid that seals the box to provide further protection. Each holds from thirty to fifty comic books.

Acid-free, archival quality Mylar envelopes and Mylar "D" Bags can be used to protect comics from dust and finger marks. Vinyl and polyethylene bags should not be used because they contain plasticizers and other additives that can damage or discolor comics. These envelopes and bags are available in a variety of sizes and thicknesses to accommodate regular, Golden Age size, Magazine, and Treasury Editions. The Mylar envelopes also are available to fit three-ring binders for book type storage.

Acid-free backer boards are available in various standard sizes. They can be inserted into the Mylar bags as stiffeners to keep the comics from buckling. Or, if envelopes are used, the cardboard can be placed between every ten comics to keep them flat and as reinforcement. Cardboard title dividers for organizing the storage boxes are also available.

### Big Little Books

The thickness of Big Little Books may preclude using Mylar sleeves, though Mylar bags may be used for irregular shapes. There also are a variety of acid-free boxes that can be adapted for storage of books of this type. Since the paper used for these books is akin to newsprint, if a little better grade, like comic books, they are subject to deterioration over a short period of time and probably not intended to last indefinitely.

## COMIC BOOKS AND BIG LITTLE BOOKS AS COLLECTIBLE

Comic books and Big Little Books are a major representation of an era — long past, but far from forgotten by the many who lived it. These books were the television of their day — picture stories in living color, if they were silent. Plots and styles spanned the spectrum from Superman to Donald Duck to Bible stories. They were a product of their environment and answered a need of their time. Who could have predicted that something that originally might have been bought for a dime now can bring prices in three or four figures on the collectible market?

# 14
# Ephemera:
# Matchbook Covers, Calendars, Etc.

## WHAT IS EPHEMERA?

The term "ephemera" is of Greek derivation, though their vocabulary did not include that word. Ephemera stems from the combination of two Greek words, "epi" meaning about or pertaining to, and "hemeris" meaning day. Eventually the combined two words "epihemeris" evolved into "ephemera" — about daily life. In modern usage, ephemera is defined as items that appear, at first glance, to be old or quaint or curious but of little value and not really very interesting. The word can be applied to items other than paper, but it has become so identified with paper that its use for other types of collectors' items is rare.

Paper ephemera were the bits and pieces of everyday life, not intended to be of value, let alone collected. But somewhere along the way, it was realized that these bits and pieces were the tangible evidence of everyday living.

Ephemera mirrors and documents the day-to-day happenings. It authenticates history. Collectors look upon it as preserving all but forgotten ways of life. The items themselves may seem ridiculous or corny or even ugly. The great minds of the day did not create them. They were meant to reach and influence the masses, and that they did, more so than their more erudite counterparts could ever hope for.

Ephemera collecting stems from other hobbies, and really isn't as new as it appears to be. Collectors of dolls or glassware or furniture or automobiles or whatever might look for brochures, vintage advertisements, original boxes or containers, patterns, blueprints, and anything that could be found related to the manufacture, sale, and use of the item. Consequently, many of the items mentioned in the preceding chapters can be classified as ephemera, and many of them have evolved into collectible categories all their own: postage stamps, greeting cards, magazines, matchbook covers. Fortunately for today's collectors, a number of these items meant to be thrown away after use were considered too nice or too pretty to end up on the trash heap and served to start the paper collectible trend which took root during the Victorian Era. Probably it was not realized at the time, but some very fine artists of the day created scores of these items. Collectors were saving what were to become much sought after works of art.

Ephemera collecting, as a hobby in itself, has received its greatest impetus within the past twenty-five or thirty years, probably urged on by the nostalgia craze of the 1960s. Collectors needn't have any pet subject, but most collect a certain kind of ephemera — matchbook covers, playbills, post cards, or by time period — Victorian valentines, Civil War military paper. Collectors with a bit more historical motivation search out truly antique ephemera which goes back to the 1800s or before.

## TODAY'S EPHEMERA

Today's ephemera is not of lesser significance than yesterday's, and it can be just as collectible. Certainly, there is much more of a selection than in its early years. The multiplicity of the human race and the complexity of lifestyles generates more and more paper, and the ephemera multiplies.

Instant printing, which put the process of image reproduction into the hands of the masses, is a major factor in this growth. Anyone with a typewriter and a photocopier can publish. With a computer, publishing is brought into the electronic age.

With such an overwhelming proliferation of paper, it is no wonder that today's ephemera is sometimes overlooked. Things so familiar and instantly available — handbills, cards, folders, notices — are too commonplace and too transient to be important. The fact that so much of it is tossed away may make it the rarities of tomorrow. In just a few years, these items will be no more.

Objections may point out that with so much to choose from, who's to know what to preserve? In reality some of it will choose itself just by the fact that, despite all adversities, it survived. Other items will be selected as representatives of today's lifestyles. The ephemerist's special instincts usually separate the wheat from the chaff.

## WHAT IS VALUABLE?

Practically any kind of paper item can have some value, but items of pictorial interest, advertising memorabilia, papers of the performing arts, American business material, and historical material in general are most likely to be of worth. Items in series or sets are usually more valuable than single pieces and, in general, earlier examples of each category are of more value than

later examples, though this is not an iron-clad rule. Books are the one exception.

### What to Collect

Limited space precludes the listing of every conceivable item that falls under the heading of ephemera, but we will hit the high spots and discuss several in detail. A mere sampling of ephemera includes almanacs, catalogs, railroad timetables, labels, blotters, punch boards, bookmarks, cigar bands, and tickets.

## CALENDARS

The calendar of very ancient times was based almost entirely on the moon. The month spanned a period from full moon to full moon, approximately twenty-nine and a half days or slightly more than four weeks. Twelve months constituted a year. Since by moon count, twelve and a quarter months constituted a year, the year gradually gave way to the four seasons.

Confusion reigned until Julius Caesar, in 45 B.C., decreed that henceforth there should be three years of 365 days each followed by one year of 366 days in perpetual cycle. The arrangement proved satisfactory for many years since there are approximately 365 and a quarter days in a year. But in the course of several centuries, the discrepancy multiplied since 365 and a quarter days was not an exact figure.

This error in the Julian calendar was corrected in 1582 by Pope Gregory XII, who omitted eleven days from that year while at the same time instituting this leap year rule: Those years whose date numbers are exactly divisible by four are leap years unless they are also exactly divisible by one hundred. In such cases they are not leap years unless they are exactly divisible by four hundred. The year 1900 was not a leap year but the year 2000 will be.

Our calendar is still far from satisfactory due to the facts that January first falls on a different day of the week each year and the months are different lengths. A year now equals fifty-two weeks plus one and one-fourth days, and therein lies the difficulty in attempting to derive a more systematic calendar.

## Collecting Calendars

Man seems to have always had a compulsion to keep track of time. These attempts were not always correct, but nearly every race on the face of the earth devised ways to count the days.

Collecting calendars is one avocation in which it pays to do one's homework. Collecting anything requires some research in order to be a knowledgeable collector and avoid costly errors. Calendar collecting has an added dimension. Collectors of original calendars may find them difficult to obtain because so many reproductions are on the market. Still, many other calendars are surfacing and are obtainable at reasonable prices.

Calendars have long been a popular means of advertising — the annual New Year's giveaway by all sorts of businesses and services. Some have special days related to the business or service marked. Others resemble mini-almanacs with all sorts of information printed on the reverse sides of the calendar pages. This, too, is often related to the business or service (Fig. 60). These are usually wall calendars.

"Year-at-a-Glance" calendars were very popular for advertising purposes, and many that date back a hundred years or more can still be found today. Some firms still utilize this form of advertising.

Antique shops, flea markets, rummage sales, swap sales, and auctions are the places to look for calendars. Stores and bookshops have them, too, where they may have spent years on a dark shelf gathering dust. Designer calendars have become popular items, with new ones coming out each year, and many of them contain some very good artwork — another variation of prints.

## Preserving Calendars

Calendars can be handled much like prints. The same storage methods can be used — acid-

*Figure 60. Brown & Bigelow calendar dated 1932. (From the archives of Brown & Bigelow.)*

free Mylar sleeves in acid-free containers. Some of the same ones used for prints should fit.

Most calendars are made from better than average paper and/or cardboard. Most also have multiple pages which should be separated occasionally to allow some passage of air. Some are constructed of one illustration at the top of a sheet of cardboard with a calendar — usually of twelve sheets, but sometimes six with two months to a sheet. Others are six to twelve pages with an illustration and a monthly calendar on each page. Some of these are constructed so that once the first six months have passed, the calendar is reversed to reveal the last six months on the back sides of the first.

*Figure 61. Vanity Fair cigarettes made in 1878 by W. S. Kimball Tobacco Co. (Photograph courtesy Cigarette Pack Collectors Assn.)*

*Figure 62. Cross-cut cigarettes in box, made in 1890s by W. Duke Sons & Co. (Photograph courtesy Cigarette Pack Collectors Assn.)*

Smaller calendars, of course, are easier to store. One sheet "year-at-a-glance" calendars can be handled like cards, utilizing the Mylar sleeves or pages with pockets of varying sizes. Album displays can be very interesting and attractive.

Calendars can be framed. Indeed, many calendar illustrations were and are so attractive that, once the calendar part was used up, the illustration or illustrations were cut from the rest of the calendar to be framed like a print. Of course, calendars, like any other collectible, should be left intact.

## CIGARETTE PACKS

One item that is not often mentioned in relation to ephemera is cigarette packs (Figs. 61 & 62). They are a popular collectible among a growing group of devotees. Collectors seek out full packs of obsolete United States brands, and the American cigarette industry has been quite prolific in the issuing of brands throughout the years of cigarette production. The choices of brand names and the graphics have been equally colorful. Names such as Zipper, Thrills, Barking Dog, Dog's Head, Smiles, and Full House all had their following. Given the throwaway nature of the product, it is surprising that so many examples of this "cigarette pack art" have survived.

The earliest cigarette packs were actually tissue papers used by shopkeepers to wrap loose cigarettes. These tissues often were stamped with the name of the shop, but very few of these wrappers are known to exist today. The "slide and shell" boxes of the late 19th century are more common. Some of the brands manufactured during this period were Duke of Durham, Cross-cut, and Pinhead, and numerous examples can still be found in private collections. The era of the standard brands which popularized the soft pack began with Camel in 1913.

### Collecting Cigarette Packs

The Cigarette Pack Collectors Association, based in Georgetown, Massachusetts and founded in 1976, forms the nucleus of a small but dedicated group of cigarette pack enthusiasts. The membership numbers about 250. See Organizations and Associations for complete address.

Old cigarette packs are not the kind of paper items one is likely to find at the usual sources for other paper items. Once the cigarettes are gone, the pack is not the kind of paper one tends to keep around, though some of the early packs were rather interesting. The association publishes a bimonthly newsletter for members to aid in the pursuit of the hobby. They also hold a convention from time to time. There have been three thus far.

### Preserving Cigarette Packs

Cigarette packs do present some rather unusual preservation problems. Tobacco beetles, which may be found in very old packs, can bore tiny holes through the cardboard or paper and destroy a collection. To resolve this problem, many collectors subject their older packs to subzero temperatures for a period of time.

Otherwise, the standard guidelines regarding heat, humidity, and light, as applied to other paper items, apply to cigarette packs as well.

## MATCHBOOK COVERS

### Matches

Matches are defined as a short slender piece of wood or other inflammable material tipped with some combustible substance that will ignite by friction. Modern matches are divided into two general classifications: safety matches, which will not ignite unless rubbed on a specially prepared surface, and matches that will strike anywhere.

One of the earliest types of matches was a long splinter of wood tipped with sulfur and lighted by pressing the tip into glowing tinder. The first true friction match was the invention of an Englishman, John Walker, in 1827. It, too, had a sulfur tip, but the tip was covered with a mixture of potassium chlorate and antimony sulfate. It was ignited by drawing the tip between folded sandpaper, which was included with each package.

Walker and other manufacturers began using white phosphorus on the tip of friction matches in 1833. Safety matches were introduced in 1855 by a Swedish man named Lundstrom. He left the white phosphorus off the tip and attached a friction surface of red phosphorus and sand to the side of the box. White phosphorus is poisonous and a hazard among match factory workers. Its use has been forbidden in many countries. A tax levied on its use in the United States in 1912 made its use commercially impossible. The exact composition now used for the tips of matches is a carefully guarded trade secret. Improved friction matches were first made in the United States in 1836 in Springfield, Massachusetts. Practically no safety matches were made in the United States prior to 1918. The complete United States supply was imported from Norway, Sweden, and Japan.

### Early Matchbook Covers

Matchbook covers have been produced in more abundance than almost any other collectible. The earliest match covers were produced by the Diamond Match Company, the granddaddy of all American match manufacturers. The age of a matchbook is determined by the manumark which contains the name of the manufacturer. On most covers, it can be found below the abrasive or inside behind the matches. The manumark of the first Diamond Match issue is located on the saddle or top of the closed book and reads: "The Diamond Match Co./Volume One." Below the abrasive it reads: "Patented Sept. 28, 1892." There are very few of these covers in existence, and collectors consider them museum pieces.

Three other manumarks besides this one were issued before Safety First's came out in 1905. They were in production until 1920. "Safety First" appears on the bottom of the front. Considering the length of time of production, few of these covers survived, and most are used and of World War I vintage. All these early covers were longer versions of regular size covers with wide irregular abrasive.

In about 1922, Diamond Match issued a series called Diamond Quality which were produced until the 1930s. Several other companies also began producing matches about this time.

### Matchbook Cover Designs

Covers are divided into three basic forms of design groups, but are not collected that way very much anymore because there are so many of them.

The original and most common form of match cover design contains twenty matches. Collectors call it "regular size" or a "twenty." Early covers of this type were slightly longer than the present ones. About 1937, the covers were shortened to fit into cigarette machines.

The second form holds thirty matches. It is the same length as the "regular," but wider. Collectors call it an "aristocrat."

The third form is even wider and holds forty matches. It is the same length as the "regular," but double the width. Collectors call them "forties," "billboards," or "royal flush."

Special matches are made in odd sizes. These are collected by size. The first odd size holds ten matches and is half the width of a regular. Collectors call them a "ten" or a "ten strike." Production of this size began in 1934 and stopped in the 1970s. Covers out of production usually attain collectible status in time.

The shortest match cover ever made was produced from 1934 to 1943 and is called a "midget." It measures 1″ by 1½″.

Several other odd sizes were made: A "twelve strike" and a "perfect thirty-six," for example, and even one called "giant" which was a shade wider than a "forty" and slightly more than nine inches long. Few of these are found.

Odd shapes, such as hourglass shaped and contoured, have also been made. Hourglass are thirty size width, but longer than a regular thirty cover. The trade calls them "jewelites." Contours are die-cut and quite distinctive. They are wider than regular size but of the same length. Thousands of hourglass covers have been produced while contours are a bit less plentiful.

The most sought after of the odd size matchbooks is the jewel size. They are the exact size of jewelite but not die-cut. Over three thousand covers are known, and some collectors specialize in jewels only. Jewels were first made in 1955, but they were not widely sold until 1963. It is thought that the first issued are from the Hotel Capri in Havana, Cuba.

These odd sizes form the accepted grouping for the match cover collecting hobby, and are the ones most often traded.

The largest cover in the world holds 240 matches, and is over a foot long. Once these covers were available only in the United States and Canada, but now they are on their way to being available worldwide. There are also covers holding two hundred matches but slightly shorter than 240s. A few eighty size covers have been produced, but probably are seen less than any others.

Color covers, resembling Kodachrome pictures, were introduced in the mid-1950s. The first ones were produced on glossy finish coated paper, but a few use other types of paper stock. They come in all sizes. Sets of souvenir covers also exist. One contains ninety-nine pieces, a collection in itself. All major match companies now produce top quality color covers on fine paper. There are also embossed designs, some impressed in colorful foil, also available in all sizes. Other styles include silktones with a fabric-like feel, uni-glos with ink that glows like neon colors, knotholes, with a hole cut into the cover, and easel backs which are cut on the back to form an easel.

Some matchbooks, called "features," have wide, flat match stems with pictures on them. These were very popular matches at one time, but many collectors don't want them because the matches, rather than the cover, are the main feature. Matchbooks cannot be stored with the matches intact because of the danger of fire, and these covers would be next to nothing without the matches. Other types of features had narrow stems and often words were printed on them instead of pictures.

## Collecting Matchbook Covers

There are numerous kinds of collecting categories — hotels, restaurants, and banks are the most common. Like stamps, there are also variations in the issues — variations in size, color, color of paper, information, manumarks, and striker width. Each of these involves a new printing and therefore, a new issue. Some of these changes may be the result of replacing a printing plate.

One must have the help of other matchbook collectors to build a collection. A collector needs not only one cover for his own collection but duplicates to trade. To get duplicates, acquire a box of matches when feasible. A box of matches contains fifty books and is called a "caddy." Hobbyists gauge their collecting efforts on how many caddies they can get on a good day's hunt. Fifteen or twenty caddies mark a successful day.

Collecting can also be done by mail. Mailers are available for all size matchbooks. These mailers are foil-lined to conform to postal regulations.

Buying all one's covers is possible, but it can be expensive, and the enjoyment of the hobby lies in swapping and trading those caddies acquired from obliging businesses.

Serious collectors may not agree, but match cover collecting can be enjoyable even if the collection is compiled of only those specimens acquired on one's daily wanderings or serious travels or from special functions — weddings, parties, etc., even if none are ever swapped or traded. Swapping and trading entail some serious office procedure and recordkeeping, and if one opts not to go that route, one can still enjoy whatever match covers happen to come one's way.

## Preserving Matchbook Covers

The preservation of a matchbook cover should start with an examination of its components, for in order for a matchbook to be collectible it must be unused, including the striker unless the cover is a rarity. Open the cover out. There is a front, a back, and a narrow strip between, called a saddle. There is an abrasive surface, usually on the front, but after 1975 mostly on the back, called a striker. The end of the cover folds up to encase the match pack on the lower end and is held in place by a staple.

The first step in the actual preservation of the cover is the careful removal of the staple. Collectors call this process "shucking" or "stripping." The staple must be extracted without damaging the cover. A staple remover can cause damage if its sharp edges dig into the cover. A small knife or tool should be used to gradually and gently pry the staple out. Loosening the prongs on the reverse side first may be advisable. Gouging the cover in any way can render it worthless. Forcing the two rows of match stems to pull the staple loose bends the cover and leaves a noticeable and very distinct crease. This also can render the cover worthless.

The stripped cover will automatically curl back up to its original shape so the next step is the flattening out process. Assemble the covers into bundles, alternating them so the striker is up one time and down the next. Bind the covers tightly with a rubber band, being careful that the band does not cut into any of them. Place them beneath a heavy object like a large book for a day or so. The covers should remain flat indefinitely, with the original crease marks to attest to their authenticity.

Early collectors cut the matches off at the base of the back. This also removed the striker. These are called bob-tailed matches and are of no value.

Matchbook covers are sometimes found already nice and flat and without matches. If there is an absence of crease lines at the saddle and below the striker, and missing staple holes, chances are these are salesman's samples, called flats or mint covers. Collectors consider them worthless, no doubt because these were never really made to cover matches. It's rather like stamps that have been issued more for collectors than for postal use. Stamp collectors consider them so much wallpaper. Match covers should always be kept in their original condition and never marked in any way.

Paper used today for the manufacture of match covers is relatively safe. Longevity expectancy is thirty to sixty years. Paper used for old matchbook covers was porous but thicker, and the components of the striker permeated the surrounding paper causing damage. Old paper is about twice as thick as the new.

### Mounting and Storing Matchbook Covers

Albums are available especially for match covers. Pre-cut slotted pages are available for regular, thirties, and forties, as well as uncut blank pages for odd sizes. Filler pages are also available in all the cover sizes.

Archival quality photo albums can be adapted for match covers. Archival mounting pages are available to which the covers can be mounted with archival mounting corners. To avoid covers catching on each other, the pages can be protected with individual Mylar sleeves. These are the size of regular three-ring binders. Match covers should never be pasted down. The inside has merit, too and may be as important as the outside if not more so. Acetate sleeves

should be used for older covers. Mounting them could prove difficult and damaging to the cover.

Gold and silver inks used on some covers will sometimes flake off, eventually to the point where the printing is not legible. Covers made from certain types of glossy paper tend to expand in normal heat and humidity in a rather brief time. Veining will appear on the striker, and it may fall off in pieces. These are unavoidable problems related to the manufacturing process and outside the province of the collector.

Covers should not be left too long before being stripped. The staples eventually rust and stain the cover, which is one reason that matchbooks are better preserved without their matches.

Older covers should be handled carefully as they tend to become brittle. Old covers sometime have brittle strikers, and some of the covers have been found with tape applied to the inside to keep the striker intact. Collectors consider these covers damaged.

Like other paper items, match covers should be handled as little as possible. Sometimes this presents a problem because the collector has to handle the covers to check out all the variations and know what specimens are needed. Careful recordkeeping may alleviate some handling, but some variations are so subtle that careful inspection is the only sure way to detect the differences.

The large 200 and 240 match covers are difficult to store because they bend and scratch. Standard match cover albums are not big enough to hold them. Some archival quality ephemera albums and Mylar pages do come in sizes large enough to accommodate the largest matchbooks, but they are rather expensive. They would also require archival mounting corners since they aren't specifically made for match covers.

Some collectors prefer to store their match covers in bundles as is done for flattening purposes. However, rubber bands should not be used for long-term storage. The preferred method for permanent storage is to wrap each bundle with a strip of paper and secure the paper with tape. A variety of acid-free archival quality paper is available that can be stripped for this type of use. A package of one hundred 12″ by 15″ sheets of acid-free tissue paper runs about ten dollars but should last for a long, long time. Archival quality polyester transparent tape is also available. As mentioned under general preservation methods, regular transparent tape should not be used. It tends to leak through the paper and will dry up and come loose in time.

## PRESERVING EPHEMERA

Most ephemera falls into three general forms: single sheets, periodicals, or books. In addition to the general preservation methods in Chapter 3, preservation methods for those items of similar form in other chapters are applicable.

A new type of archival quality Mylar envelopes is available for the storage and protection of letters, photographs, pamphlets, periodicals, and other paper items. Sizes run from 6″ by 9″ up to 9½″ by 12½″. All sizes are available with the opening on either the wide side or the narrow side, a nice option considering the diversity of ephemera.

Collectors should ever bear in mind the fragility of paper, and that a major cause of deterioration is the touch of the hand.

## EPHEMERA AS COLLECTIBLE

Ephemera is looked upon as the small, inconsequential things of life, but the small and inconsequential comprise a significant part of one's life. Often, they are the things that make life worth living. Though much ephemera is and was created for advertising purposes, it is the tangible evidence of living. It documents memories of time past and gives insight into the living of those times past. Ephemera is the stuff of which daydreams are made. Best of all, much of it is free!

# 15
# An Ounce of Prevention

This may be the most important chapter in this book. A collector may take infinite pains to ensure that his paper treasures are protected against all exigencies and still miss the biggest obstacle of all against the safeguarding of his collection.

While the preceding chapters pointed out the aesthetic values in preserving paper memorabilia and the proper preservation methods for an ongoing collection, this chapter deals with the preservation of a collection when the collector is not in a position to maintain it himself.

Too many collections have been cannibalized through the ignorance of estate executors and/or relatives, well-meaning though they may be, because the owner failed to provide detailed instructions for the disposition of the collection if he is disabled or has gone to his reward. One relative might opine, "This old map would look great over my fireplace." Another, "This pretty bird print would look nice in my den." The executor may consider any paper items frivolities among fine antiques and bric-a-brac. "Let's sell these old post cards cheap to get rid of them fast." "Imagine a grown man saving comic books." Bargain hunters may be elated, but the heirs may lose more than they bargained for, and a fine collection may be lost to posterity.

## PREPARING INSTRUCTIONS

### Inventory Sheet

Most serious collectors keep some sort of inventory of their acquisitions. They want to know what they have either to avoid duplication or to update when a better example is available. An inventory is also necessary for insurance purposes. How detailed the inventory is depends on the nature of the collection. There are so many varieties of postage stamps that it is necessary to be specific. Two stamps may look the same, but one may be worthless while the other is a rarity of inestimable value. Original prints, first editions, and other one-of-a-kind items should be listed with any special descriptions. Documents of authenticity should be included with the listing. It may be advisable to list rare items on a separate sheet and attach the authentication to the proper sheet.

Some collectors now use computers to keep track of their treasures, and they appear very pleased with the results. It does facilitate changes — keeping track of values, updating to better specimens, purchases, and sales, etc. If a computer recordkeeping process is used, do include instruction for access to any computer coding.

### Instruction Sheet

Even if the collector has confided in someone his ultimate intentions for his collection, he should also put it in writing. Written instructions avoid misunderstandings and the possibility that the executors and/or heirs may not want to "take someone's word for it." Hard feelings also may result because the collector told one person and didn't tell others.

These instructions should include the collector's specific wishes for the disposal of the collection, whether it is to be sold or donated to a museum or other institution.

Ideally, the collector should make arrangements beforehand for the museum or institution to receive the collection from the estate. The collector is in the best position to know what type of museum or institution could benefit most from the collection, and if his wishes aren't known, who can say what will happen to the collection? If arrangements are not made beforehand, then the collector should be very specific in his instruction about who the receiver should be, or at least suggest what type of receiver it should be. It may be wise to include the donation of rare and valuable items in one's will to ensure that the collector's wishes are carried out.

If the collector knows a reputable dealer or dealers he wishes to handle his collection, he should list them in his instructions. If he has made arrangements with a dealer for the disposition of the collection, he should say so.

If the collection has been appraised, that should be mentioned, and a copy of the appraisal attached to these instructions. The name of the appraiser should be included.

Along with the inventory and detailed instructions, it may be advisable to include photographs or photocopies of the most valuable items. Photocopies may be a wise alternative anyway, if it is necessary to refer to the contents of a document or manuscript or other written material frequently. Photos of these items could prove invaluable should a theft occur.

The instruction papers should be attached to the inventory sheets, and all these papers should be put with the collector's will. Another set of these papers, with another copy of the will, should be placed in a safe location outside of the home. A safe deposit box or an attorney's office are possibilities.

Instructions also should include proper handling of the collection in moving it, or in the event temporary storage is necessary before final disposition.

## If No Instructions Were Left

Executors and/or heirs should not be overly anxious to dispose of a collection or to relegate it to the sidelines to get it out of the way. The tendency is to gather up paper items and shove them anywhere so the "important stuff" can be arranged to the best advantage for an estate sale or to make room for movers. This is especially true if the collection or any part of it happens to occupy some items of furnishings to be sold.

The collection should be moved intact to a dry area of moderate temperature, away from direct light, and off the floor. If the collection has been stored on its own shelving, then that should be moved with it, and the collection reset up as it was originally, or as close to the original as possible. Care should be taken to keep the items in the same position as they were originally stored. Books and albums should be stored upright without leaning, otherwise they could warp. Boxes of items should be stored as they were shelved.

A word of caution: No one should be allowed to rummage through a collection helter skelter. As mentioned, paper is delicate, and inexperienced hands could cause irreparable damage and diminish the value of the collection.

Ideally, several months should be allowed to pass before disposing of a collection. It may take that long to secure appraisals, and more than one may be advisable, and decide which, if any, should be accepted. If the executor and/or heirs are too anxious to "dispose of the clutter," they could end up cheating themselves.

With some collections, disposition may take even longer-even a year or more. When rare books and documents, original works of art, one-of-a-kind manuscripts, and like items are involved, selling them at auction may be the only way. Setting up an auction with a reliable dealer and getting the word out to prospective bidders takes time. The bidding alone may be time consuming. When high stakes bidding is involved, confirming authenticity may be an added factor, and that takes time, too.

In most circumstances, it is best to sell a collection intact, though the value of some items may prohibit selling the whole collection as a unit. Postage stamps are a prime example. Learned philatelists know which stamps are the hallmarks of a collection, and those may constitute only a dozen or so out of hundreds. With those dozen or so removed, the collection may still appear reasonably intact, but the value has been diminished considerably.

### Taking Inventory

If no inventory has been kept by the collector, the executor and/or heirs should do this, most preferably before the collection is moved. Nothing should be moved or removed from an estate without first making an inventory. To know if anything is eventually missing, one must first know what is there. That is protection for the executor and the heirs. Knowing what's there from the beginning also can avoid hassles later.

### Insuring a Collection

Homeowners' (and renters') policies can be obtained to cover collections to some extent against fire, theft, and natural disasters. But the extent and the value of the collection may dictate additional insurance. Those rarities and originals and one-of-a-kinds, and very valuable collections, may require much more coverage than the homeowners' (renters') policy will allow.

An insurance adviser can steer the collector to the right policies. For certain types of collectible, there are collectors' organizations that offer insurance coverage for whatever type of collection is involved. The American Philatelic Society (APS) offers advice and coverage for stamp collections. Scouts On Stamps Society International (SOSSI) offers advice related directly to the protection and disposition of collections of stamps related to the scouting movement.

## SECURITY MEASURES FOR THE HOME

### Outside the Premises

Outside security entails keeping the yard free of hiding places for burglars as well as not advertising when no one is at home.

1. Trees. Keep the lowest branches of mature trees trimmed at least seven feet from the ground. In addition to providing hiding places for intruders, low tree branches allow an easy means for climbing a tree which may in turn allow access to a second-story window.

2. Shrubs. Keep shrubs trimmed to a three-foot or less height. Tall shrubs provide good protection for burglars.

3. Light. Sufficient light is sound security. Spotlights should be mounted on the four corners of the house and installed over each door out of reach of a tall person. An ideal option are lights that go on automatically at sundown.

4. House Numbers. House numbers should be readily visible so the police and fire department can find the house quickly in the event of an emergency.

5. Ladders, etc. Do not leave ladders, or anything else that could aid in providing access to second-story windows, standing around outside the house.

6. Notes on Doors. Do not leave notes on doors indicating your absence and stating the time of your return.

7. House Keys. If it is considered necessary to have a spare key on or near the premises, give one to a neighbor and keep one for him.

8. Visible Valuables. Do not keep a valuable collection, or parts thereof, or any other valuables in a location that is visible from a window. As mentioned in previous chapters, direct light can be damaging to paper anyway.

9. Unlocked Doors. Do not leave doors unlocked when working outside. Thieves have entered and done their dirty work while homeowners were occupied in an area away from the unlocked door. Do not even leave the door unlocked to retrieve a newspaper or take out garbage, if you must be away from the vicinity of the

door to do so. All a thief needs is for a back to be turned for a few seconds.

**Inside the Premises**

A good way to discourage burglaries is to increase the time it takes to break in and the time it takes to find and gather up whatever the thief has in mind to steal.

1. Doors. Solid wood or metal doors about two inches thick are more secure than hollow wooden doors.

2. Door Locks. Double-cylinder deadbolt locks are recommended. This type of lock requires a key to unlock the door from both the inside and the outside of the house.

3. Double-Hung Windows. This type of window can be secured by drilling a hole at an angle through the top frame of the lower window and through the bottom frame of the upper window. Then insert a long nail with the head sawed off into the holes.

4. Window Locks. Key locks can be installed on all windows. Normal thumb-turned window locks can be pried open easily with a screwdriver.

5. Home Safes. Some collectors have safes installed in their homes to store valuables, but unless it is a "Burglar Class Safe," it may invite trouble. Burglar Class Safes are the most secure places for securing valuables in the home. Non-Burglar Class Safes must weigh at least 300 pounds empty. Anything lighter than that can be opened with a crowbar or an ax or just carted off with the contents intact. Obviously, a safe of any kind may be impractical for storing large items. Very high-value items are best in a bank vault when not being worked with or used. Photocopies or photographs should be retained at home for reference.

6. Storing a Collection. Storing a collection in different areas of one's home can deter bur-

glars. If the collection is all in one room, the thief can grab it and run. Most burglars want to spend no more than fifteen or twenty minutes getting in, getting the loot, and getting out. If the collection is spread out in several rooms, chances are the burglar will miss a good part of his intended target.

**When No One is Home**

When no one is home for several days or longer, try to make it appear as if someone will be back any minute.

1. Temporary Storage. It may be advisable to transfer very valuable items to a bank vault, if the home doesn't have the equivalent of a burglar-class safe.

2. Shades and Draperies. Leave shades and draperies open as they normally are when the house is occupied.

3. Deliveries. Stop all deliveries such as mail and newspapers or have someone pick them up every day.

4. Maintain the Yard. Arrange to have the grass cut or snow shoveled while you're away.

5. Leave a Car in the Driveway. If you are a two or more car family, leave one of them parked in the driveway. A child's toy left in the yard also gives the appearance of a brief absence.

6. Timers. Have timers set to turn the lights on and off at the times they are normally turned on and off. Timers to turn radios and televisions on at times they are in normal use is also a good idea.

7. Have Someone Check Your Home Daily. Have a friend, neighbor, or relative take a quick check inside the house daily.

8. Leave an Itinerary with Someone. Leave an itinerary with that same friend, neighbor, or relative. Include phone numbers and names where you can be contacted in the event of an emergency.

# Bibliography

## Books

*American Card Catalog, The. The Standard Guide on all Collected Cards and Their Values.* Nostalgia Press, Inc., Franklin Square, NY, 1967.

*Autographs: A Collector's Guide.* Jerry E. Patteson, Crown Publishing, Inc., New York, 1973.

*Collecting Comic Books.* Marcia Leiter, Little Brown & Company (Canada), Ltd., Boston, Toronto, 1983.

*Collecting Historical Documents.* Todd M. Axelrod, T.F.H. Publishing, Inc., Neptune City, NJ, 1984.

*Collecting Paper Money and Bonds.* Colin Narbeth, Robin Hendy, and Christopher Stocker, Mayflower Books, Inc., New York, 1979.

*Collecting Paper Money — A Beginner's Guide.* Colin Narbeth, American edition published by Henry Regney Company, Chicago, 1973, by arrangement with Lutterworth Press, London.

*Collecting Photographs — A Guide to the New Art Form.* Landt and Lisl Dennis, E.P. Dutton, New York, 1977.

*Collecting Postcards.* Valerie Monahan, Blandford Press, Ltd., England, 1980.

*Collecting Postcards — 1894-1914.* William Duval and Valerie Monahan, Brandford Press, Ltd., England, 1978.

*Collecting Printed Ephemera.* Maurice Rickards, Abbeville Press, New York, 1988.

*Collecting Today for Tomorrow.* David Alan Herzog, Arco Publishing, Inc., New York, 1980.

*Compleat Philatelist, The.* Herman Herst, Jr., The Washington Press, Florham Park, NJ, 1979.

*Complete Book of Baseball Collectibles, The.* George E. Sullivan, Arco Publishing, Inc., New York, 1983.

*Complete Book of Paper Antiques, The.* Adelaide Hechtlinger and Wilbur Cross, Coward, McCann & Geoghegan, Inc., New York, 1972.

*Concise History of Posters, A.* John Barnicoat, Thames and Hudson, London, 1972.

*Conservation of Books and Documents, The.* W.H. Langwell, F.C. I.C., P. Himan, London, 1957.

*Fine Books.* Alfred W. Pollard, first published London, 1912, republished E.P. Publishing Ltd., Yorkshire, England, 1973.

*Great American Baseball Card Flipping, Trading and Bubblegum Book.* Brendan C. Boyd and Fred C. Harris, A Sports Illustrated Book, Little Brown & Co., Boston, 1973.

*Guide to Collecting and Care of Original Prints, A.* Sponsored by The Print Council of America, Crown Publishing, Inc., New York, 1965.

*Guide to Collecting Trade and Cigarette Cards, A.* Roy Genders, Pelham Books Limited, London, 1975.

*Introducing the Song Sheet.* Helen Westin, Thomas Nelson, Inc., Nashville, TN, 1976.

*Investing in Paper Money.* Kenneth R. Lake, Pelham Books, London, 1972.

*Linn's World Stamp Almanac.* Second edition. Compiled and edited by the staff of *Linn's Stamp News*, Amos Press, Inc., Sidney, OH, 1978.

*Maps and Prints for Pleasure and Investment.* D. C. Gohm, Arco Publishing Co., Inc., New York, 1969.

*Maps — A Historical Survey of Their Study and Collecting.* R.A. Shelton, The University of Chicago Press, Chicago, 1972.

*Match Covers — A Guidebook for Collectors.* Esther Rancier, Century House, Watkins Glen, NY, 1976.

*More Precious than Gold and Philately.* Bruno J. Forster, 1971.

*Official Price Guide to Collectors Prints, The.* Second edition. Ruth M. Pollard, The House of Collectibles, Inc., Orlando, FL, 1981.

*Official Price Guide to Paper Collectibles, The.* The House of Collectibles, Inc., Orlando, FL, 1980 and 1981 editions.

*Pamper Your Possessions.* Vera Penick Wright, Barre Publishing, Barre, MA, 1979.

*Paper Collectibles.* Robert D. Connolly, Books Americana, Inc., Florence, AL, 1979.

*Paper Money.* Ian Angus, St. Martin's Press, New York, 1974.

*Philatelic Terms Illustrated.* Compiled by Russell Bennett and James Watson, Stanley Gibbons, Ltd., London, 1972.

*Picture Postcard and Its Origins.* Frank Staff, Frederick A. Prager, Inc. Publishers, New York, 1966.

*Playing Cards — History of the Pack and Explanations of Its Many Secrets.* W. Gurney Benham, Spring Books, London.

*Postcard Collecting.* Thomas E. Range, E.P. Dutton, New York, 1980.

*Preservation of Paper and Textiles of Historic and Artistic Value.* John C. Williams, American Chemical Society, 1977.

*Romance of Greeting Cards, The.* Ernest Dudley Chase, Rust Craft Publishers in Commemoration of the Fiftieth Anniversary of Rust Craft Greeting Cards 1906-1956, Printed by The University Press of Cambridge.

*Scott Standard Postage Stamp Catalogues.* Scott Publishing Co., New York, 1989.

*Stamp Collector's Encyclopedia, The.* Revised edition. R.J. Sutton, Bonanza Books, a division of Crown Publishing, Inc., 1946.

*Story of Paper Money, The.* Yasha Beresiner and Colin Narbeth, Arco Publishing Company, Inc., New York, 1973.

*This is Ephemera.* Maurice Rickards, The Gossamer Press, Brattleboro, VT, 1977.

*Those Fascinating Paper Dolls.* Marian B. Howard, Dover Publications, Inc., New York, 1981.

*Word Shadows of the Great.* Thomas F. Madigan, Facsimile reprint of 1930 edition published in New York by Frederick A. Stokes Co., Gale Research Co., Detroit, 1971.

*World War II Allied Military Currency.* Fourth edition. Raymond Toy and Carlton F. Schwan, Carlton F. Schwan, Portage, OH, 1974.

## Articles

"Brittle Books and Journals," *Science*, October 30, 1987.

"From Rags to Ruin," *Atlantic Monthly*, June 1979.

"Making Books That Last," *Publishers Weekly*, May 29, 1981.

"Millions of Books are Turning to Dust — Can They Be Saved?", *New York Times Book Review*, March 29, 1987.

"Putting It on Paper Permanently," *Science News*, September 6, 1986.

# Suppliers, Organizations, and Associations

## Suppliers of Archival Materials

Conservation Materials, Ltd.
1165 Marietta Way
Sparks, NV 89431
(702) 331-0582

University Products
P.O. Box 101
Holyoke, MA 01041
(413) 532-9431

## Organizations and Associations

American Business Card Club
31759 Stricker
Warren, MI 48093
President: Darrell Christopher

American Game Collectors Association
4628 Barlow Drive
Bartlesville, OK 74006
Editor of publication: Bill Alexander

American Historical Print Collectors Society
P.O. Box 1532
Fairfield, CT 06430
Secretary: William F. Stickle

American Philatelic Society
P.O. Box 8000
100 Oakwood Avenue
State College, PA 16803
Executive Director: Keith A. Wagner

Chicago Map Society
c/o Newberry Library
60 W. Walton Street
Chicago, IL 60610
President: Mary E. Fortney

Chicago Playing Card Collectors
1559 W. Pratt Blvd.
Chicago, IL 60626
Director: Bernice DeSomer

Cigarette Pack Collectors Association
61 Searle Street
Georgetown, MA 01833
President: Richard W. Elliott

Deltiologists of America (postcards)
P.O. Box 8
Norwood, PA 19074
Director: James L. Lowe

Ephemera Society of America
P.O. Box 37
Schoharie, NY 12157
President: William Frost Mobley

National Valentine Collectors' Association
Box 1404
Santa Ana, CA 92702
President: Evalene Pulati

Newspaper Collectors Society of America
P.O. Box 19134
Lansing, MI 48901
Contact: Rick Brown

Postcard History Society
Box 1765
Manassas, VA 22110
Executive Secretary: John McClintock

Poster Society
P.O. Box 43171
Upper Montclair, NJ 07043
Executive Director: Richard C. Allen

Railroadiana Collectors Association, Inc.
795 Aspen Drive
Buffalo Grove, IL 60089
Secretary: Joe Mazanek

Society of Paper Money Collectors
P.O. Box 1085
Florissant, MO 63031
Secretary: Bob Cochran

Universal Autograph Collectors Club
P.O. Box 467
Rockville Centre, NY 11571
President: Herman M. Darvick

# Acknowledgments

Any book is a compilation of research from many sources. The response from sources for this book was most rewarding, and each deserves special thanks for so generously giving of their time to provide information and/or illustrations.

American Philatelic Society Insurance Plan Manager
American Business Card Club
Brown & Bigelow
Rick J. Brown of the Newspaper Collectors Society of America
Canadian Conservation Institute
Cigarette Pack Collectors Association
Commission on Preservation and Access
Conservation Materials, Ltd.
Council on Library Resources
H. S. Crocker Co., Inc.
Deltiologists of America
Eastman Kodak Co.
Ephemera Society of America
Finch, Pruyn & Co., Inc.
P. H. Glatfelter Co.
Hallmark Cards, Inc.
The Library of Congress
Milton Bradley Company
Mohawk Paper Mills, Inc.
National Archives and Records Administration
National Archives of Canada
National Audubon Society
Newberry Library
Playboy Enterprises, Inc.
Postcard History Society
Railroadiana Collectors Association Incorporated
Bill Retskin of *The Front Striker Bulletin*
Ralph Roberts, Writer-Editor
Scouts on Stamps Society International Heirs Committee
Scott Publishing Co.
Society of Paper Money Collectors
The Topps Company, Inc.
United States Playing Card Co.
University Products
S. D. Warren Co.
Wei T'o Associates, Inc.

# Index

**A**

Acid-free paper, 19
Acid-free storage, 31-2
Acids, as enemies of paper, 17
Advertising cards, 8, 81, 82, 90-1
  collecting, 90-1
Advertising on envelopes, 100
*Age of Innocence, The*, 137
*Ainsworth Psalter*, 118
Albums, for postage stamps, 52
Albums, for postal cards, 53
Alum, as enemy of paper, 17
American Business Card Club, 97, 179
American colonial paper money, 106
American Game Collectors Association, 179
American Historical Print Collectors Society, 179
American literature, 135-8
  19th century, 136
  20th century, 137-8
  at the turn of the century, 137
  beginnings, 135
  Revolutionary period, 136
*American Magazine*, 131
*American Minerva*, 129
American music, 118-9
American National Standards Institute, 72, 74
American paper money, 105-7
American Philatelic Society, 175, 179
Amman, Josh, 14
Aquatint, 56
Archer, Scott, 67
Archival-quality storage, 31-2
Armat, Thomas, 123
*Around the World in 80 Days*, program, 9
Arrowsmith, Aaron, 65
Art Deco, 61
Art Nouveau, 60
Association of Research Libraries, 24
Atmospheric conditions, as enemies of paper, 18
Audubon, John James, 59
  print reproduction, 59
Autographs, 6, 35, 37-9, 123
  collecting, 37-9
  content, 38-9
  rare, 39
  rarity, 38
*Avisa Relation oder Zeitung*, 127

**B**

Bache, Richard, 48
Bacon, Nathaniel, 135
Baker, Howard H., Jr., 40
Bank notes, national, 107
Barker, James N., 136
Barlow, Joel, 136

Baseball cards, 8, 81, 84, 85, 91
  collecting, 91
  valuing, 85
*Bay Psalm Book*, 16, 118
Behaim, Martin, 64
Belcher, J., 149
Belize postal issue, 10
Berlin, Irving, 119
Bernstein, Leonard, 119
Besnardeau, M. Leon, 89, 90
Bewick, Thomas, 56
Bibliography, 177-8
Big Little Books, 160-1
  as collectible, 161
  collecting, 160
  preserving, 161
Billheads, 96
*Birds of America, The*, 59
Black-and-white photographs, see Photographs, black and white
Blake, Eubie, 120
Books, rare, 141
Borge, Victor, concert program, 9
*Boston News-Letter*, 129
Bradford, Andrew, 131
Bradford, William, 16
Bradley, Will, 60
Broadcasting, 124-5
  radio, 124
  television, 124-5
Broadcasting memorabilia, collecting, 125
Broadsides, 56-7, 127
Brooks, Jack, 40
Brown, Charles Brockden, 136
Brown, Rick, 131
Brown, Taggart & Chase, 149
Brown & Bigelow calendar, 165
Bubblegum cards, 8, 81, 84-5
  Topps, 84-5
Buck, Dudley, 119
Business cards, 97
  collecting, 97

**C**

Cadman, Charles Wakefield, 119
Calendars, 11, 164-6
  collecting, 165
  preserving, 165-6
Calhoun, John C., 137
Campbell, John, 129
Canadian Conservation Institute, 75
Cards, 8, 81-94
  advertising, 8, 81, 82
    collecting, 90-1
  as collectible, 94
  baseball, 8, 81, 84
    collecting, 91
    valuing, 85
  bubblegum, 8, 81, 84

Topps, 84-5
  business, 97
    collecting, 97
  Christmas, 88-9
  cigarette, 81
    collecting, 90-1
  greeting, 85-9, 91-2
    collecting, 91-2
    modern, 89
  insert, 82, 91
    collecting, 91
  Mother's Day, 86
  New Year's, 85-6
  playing, see Playing cards
  post, see Post cards
  preserving, 93
  souvenir, 8, 81-2, 85, 91
    collecting, 91
  store, 81
  tobacco, 82-4
  trade, 81, 82
  Valentine's Day, 86-8
  visitors, 89
Carpenter, John Alden, 119
Caxton, William, 57
Chadwick, George W., 119
Charlton, John, 90
Checks, 98
  collecting, 98
Cheret, Jules, 57, 58
  poster reproduction, 58
Chevalier, Guillaume, 58
*Chicago American*, 157
  front pages, 128
Chicago Map Society, 179
Chicago Playing Card Collectors, 179
Children's books, 143-5
Children's items, 11, 150-1
  as collectible, 151
  collecting, 150
  preserving, 150-1
Christmas cards, 88-9
Cigarette cards, 81
Cigarette Pack Collectors Association, 167, 179
Cigarette packs, 11, 166-7
  collecting, 167
  preserving, 167
Civil War paper currency, 106-7
*Cleveland News*, front page, 128
Coin notes, 107
Cole, Henry, 88
Collecting, 5, 7-8, 33, 173-4, 175
  deciding what to collect, 7-8
  insuring, 175
  reason for, 5
  housing, 33
  instructions for, 173-4
  inventory, 173, 175

Color photographs, see Photographs, color
Comic books, 157-161
    as collectible, 161
    collecting, 160
    Golden Age, 157
    origins, 157
    preserving, 161
Comics Code Authority, 159
Commercial paper, 8-9, 95-101
    as collectible, 101
    preserving, 100
Committee on Preservation and Access, 28
Como, Perry, autograph, 7
Compound interest treasury notes, 107
Condition, 6
Confederate currency, 106
Congin Paper Mill, 16
Conservation, definition, 24
Conservation Materials, Ltd., 179
Content, preserving, 28
Correspondence, 95-7
    collecting, 96-7
    printed, 95
Council for Library Resources, 24, 28
Cross-cut cigarettes, 166
Currency, 9, 93, 103-9
    American colonial, 106
    American paper, 105-7
    as collectible, 109
    Civil War, 106-7
    coin notes, 107
    collecting, 108
    compound interest treasury notes, 107
    Confederate, 106
    demand notes, 107
    federal reserve notes, 107
    French Revolution, 105
    gold certificates, 108
    greenbacks, 107
    national bank notes, 107
    preserving, 108-9
    promissory notes, 107
    silver certificates, 107
    small-sized notes, 108
    state-issued, 106
    treasury notes, 107
Curt Teich Company, 93

**D**

Daguerre, Louis Jacques, 67
Daguerrotype, 67
Dance memorabilia, collecting, 121
Dates, 6
    in proving authenticity, 6
DC Comics, 159
Deacidification process, 26
DeForest, Lee, 124
Deltiologists of America, 179
Demand notes, 107
Detective Comics, 157
Diamond Match Company, 167-8
Diethyl zinc, 26
Dockwra, William, 46
Dolls, paper, see Paper dolls
Dolly Dingle paper doll, 145
Donahey, William, 145

Donenfeld, Harry, 157
Draper, John W., 67
Durer, Albrecht, 55, 56
Dust, as enemy of paper, 18

**E**

Eastern Color Printing Company, 157
Eastman Kodak Company, 68, 72
Eastman, George, 67
Edison, Thomas, 123
Educational Comics, 157
Egley, W. M., 88
Entertaining Comics, 157
Envelopes, advertising on, 100
Environmental conditions for preserving paper, 31
Ephemera, 11, 163-171
    as collectible, 171
    definition, 163
    modern, 164
    preserving, 171
    value, 164
    what to collect, 164
Ephemera Society of America, 179
Etchings, 56
Evans, Lewis, 65

**F**

Federal reserve notes, 107
Finch, Pruyn & Company, Inc., 20
First editions, collecting, 139
First-day covers, 51
Fourdrinier, Sealy and Henry, 17
Foxing, 18
Framing, glazing materials, 77
Framing historical documents, 43
Franklin, Benjamin, 16, 48, 129, 131, 151
Franklin, James, 129
Franks, free, 39-40
*Free Exchange, The*, 90

**G**

Gaines, Max, 157
Gaines, William, 157
Games, 11, 147-8
General Postal Conference, 48
General Postal Union, 47
*Geographia*, 62
Glass, as glazing material, 78
Glassine envelopes, for stamps, 52
Glazing materials for framing, 77
    glass, 77-8
    plastic, 77-8
Godfrey, Thomas, 136
Gold certificates, 108
Goodal, Thomas, 68
Goodwin, Hannibal, 67
Greenaway, Kate, 132, 145
    reproduction of illustration, 146
Greenbacks, 107
Greeting cards, 85-9, 89, 91-2
    collecting, 91-2
    modern, 89
Guidelines for preserving literary items, 139-141
Gutenberg Bible, 15
Gutenberg, Johann, 15, 16

Gwinnett, Button, 40
    signature, 40

**H**

H. S. Crocker Co., Inc., 93
Haas, Warren J., 25
Hanson, Howard, 119
Harris, Benjamin, 16, 127, 129
Harris, Roy, 119
Hayne, Robert Y., 137
Hermann, Emmanuel, 48
Herrick, Henry, 144
Hiatt, Charles, 57
Hill, Rowland, 46, 49
Hillyer, Robert, 138
Hinges, for stamps, 50
Historical documents, 35, 41-43
    as collectible, 43
    framing, 43
    keeping records of, 42-3
    preserving, 41-2
    repairing, 42
    restoring, 42
    storing, 42
Historical papers, 8, 35-43
    collecting, 36
    definition, 35
Homemaking brochures, 11
Honegger, Arthur, 119
Horsley, Calcott, 88
Howland, Esther A., 88
    valentine, 87

**I**

Inks, aniline, 17
Inks, as enemies of paper, 17
Insects, as enemies of paper, 18
Insert cards, 82
    collecting, 91
Instructions for collection, 173-4
Insuring a collection, 175
*Interesting Cartophile, The*, 90
International Postal Association, 47
Inventory of collection, 173, 175
Isaacs, John D., 122

**J**

Jigsaw puzzles, 146-7

**K**

Kelley, Edgar Stillman, 119
King, Jonathan, 88
    valentine, 87
Klein, C., 92
Kremer, Gerhard, 64
Kurtzman, Harry, 159

**L**

Lambert, Johann, 64
Law, John, 105
Le Prince, Jean Baptiste, 56
Lee, Stan, 159
Leidenberg, Harry Miller, 24
Letterheads, 96
Library of Congress, 25-7, 28
    national preservation program, 25-7
*Life* magazine, 133
Light, as enemy of paper, 18

Lignin, 19
Lincoln, Abraham, 137
   signature, 7
Lipman, H., 90
Literary items, 10, 135-142
   as collectible, 142
   collecting, 138-9
   first editions, 139
   guidelines for preserving, 139-141
   preserving, 139-142
Literature, American, see American
      literature
Lithographic prints, 56
Lupino, Ida, autographed photograph, 38
Lynch, Thomas, Jr., 40
   signature, 40

**M**
MacDowell, Edward A., 119
*MAD*, 159
Maddox, R. L., 67
Magazines, 10, 131-4
   as collectible, 134
   collecting, 132-3
   covers, 132
   "first editions," 132
   preserving, 133-4
   sources, 133
Man, as enemy of paper, 18-9
Manuscripts, 35
   storing, 141-2
Map making, 62-3, 64, 65
   early American, 65
   early techniques, 63
   European, 62-3
   in the 1900s, 65
Map of the World in 1638, 64
Maps, 62-6
   ancient, 62
   collecting, 66
   coloring, 63-4
   early, decoration, 63
Marvel Comics, 159
Mat sizes, 74-5
Mat, preparing, 75
Matchbook covers, 11, 167-171
   collecting, 169
   designs, 168-9
   early, 167
   manufacturing, 167
   mounting and storing, 170-1
   preserving, 169-170
Matting and framing prints, 74-9
McLoughlin Brothers, 144-5, 148, 149
Mercator, 64
Meunier, Henri, 60
Military items, 36
Milton Bradley, 145-6, 147, 148, 150
   puzzle, 147
   game, 146
Mitchell, John, 65
Mohawk Paper Mills, Inc., 20
Money, paper, see Paper money
Motion picture memorabilia, collecting,
      123
Motion pictures, 122-3
Mucha, Alphonse, 60
Mulready, William, 46

Music, 116-121
   19th century opera, 117
   20th century, 117-8
   American, 118-9
   folk, 119-120
   of Middle Ages, 116-7
   of Romantic era, 117
   post-Romantic, 117
Music memorabilia, collecting, 120-1
Musical scores, collecting, 120-1
Mylar mounts, for stamps, 50, 52

**N**
Nast, Thomas, 129, 144
   illustration, 145
National Academy of Sciences, 30
National Aeronautics and Space
      Administration, 26
National Archives and Records
      Administration, 30
National Archives, 28, 30
National bank notes, 107
National Endowment for the Humanities,
      28
National Information Standards
      Organization (NISO), 20
National Valentine Collectors' Association,
      179
Newberry Library, 28
Newspaper Collectors Society of America,
      131, 179
Newspapers, 10, 127-131, 134
   as collectible, 134
   collecting, 130
   preserving, 131
   sources, 130-1
Noh theater, 115

**O**
O'Neill, Rose, 132, 145
One-penny black, 46
Organizations and Associations, 179
Ortelius, Abraham, 64
Osgood, Samuel, 49

**P**
P. H. Glatfelter Co., 20
Page, Thomas Nelson, 137
Paine, John Knowles, 119
Pamphlets and flyers, 11
Pantin, 148
Paper, 8-9, 13-22, 30-2, 67
   acid-free, 19
   American national standard for, 20, 22
   bark, 14
   commercial, 8-9
   deacidification process, 26
   definition, 13-22
   enemies, 17-9
      acids, 17
      alum, 17
      atmospheric conditions, 18
      dust, 18
      inks, 17
      insects, 18
      light, 18
      man, 18-9
      temperature, 18

   future of, 19-20
   introduction of, 14-5
   permanent, 19
   photographic, 67
   preparing to store, 32
   preserving at home, 30-2
   preserving content, 28
   preserving, environmental conditions,
      31
   storage methods, 32
Paper collectibles, 5-6, 8
   how value is determined, 5-6
   reason for collecting, 5
   types, 8
Paper dolls, 8, 148-50
   American, 149
   celebrity, 149-150
   in *Godey's Ladies' Book*, 149
Paper making, 14-5, 16-7
   beginnings in China, 14-5
   in the New World, 16
   methods, 16-7
Paper money, 104-9
   American colonial, 106
   American, 105-7
   as collectible, 109
   collecting, 108
   early English, 105
   first European, 104
   first, 103-4
   French Revolution, 105
   preserving, 108-9
   state-issued, 106
Papers, historical, 35-43
Parker Brothers, 147, 149
Paterson, William, 105
Payne, John Howard, 136
Penfield, Edward, 60
   poster reproduction, 60
Performing arts memorabilia, 125-6
   as collectible, 126
   preserving, 125-6
Phillips, Wendell, 137
Photographic paper, 67
Photographs, 66-9, 70-4
   black and white, 70
      categories, 70-1
      fiber-based, 71
      handling, 71
      preserving and storing, 71-2
      resin-coated, 71
      salted paper, 71
   collecting, 68-9
   color, 72-4
      handling, 74
      permanence characteristics, 73
      preservation and storage, 74
   preserving, 70-4
Photography, beginnings of modern, 67
Photography, color, processes, 72-3
Picture post cards, first, 89-90
Plastic, as glazing material, 77-8
*PLAYBOY*, 10, 133
Playing Card Museum, 156
Playing cards, 11, 151-6
   American souvenir, 155
   American, 154
   as collectible, 156

(playing cards, continued)
  children's, 155
  collecting, 155-6
  decorative backs, 154
  designs, 151-3
  double-ended, 153-4
  German, 152
  presentation packs, 154
  preserving, 156
  "squeezers," 155
Portolano, 63
Post card, top selling, 93
Post cards, 89-90, 92-3
  collecting, 92-3
  linen, 93
  picture, first, 89-90
Postage stamp, first, 46
Postage stamp albums, 52
Postage stamps, 49, 50, 52, 53
  first U.S., 49
  glassine envelopes, 52
  hinges, 50
  mounting, 50
  Mylar mounts, 50, 52
  paper, 49
  stock book, 53
  stock pages, 50, 53
Postal cards, albums, 53
Postal cards, first, 47-8
Postal items, 8, 45-54
  as collectibles, 52, 54
  preserving, 50, 52
Postal system, beginnings, 45
  European beginnings, 46
Postcard History Society, 179
Poster Society, 179
Posters, 56-61
Postmasters' Provisionals, 49
Preparing to store paper items, 32
Preservation, definition, 23-4
Preserving historical documents, 41-2
Preserving paper items at home, 30-2
*Primer on Collecting Old & Historic
  Newspapers, A*, 131
Print, 55, 76-9
  definition, 55
  framing, glazing materials, 77
  matting, 76-9
Print storage boxes, 70
Prints, 8, 55-79
  aquatint, 56
  as collectible, 79
  collecting, 61
    older, 62
  etched, 56
  handling, 69
  lithographic, 56
  matting and framing, 74-9
  old mats and, 69-70
  oversize, preserving, 70
  preserving, 69
  protecting surface of, 70

storage, 70
  tears, 69
  wood block, 55-6
Programs, souvenir, 123
Promissory notes, 107
  European, 104
Puzzles, 11

**Q**
Queen Kristina, letter, 37

**R**
Radio broadcasting, 124
Railroadiana Collectors Association, Inc.,
  179
Rare books, 141
Rare paper items, treating, 27-8
Rarity, 6-7, 38
  autographs, 38
Repairing historical documents, 42
Restoration, definition, 24
Restoring historical documents, 42
Robert, Nicolas-Louis, 17
Romberg, Sigmund, concert program, 119

**S**
S. D. Warren Company, 16, 20
Schultz, J. H., 67
Schuman, William, 119
Scouts On Stamps Society International,
  175
Security in home, 175-6
Sheet music, 9, 10, 120-1, 126
  collecting, 120-1
Shih Chang-ju, 15
Signature collecting, 40-1
Signatures, 6
Silver certificates, 107
Small-sized notes, 108
Smith, Jedediah, 65
Smith, Richard D., 27
Society of Paper Money Collectors, 179
Solander box, 32
*Sound of Music, The*, souvenir program,
  124
Souvenir cards, 8, 81-2, 85, 91
  collecting, 91
Souvenir programs, 123
Spilsbury, John, 146
Stamp collecting, 49-50
Stamp tongs, 52
Stamped envelope, first, 46
Stampless covers, 95
Stamps, see Postage stamps
State-issued currency, 106
Stock book, for stamps, 53
Stock pages, for stamps, 50, 53
Stocks and bonds, 98-100
  collecting, 99-100
Storage boxes, for prints, 70
Storage methods, paper, 32
Store cards, 81

Storing historical documents, 42
Sumner, Charles, 137
Suppliers of Archival Materials, 179

**T**
Television broadcasting, 124-5
Temperature, as enemy of paper, 18
Theater, 111-5
  18th and 19th century, 114
  20th century, 114-5
  early history, 111-2
  English, 114
  French, 114
  Greek, 112
  medieval, 113
  Noh, 115
  Oriental, 115
  Renaissance, 113-4
  Roman, 112-3
Theatrical and entertainment items, 9
Theatrical memorabilia, collecting, 115
Tobacco cards, 82-4
Topps bubblegum cards, 84-5
Toulouse-Lautrec, Henri de, 58-9
  poster reproduction, 59
Trade cards, 81, 82
Treasury notes, 107
Ts'ai Lun, 14, 15
Two-penny blue, 46

**U**
United States Geological Survey, 65
United States Postal Service, 36, 48
  beginnings, 48
Universal Autograph Collectors Club, 179
Universal Postal Union, 47
University Products, 179

**V**
Valentine's Day Cards, 86-8
Valentines, 87, 88
  Victorian, 87
  "vinegar," 88
Value, how determined, 5-6
Vanity Fair cigarettes, 166
Visitors cards, 89
Von Stephen, Heinrich, 48

**W**
Waldseemuller, Martin, 64
Wallace, Lew, 137
Wand, A. R., 129
Warren Publishing Company, 160
Warren, Dennis, 16
Webster, Noah, 129
Wedgewood, Thomas, 67
Wei T'o System, 27
Wertham, Frederic, 159
Wildenburg, Harry, 157
Williams, Gordon, 24, 25